CONTENTS

SPOILER WARNING!

This Piggyback™ guide is designed to enhance your Halo 2 experience with tips, strategies and inside information. It is not our intention, however, to ruin Halo 2's captivating storyline for you. This guide has been carefully designed to minimize annoying spoilers, with plot-sensitive information positioned carefully in the relevant sections of the Campaign chapter. If you value the Halo 2 narrative experience – and you *really* should – please don't read level walkthroughs until you arrive at the corresponding point in the game!

Index Tab

For ease of orientation, you will find an index tab on the right-hand margin of each double-page spread. Use it to see at a glance which subjects are featured in each chapter. The upper index indicates the different chapters within the guide. The lower index denotes the different sections within the actual chapter.

CHAPTER 1

HOW TO PLAY

Halo 2 is not just bigger than its predecessor: it's more complicated, too, with new weapons, enemies, vehicles and innumerable new experiences. This section explains the fundamental skills required to control the Master Chief and how to put his many abilities to best use. From basic controller functions to expert hints and tips, the following pages are an essential read for Halo: Combat Evolved graduates and new recruits alike.

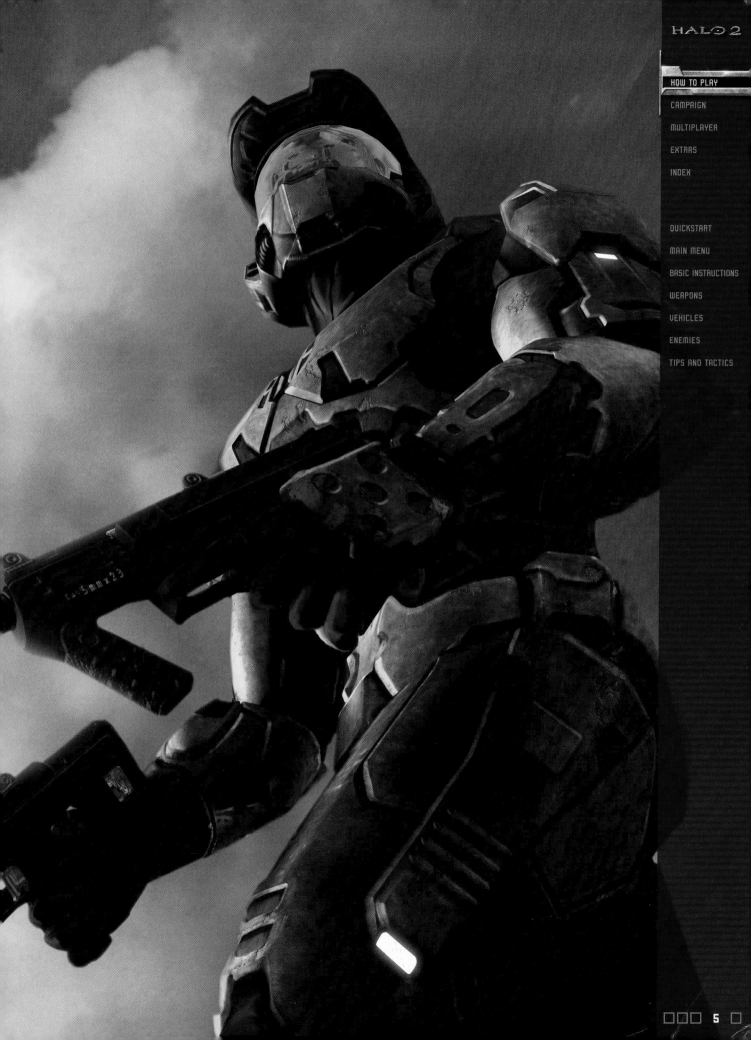

SECTION 10

Quickstart

For Beginners

Even if you're keen to leap feet-first into Halo 2's Campaign or multiplayer mode, you should at least read the following steps first.

- Press ▷ or Ⓐ on the title screen. If this is your first game, you'll need to create a new Profile before you can play. Your Profile tracks your individual settings and information, such as controller configuration (see page 10) and Campaign progress. Creating one is simple: a name will suffice. You can return to your Profile at any point to change your personal settings.

- If you want to sign in to Xbox Live, you can refer to page 158 for more details. Having second thoughts? Simply select Don't Sign In.

- The Main Menu allows access to the Campaign mode, the Settings menu (see below) and three flavors of multiplayer: via Xbox Live (online gaming), Split Screen (up to four players on a single Xbox) and System Link (multiple connected Xbox consoles). A chapter dedicated to Halo 2's extraordinary multiplayer component can be found on page 156.

- The Settings menu allows you to edit (or create) Profiles. If you're concentrating on Halo 2's Campaign mode, you can choose to have Subtitles on or off and fine-tune your controller setup. Don't feel obliged to configure the latter right now, though – you can also change controller options via the Pause Menu during play. The Game Variants option allows you to create specific multiplayer game types to enjoy at a later date. You can find an exhaustive explanation of this menu's many settings and features on page 170.

- Select Campaign if you want to fight the Master Chief's war against the Covenant. You can play this mode alone (New Campaign), or via a split-screen display with a friend (Cooperative). On starting a new Campaign, you'll be asked to choose a difficulty setting (see page 8). Ask yourself honestly: how skilled are you? Most players will be best served by selecting Normal, but don't be embarrassed to select Easy if you're not a particularly experienced gamer.

Halo 2 begins with a short training section which allows new players to become accustomed to controlling the Master Chief. With the default control setup, the left thumbstick allows you to move forward, back, left and right. The right thumbstick allows you to look around: up, down, left and right. If this dual-stick system is new to you, it may initially feel quite strange and confusing. Worry not: with practice, you'll discover that it's a flexible and instinctive means of control. R fires your weapon once you have one, and you can press ▶ to pause the game. The Pause Menu offers access to the Controller Settings screen. If you want to tweak your controls – for example, to invert the vertical axis on the right thumbstick, a popular choice for some gamers – you can do so here at any time.

As you begin to play through Halo 2, you'll notice that you reach regular Checkpoints – signaled by the onscreen text "Checkpoint... Done" – when arriving at certain areas or having achieved certain goals. Should the Master Chief die at any point, you will automatically return to the last saved Checkpoint. If you want to stop play for any reason, you will need to manually save your game before powering down your Xbox. Press ▶ and choose Save and Quit. Your progress up to the last Checkpoint will be saved in your Profile. The action will be resumed at this point next time you play.

For Halo Veterans

If you're a seasoned Halo: Combat Evolved campaigner, you'll already be aware of many basic Halo 2 ingredients – like its control system and Checkpoints. There are some important new features that you should familiarize yourself with.

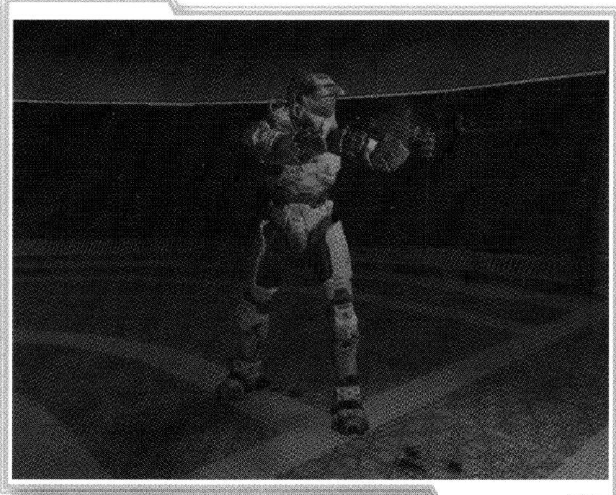

01

You can now use two weapons at once. While holding a small weapon like a pistol, you can choose to pick up a similar or identical weapon and use both simultaneously. This is known as dual-wielding (see page 17). The weapons in the Master Chief's left and right hands can now be fired with L and R respectively. This additional firepower is not without an attendant cost, though: while you dual-wield, you will be unable to throw grenades without first dropping one weapon. You can do this by pressing Y or B (Fig. 1).

02

You can now hijack or board enemy vehicles. Press and hold X to dislodge a vehicle's current driver from his seat, but only when it is moving at a non-lethal pace. This new feature is something of a double-edged sword: in both multiplayer and Campaign modes, your enemies can do the same to you. See page 21 for a more detailed explanation (Fig. 2).

Weapons generally work as they did in Halo: Combat Evolved, but there are several small changes in detail. For example, the pistol – the M6C Magnum – no longer has a built-in scope and is less powerful now. The addition of new Covenant foes also means that there are more variables to consider when choosing your primary and secondary firearms.

The Master Chief's MJOLNIR Mark 6 battle suit has been upgraded and now offers, among other details, a built-in zoom function. This can be activated by pressing the right stick button. If the Master Chief is carrying a weapon with its own scope – like the Battle Rifle – then its optics will take priority.

The onscreen display has been modified. You'll find an authoritative overview of the new HUD on page 12.

SPLIT SCREEN: COOPERATIVE SETUP
Change Level...
CURRENT LEVEL:
Delta Halo
Choose a different campaign level for your co-op game. Only levels unlocked by the host are available.
SELECT BACK

01

SECTION 2

Main Menu

Campaign

The story mode of Halo 2 is called Campaign. Select the option New Campaign to start the single-player mode; if you've already got a saved game, you can continue with Resume. You can also revisit previously completed levels by opting for Select Level.

When you're starting a Campaign or replaying a level, you can also select a difficulty level: Easy, Normal, Heroic or Legendary. The higher the setting, the more dangerous your adversaries are: they will attack with greater ferocity, in greater numbers, and their positioning in any given area may vary. Experienced gamers and Halo veterans should opt for the default Normal mode, while those unfamiliar with the first-person shoot 'em up genre may prefer to choose Easy.

You can play the Campaign mode with a friend, too: select Cooperative to do so. Once the second player has selected a Profile, you can start the game in the Pregame Lobby. The option Game Setup allows you to select a level of difficulty and begin your co-op Campaign from a different (but previously unlocked) mission should you wish (Fig. 1).

Xbox Live, Split Screen, System Link

These options allow access to Halo 2's multiplayer modes on a single Xbox, through networked Xbox consoles, or online with Xbox Live. You can find a comprehensive overview of the massive number of multiplayer settings, a wealth of useful strategy tips and guides to each map in a dedicated section beginning on page 158.

Settings

The Settings menu allows you to change options for both Campaign and multiplayer modes. Some options are exclusive to a particular game mode; others, like Control Settings, can be found inside the in-game Pause Menu.

Player Profiles

Using this option you can create, edit, change or delete profiles (Fig. 2). Appearance, Voice Output, Voice Masking, and Online Status are specific to the multiplayer mode (see page 180). Enabling Subtitles will, much as its name suggests, display character dialogue during cinematic interludes as onscreen captions. The Controls menu enables you to adjust the default controller configuration.

- **Thumbstick Layout:** Tailor each thumbstick to suit you. Southpaw will exchange the functions of the right and left stick, which makes it a good choice for left-handed players. Legacy is a very different way of controlling Halo 2: the thumbstick directions for strafing and turning to the right or left are swapped. There is also a permutation of Legacy for left-handed players.

- **Button Layout:** You can change the layout for your controller's buttons and triggers. Note that button references in this guide will always refer to the default configuration.

- **Look Sensitivity:** You can increase and decrease the speed at which you look around with the right thumbstick. If you have yet to actually play Halo 2 you should probably leave this setting alone for now: it's better to fine-tune it at a later point once you have a better "feel" for the way the Master Chief moves.

- **Look Inversion:** By default, moving the right thumbstick up or down will make the Master Chief look in those directions. However, a number of first-person shooter aficionados prefer to invert this vertical axis: therefore, moving the thumbstick down will make you look up, and vice versa.

02

- **Automatic Look Centering:** If you activate this function, the Master Chief's view will return to a central point as you begin to move. This is a useful option for FPS (first-person shooter) novices, but many will find its effect a little too intrusive. If you're having difficulties reorienting your view to center on a regular basis, you should give this option a test drive.

- **Controller Vibration:** If you don't want your controller to vibrate in accordance with various game events, you can deactivate it here.

Game Variants

Halo 2 has an outstanding wealth of multiplayer options and settings. In the Game Variants menu, you can create your very own match types for future play. You'll find the manifold possibilities described in detail on page 170.

Basic Instructions

Before you enter combat, it's important to have a reasonable grasp of Halo 2's control system and various game concepts. The Master Chief is a powerful, versatile warrior (as, indeed, are his Elite equivalents if you opt to play as one in multiplayer mode), but he's not invincible. To help him survive against a tide of Covenant foes, you'll need to learn and utilize every conceivable skill. Even those who have braved the horrors of Installation 04 in Halo: Combat Evolved should take the time to reacquaint themselves with SPARTAN-117 and his revised MJOLNIR Mark 6 battle suit.

THE CONTROL PAD

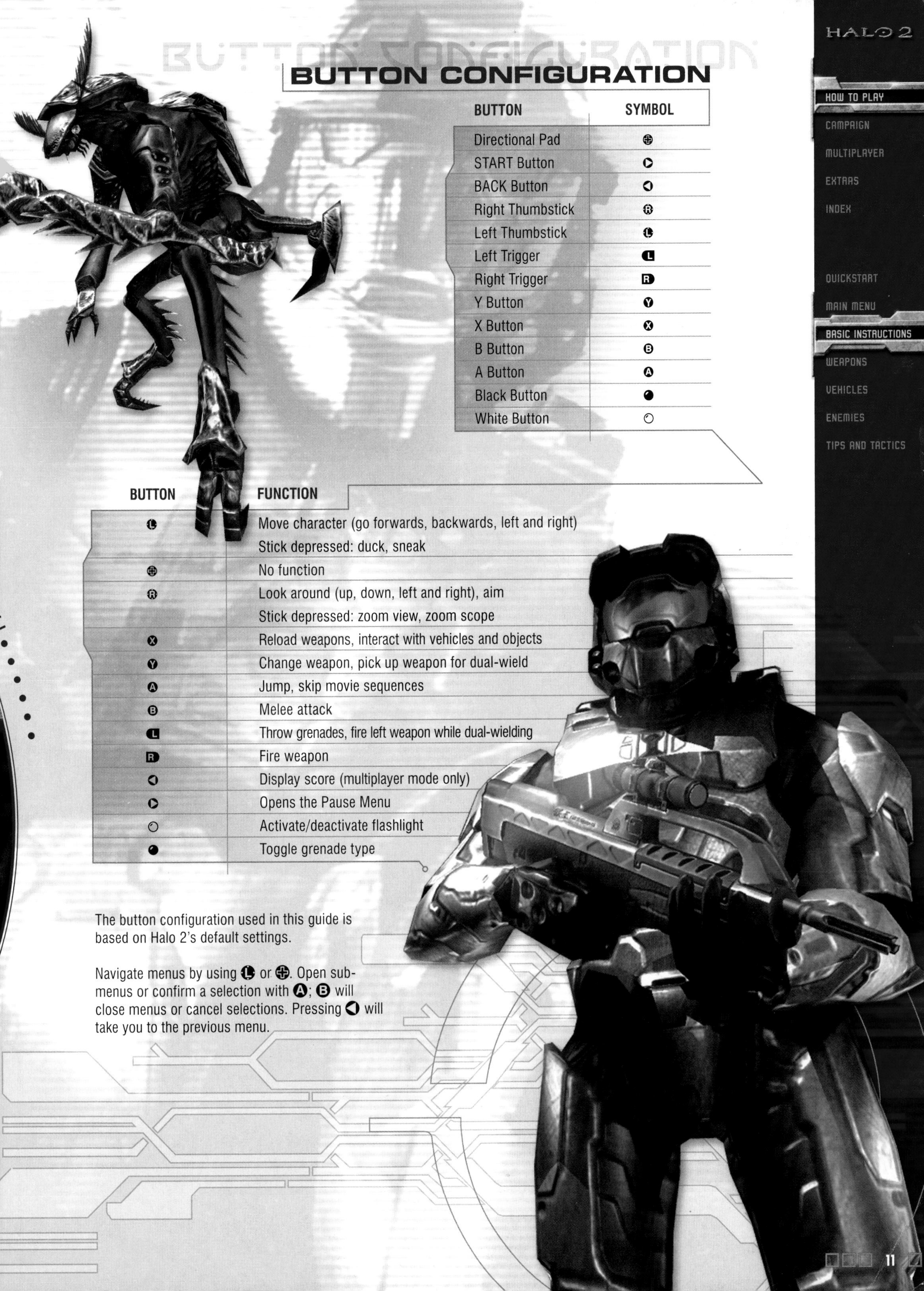

BUTTON CONFIGURATION

BUTTON	SYMBOL
Directional Pad	⊕
START Button	▶
BACK Button	◀
Right Thumbstick	Ⓡ
Left Thumbstick	Ⓛ
Left Trigger	L
Right Trigger	R
Y Button	Ⓨ
X Button	Ⓧ
B Button	Ⓑ
A Button	Ⓐ
Black Button	●
White Button	○

BUTTON	FUNCTION
Ⓛ	Move character (go forwards, backwards, left and right) Stick depressed: duck, sneak
⊕	No function
Ⓡ	Look around (up, down, left and right), aim Stick depressed: zoom view, zoom scope
Ⓧ	Reload weapons, interact with vehicles and objects
Ⓨ	Change weapon, pick up weapon for dual-wield
Ⓐ	Jump, skip movie sequences
Ⓑ	Melee attack
L	Throw grenades, fire left weapon while dual-wielding
R	Fire weapon
◀	Display score (multiplayer mode only)
▶	Opens the Pause Menu
○	Activate/deactivate flashlight
●	Toggle grenade type

The button configuration used in this guide is based on Halo 2's default settings.

Navigate menus by using Ⓛ or ⊕. Open sub-menus or confirm a selection with Ⓐ; Ⓑ will close menus or cancel selections. Pressing ◀ will take you to the previous menu.

HEADS-UP DISPLAY

Heads-Up Display

The game environment is viewed through the visor of the Master Chief's battle suit. You should familiarize yourself with the information provided by the overlaid Heads-Up Display (or HUD) as soon as possible. The Master Chief's HUD is blue. If you're playing as a Covenant Elite in multiplayer mode, the display will be purple.

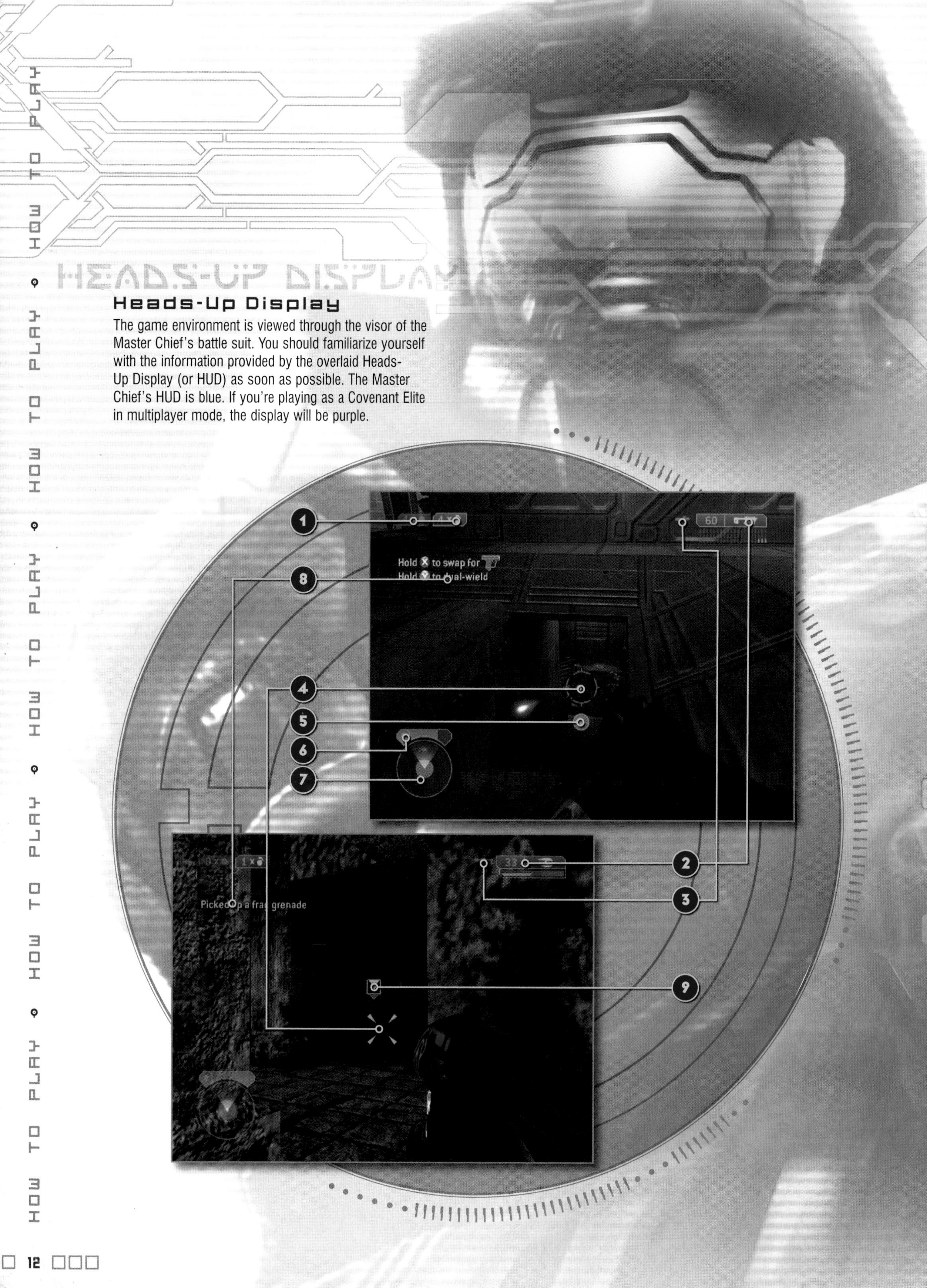

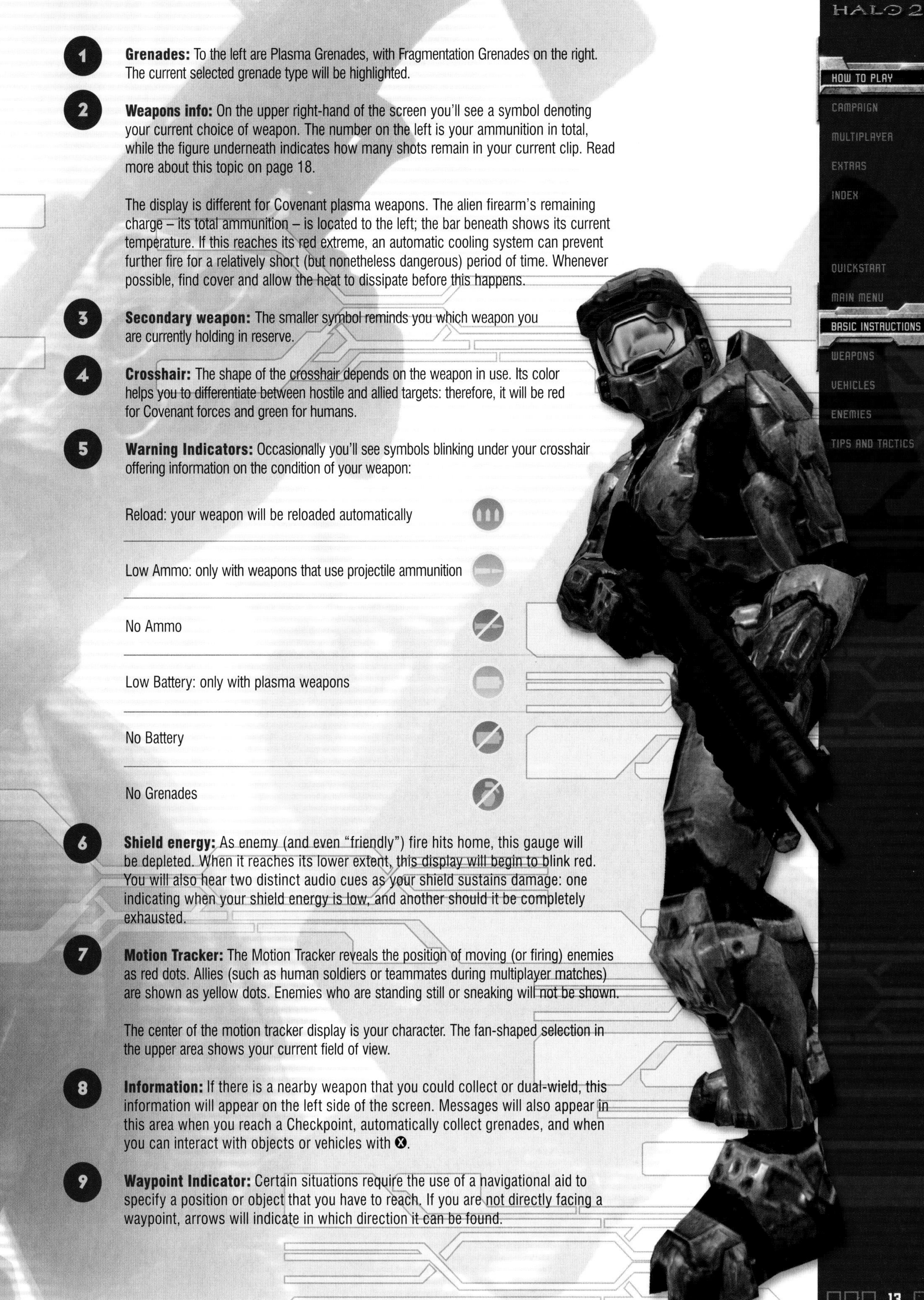

1 **Grenades:** To the left are Plasma Grenades, with Fragmentation Grenades on the right. The current selected grenade type will be highlighted.

2 **Weapons info:** On the upper right-hand of the screen you'll see a symbol denoting your current choice of weapon. The number on the left is your ammunition in total, while the figure underneath indicates how many shots remain in your current clip. Read more about this topic on page 18.

The display is different for Covenant plasma weapons. The alien firearm's remaining charge – its total ammunition – is located to the left; the bar beneath shows its current temperature. If this reaches its red extreme, an automatic cooling system can prevent further fire for a relatively short (but nonetheless dangerous) period of time. Whenever possible, find cover and allow the heat to dissipate before this happens.

3 **Secondary weapon:** The smaller symbol reminds you which weapon you are currently holding in reserve.

4 **Crosshair:** The shape of the crosshair depends on the weapon in use. Its color helps you to differentiate between hostile and allied targets: therefore, it will be red for Covenant forces and green for humans.

5 **Warning Indicators:** Occasionally you'll see symbols blinking under your crosshair offering information on the condition of your weapon:

Reload: your weapon will be reloaded automatically

Low Ammo: only with weapons that use projectile ammunition

No Ammo

Low Battery: only with plasma weapons

No Battery

No Grenades

6 **Shield energy:** As enemy (and even "friendly") fire hits home, this gauge will be depleted. When it reaches its lower extent, this display will begin to blink red. You will also hear two distinct audio cues as your shield sustains damage: one indicating when your shield energy is low, and another should it be completely exhausted.

7 **Motion Tracker:** The Motion Tracker reveals the position of moving (or firing) enemies as red dots. Allies (such as human soldiers or teammates during multiplayer matches) are shown as yellow dots. Enemies who are standing still or sneaking will not be shown.

The center of the motion tracker display is your character. The fan-shaped selection in the upper area shows your current field of view.

8 **Information:** If there is a nearby weapon that you could collect or dual-wield, this information will appear on the left side of the screen. Messages will also appear in this area when you reach a Checkpoint, automatically collect grenades, and when you can interact with objects or vehicles with Ⓧ.

9 **Waypoint Indicator:** Certain situations require the use of a navigational aid to specify a position or object that you have to reach. If you are not directly facing a waypoint, arrows will indicate in which direction it can be found.

Abilities and Actions

The authorities behind the SPARTAN-II project sought to create the ultimate augmented human warriors. The Master Chief, as the sole survivor of this unique caste, is blessed with outstanding agility, strength and skills. As you guide him through Halo 2, you'll soon learn that an appreciation of his many abilities – and, at times, his limitations – is essential.

Movement

L

While you obviously know that you can move the Master Chief with the left thumbstick and look around with the right thumbstick, it's vital to remember that these controls are **analogue**. The speed at which he walks depends on the extent that you move the thumbstick. Move either by a small amount and he will creep forward, or turn slowly. It's not necessary to run at all times and nor, indeed, is it advisable. When in doubt of the position of local enemy forces, walking around a corner can give you a split-second opportunity to return to cover before you are spotted by your foes.

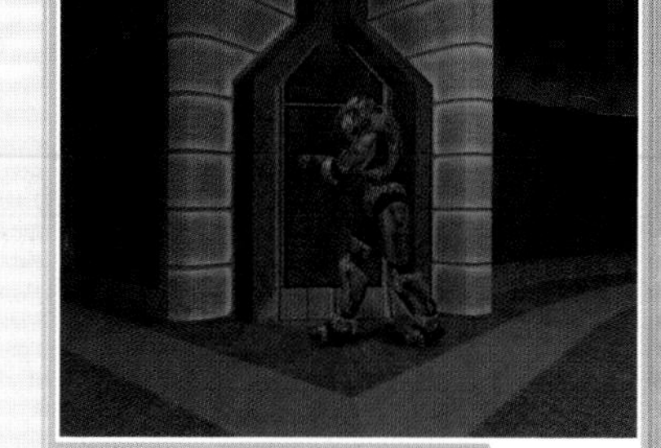

Angle of Vision

R

If you want to see what's going on to your left or right side without moving an inch, use the right thumbstick (see Aiming on page 18). The practice of moving with one thumbstick while looking around and aiming with the other can be quite tricky for novices. Don't worry: with a little practice, this soon becomes entirely instinctive.

If this is your first-person shooter debut, take the time to become accustomed to basic movement techniques before rushing into battle. As you approach a right-hand corner, for example, you can glide smoothly around it by steering the left thumbstick stick to an up-left position, and the right thumbstick gently to the right. By pressing up-left on the movement thumbstick, you are moving the Master Chief both forward and to the side; the right thumbstick controls your orientation.

Jump

A

Press A to jump. The MJOLNIR Mark 6 battle suit augments the Master Chief's innate agility, allowing him to leap an impressive height. To jump longer distances you should keep the left thumbstick held until he lands. You should also note that you can reorient him while airborne.

CROUCHING

Crouching

Press the left thumbstick button to make the Master Chief crouch. While holding this down you can move under obstructions and, more importantly, stealthily creep up to or sneak past foes that are oblivious to your presence. In Halo 2's multiplayer mode, moving while crouched will render you invisible to your opponents' motion trackers.

CLIMBING

Climbing

It's not something that the Master Chief is required to do on a regular basis, but there are occasionally instances where he must climb ladders. To do so, simply walk towards one to mount it. Move forward while looking up with the right thumbstick to ascend.

ACTIVATE

Activate

When you encounter a device that can be used – to call an elevator or open certain doors, for example – you will be advised of this fact by an onscreen prompt. Press and hold Ⓧ to interact with the object in question.

Equipment

SHIELDS

Shields

The MJOLNIR Mark 6 battle suit is protected by a powerful energy shield. Gunfire, explosions, melee attacks and collisions with flying objects – knocked in your direction by a belligerent Hunter, for instance – will all reduce its ability to protect SPARTAN-117 from harm. Should its energy be completely depleted, the MJOLNIR Mark 6 armor and, ultimately, the Master Chief himself will sustain damage. The shield indicator on the HUD will flash red to warn when it is dangerously weak or compromised. Should a lethal shot cut a particular battle short, play will resume at the last activated Checkpoint (see page 21).

When the shield's energy becomes dangerously low, you should take cover and allow it time to recharge. While pinned down by Covenant forces this can seem to take a lifetime rather than, in actuality, mere seconds.

FLASHLIGHT

Flashlight

You can toggle your flashlight on and off by pressing ○. This source of illumination will always be directed at the area you are facing. Unlike its equivalent in Halo: Combat Evolved, this flashlight will not cut out at inopportune moments during battles in poorly-lit areas. It will automatically turn itself off should its sensors detect a suitable increase in local lighting.

SCOPE

Scope

Press the right thumbstick button to activate a zoom function. There is only one level of magnification. Press the thumbstick again to disable it. When brandishing a weapon with a facility for zooming in on distant targets – such as the Battle Rifle – its scope will take priority over this built-in capability.

MOTION TRACKER

Motion Tracker

The Motion Tracker is displayed at the lower left-hand area of the screen. This essential device will save the Master Chief's life on many occasions during combat, but be warned: it is not a radar. An enemy must fire or move to betray their position to the device; static or stealthy assailants will not be displayed. The Motion Tracker can be an invaluable aid, but only when complemented by sharp visual acuity and battle-honed tactical insight.

The symbols that appear on your Motion Tracker are:

LARGE RED DOT:	Enemy vehicles
SMALL RED DOT:	Enemy on foot
LARGE YELLOW DOT:	Allied vehicles
SMALL YELLOW DOT:	Ally on foot

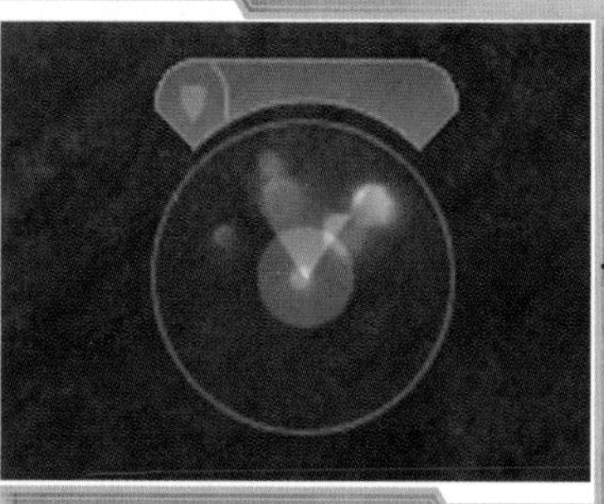

COLLECTING WEAPONS

Collecting Weapons

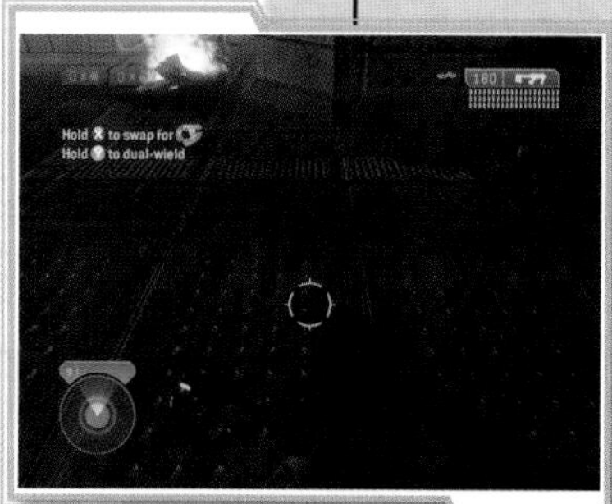

X

You will be notified on your HUD if you can collect a nearby weapon. Press and hold (X) to collect it and discard the one you are carrying. You can either use one weapon with another held in reserve, swapping between the two with (Y), or dual-wield two guns (more on which in a moment) with a third stored elsewhere. There is a caveat: the Master Chief will not collect a weapon of a type he already has unless he intends to (and can) dual-wield them. Additionally, he will not swap his current, battery-powered Covenant weapon for an equivalent with less energy. As a seasoned warrior, he fully appreciates the tactical opportunities that two distinct firearms can provide – and so should you.

DUAL-WIELD

Dual-Wield

To dual-wield is to hold two firearms at once, each fired by the corresponding left and right triggers on your controller. A third weapon is kept in reserve. Not all weapons can be dual-wielded: you can find out more about this in the Weapons section. This can be a phenomenally effective combat technique. You can pack a tremendous punch while firing two SMG "bullet hoses". Furthermore, using a charged Plasma Pistol shot to take down an Elite's shields before firing a M6C Magnum Sidearm to dispatch it is a rapid and effective technique. This trick is an evolution of a popular tactic from Halo: Combat Evolved – but, thanks to the new dual-wield ability, you no longer need to endure a pause while changing weapons.

There are drawbacks to dual-wielding, of course. You cannot throw grenades while holding weapons in both hands, although you can discard the left gun – and therefore regain these abilities – by pressing (Y) at any time. Additionally, should you perform a melee attack, the Master Chief will automatically drop the second weapon.

If you are dual-wielding two weapons and would like to collect another, there are a few possibilities.

- If the new weapon cannot be dual-wielded, you will drop your two active firearms when you pick it up.
- If it's possible to dual-wield the weapon, you can press and hold (X) to swap it with the weapon in your right hand or (Y) for your left hand.

SHOOTING

Shooting

Use (R) to fire a weapon. Every firearm in Halo 2 has its own features – you can read about their individual strengths and shortcomings from page 22 – and may require you to tap or hold the trigger to access individual fire modes. While dual-wielding, use (L) to fire the weapon in your left hand.

AIMING

Aiming

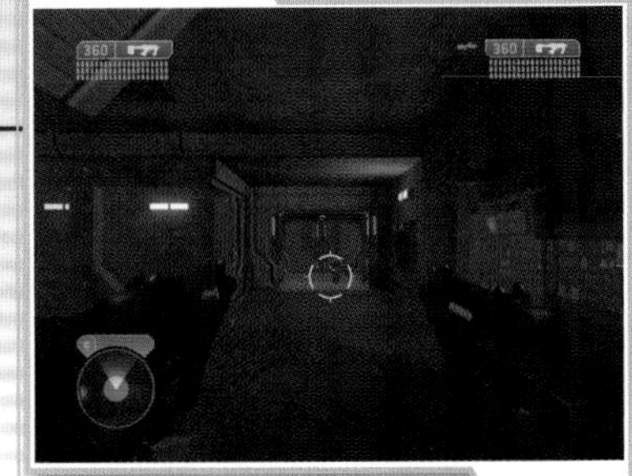

The reticule may change from weapon to weapon, but the principle remains the same: take aim and fire. You could say it's a simple point 'n' click interface. The Master Chief's HUD provides a modicum of assistance by changing the color of the crosshair to indicate whether the target is hostile or allied. Point at a Grunt's head, and it will be red; direct it at a Marine, and it will be green. It's as simple as that.

There is an exception. Over long distances, your reticule will retain its neutral color while pointed at friend and foe alike. This does not necessarily mean that your shots will not reach, but merely that the Master Chief's software cannot identify the target at that range. If you're a confident marksman, feel free to fire away.

RELOAD

Reload

Human weapons must be reloaded when their current clip is depleted. If you attempt to fire (or, with an automatic weapon, continue to fire) when their bullet count reaches zero, the Master Chief will perform an immediate reload. You can perform this action manually by pressing Ⓧ. As a rule of thumb it's extremely bad practice to allow the Master Chief to automatically reload during a firefight, as doing so leaves him momentarily vulnerable. If your current clip is almost depleted you should either switch to your secondary weapon, or dive behind available cover to manually reload before this happens. While it may appear that the Master Chief discards unused bullets when he throws away a partially depleted clip, this is not actually the case. Don't be shy to reload, and always do so after battles.

Plasma-based Covenant weapons have built-in power sources and cannot be reloaded. This is not quite the advantage it could be, though: they are highly prone to overheating. When the temperature gauge rises, it's advisable – unless, perhaps, you're one shot away from dispatching a final Elite – to hold your fire for a moment and allow it to cool down.

Collecting Ammunition

To collect ammunition, simply walk over an available clip or weapon and the Master Chief will automatically add what he finds to his current stocks. The amount found will be indicated on the upper left of the screen. There is a limit on the amount of ammo that can be carried at any given time. If you're dual-wielding two guns of the same type, though, your stores will be cumulative.

Close Combat

Even with the combined weapons technology of the human and Covenant races at your disposal, you should never underestimate the potency of a well-aimed melee attack. Press Ⓑ to unleash your inner barbarian and use your right-hand weapon as a crude (but effective) cudgel. If you're holding two active weapons, the left one will be thrown away to enable you to perform the attack.

Don't regard close-quarters combat as a last resort. A blow to the head can often offer the most trenchant conclusion to the life of a fleeing Grunt or troublesome, shield-bearing Jackal. Combine melee attacks with stealth tactics (plus a small amount of patience), and you can devastate an unprepared combat group without firing a single shot. Expert Halo 2 players will, for example, try to thin the numbers of a patrolling force of Covenant Elites by creeping behind each and delivering a single, solid blow to their backs.

Collecting Grenades

As with ammunition, grenades are collected automatically as the Master Chief walks over them. You can only carry four of each type. When your stocks are full, it's worth noting the positions of large amounts of free grenades. You could, should you wish, use your collection with wild abandon during your next combat encounter, then backtrack to replenish your supplies (if required) when the battle ends.

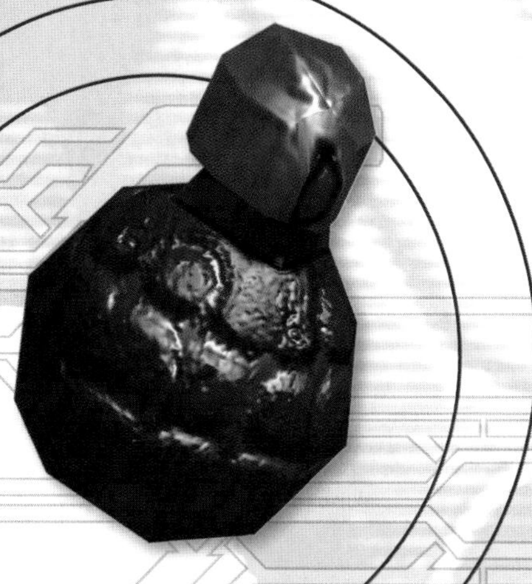

THROWING GRENADES

Throwing Grenades

Press the left trigger to hurl a grenade. If you're dual-wielding, you'll need to drop your second weapon first. The trajectory of your shot depends on the direction that you're currently facing. If you're aiming for a distant enemy, you should aim high. For a nearby group of Covenant foes, aim low and try to bounce it towards their feet.

You should familiarize yourself with the properties of available grenades. For example, the Frag Grenade can be bounced from walls and objects. Knowing this, you can disrupt forces from oblique (and unexpected) angles. The Plasma Grenade "sticks" to creatures and vehicles – but not walls or furniture – so a well-judged throw can mean certain death for an unfortunate Covenant warrior, not to mention his immediate companions.

In Campaign mode, should an inactive grenade – dropped, for example, by a slain Marine or Covenant Grunt – be caught in an explosion, it will immediately detonate. If there is more than one, the resultant chain reaction can be both awe-inspiring and deadly. Knowing this, you should use this feature to your advantage. If facing an awkward and entrenched group of enemies, try diving from cover to pick off a few Grunts. Now hurl a grenade at the position their corpses and, hopefully, a few dropped grenades lie. The resultant pyrotechnics will, at very least, distract and scatter nearby enemies.

TOGGLE GRENADES

Toggle Grenades

Use ● to toggle between the two varieties of grenade in your inventory. Should you exhaust your stock of a specific type, this will occur automatically.

TURRETS

Turrets

X, R

To man a stationary turret, press and hold X. You can fire with R and should do so with gusto: you're blessed with unlimited ammunition at all times. Press X once more to leave.

Vehicles

ENTERING

Entering

X

To enter a vehicle, approach it then press and hold X – an onscreen prompt will inform you when you are sufficiently close. The same button allows you to jump out. You should try to master the "priming" technique. It's really very simple: if you press and hold X just before you reach the required hot-spot on a vehicle, you will immediately jump aboard once in range. When fleeing an angry Covenant mob or rival team in a multiplayer battle, this trick could save your life. In some vehicles you can even use a passenger seat or – better still – a fixed weapon. You can learn more about this from page 32.

Boarding

If the velocity of an enemy-controlled vehicle is sufficiently low you can attempt to hijack it. Move yourself quickly and safely to a close distance, then press and hold Ⓧ when prompted to do so. You can also board vehicles from above after jumping from a raised vantage point.

The boarding of larger vehicles, on the other hand, is not so simple. As the driver of a Wraith or Scorpion is covered by a steel hatch, you cannot evict him by merely holding Ⓧ. However, it is possible to plant a grenade inside the vehicle. Turn to page 54 for further details.

Flipping Vehicles

Using his natural strength and the power of his battle suit, the Master Chief can flip an overturned vehicle to restore it to working order. Press Ⓧ when the onscreen prompt appears to achieve this Herculean feat with casual ease. If the vehicle is beyond serviceable use, the prompt will not appear.

Essential Information

Checkpoints

Rather than diluting its appeal by allowing players to save their progress at any position, or inflicting the old-school horror of sending players back to the very beginning of a level when they die, Halo 2 uses a "Checkpoint" system. At key points on every mission – generally after a battle, or after reaching a certain area of the map – the text "Checkpoint… done" will appear. Should you subsequently die, you will restart at this very point (and will begin with the same equipment). Consider it a leap back in time: having established in an inept manner what the Master Chief should not do while attempting to save humanity, you have a second, fifth or even thirtieth opportunity to put things right…

Saving your Game

Passing a Checkpoint creates a temporary save position. If you turn off your Xbox you will lose your progress. To make a permanent save, press ▷ and choose Save and Quit. Your position – from your last Checkpoint – will be stored in your Profile. You can continue this game at a later date by selecting the Resume option. Remember: you cannot have more than one saved game on a single Profile. If you choose to replay a previous level – they are unlocked after completion in Campaign mode – you will overwrite any other save position that you have.

Mission Objectives

If you forget what your last order was, you can refer to the Pause Menu. This will list the known objectives for your current level. Additional objectives will be added as you progress through a mission, while completed tasks will be suitably marked as being just that.

Pause Menu

Use ▷ to bring the action to a halt. The Pause Menu offers the following options:

- Continue
- Revert to Last Checkpoint
- Restart Level
- Controller Settings
- Save and Quit

You can return to your last stored position with Revert to Last Checkpoint. This is useful if an encounter has gone particularly FUBAR, or even if you simply want to experience a spectacular set-piece again. Restart Level takes you back to the very beginning of the mission. Controller Settings allows you to tweak your controller configuration while, incredibly enough, Save and Quit does as it says. Knowing how keen you'll be to continue, Bungie has gifted you with three means to return to the fray: select Continue, press ▷ or tap Ⓑ to resume play.

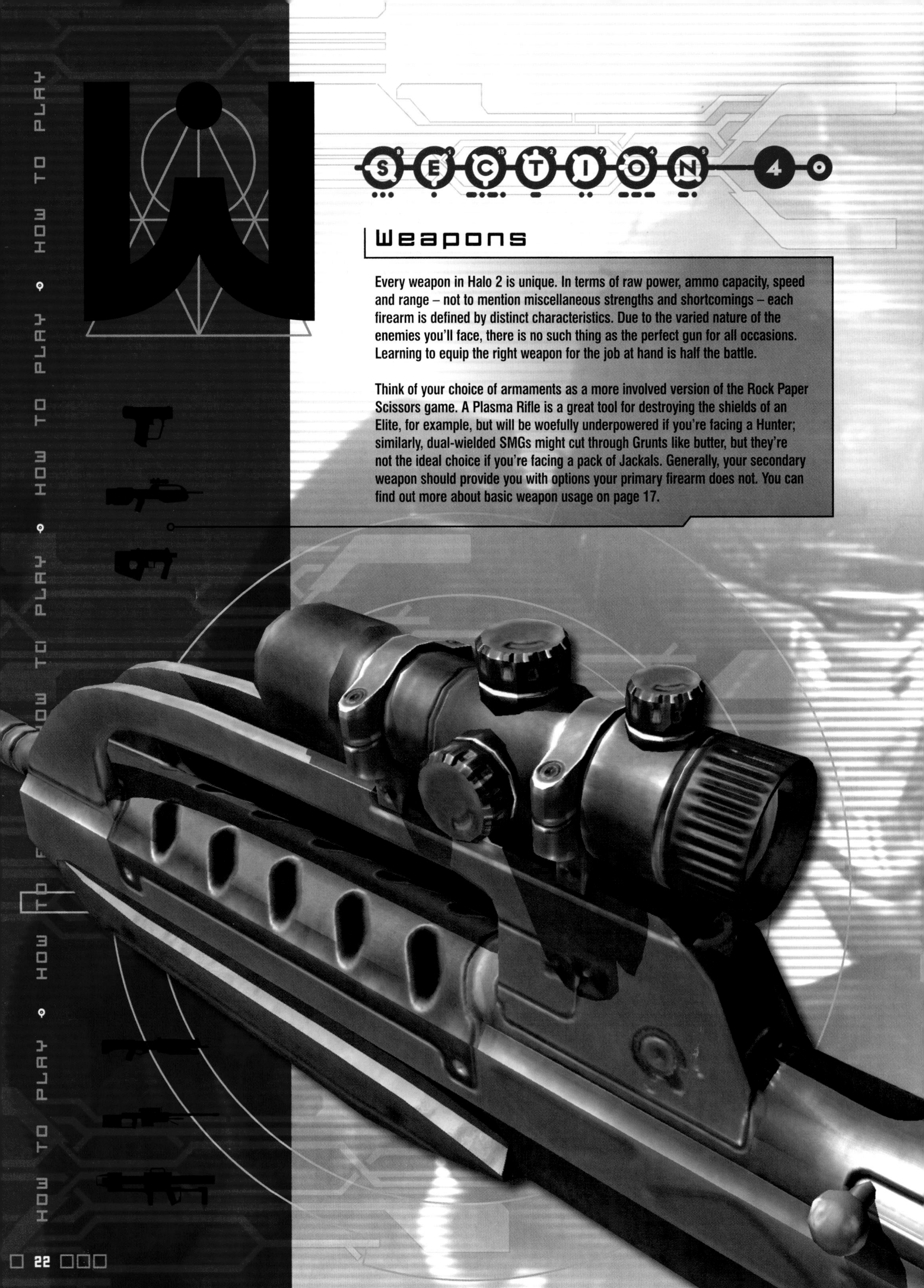

SECTION 4

Weapons

Every weapon in Halo 2 is unique. In terms of raw power, ammo capacity, speed and range – not to mention miscellaneous strengths and shortcomings – each firearm is defined by distinct characteristics. Due to the varied nature of the enemies you'll face, there is no such thing as the perfect gun for all occasions. Learning to equip the right weapon for the job at hand is half the battle.

Think of your choice of armaments as a more involved version of the Rock Paper Scissors game. A Plasma Rifle is a great tool for destroying the shields of an Elite, for example, but will be woefully underpowered if you're facing a Hunter; similarly, dual-wielded SMGs might cut through Grunts like butter, but they're not the ideal choice if you're facing a pack of Jackals. Generally, your secondary weapon should provide you with options your primary firearm does not. You can find out more about basic weapon usage on page 17.

UNSC Weaponry

By the year 2552 (Military Calendar), human weapons science has undergone an evolution, not revolution. UNSC armaments utilize technology first conceived centuries before and are based on what is, by Covenant and Forerunner standards, the almost archaic principle of accelerating crude metal projectiles. Still: as the saying goes, "if it hurts, it works". While spaceborne combat exchanges have invariably led to the decimation of its fleets, homo sapiens has fared a little better when given the opportunity to launch its latter-day spears at the Covenant on solid ground.

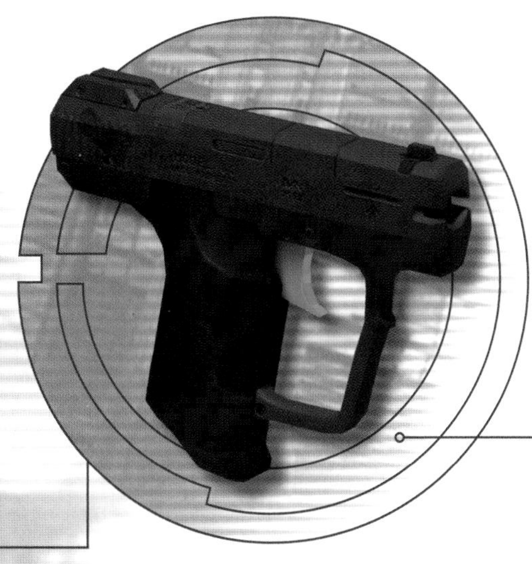

MAGNUM

A stripped-down version of the M6D Pistol equipped by the crew of the Pillar of Autumn during their battle with the Covenant on Installation 04, the Magnum does not have a scope – and therefore lacks the very feature that made its counterpart so deceptively deadly in Halo: Combat Evolved.

The magazine of this handgun can hold 12 bullets and has moderate stopping power. In close quarters with a dual-wield configuration, it can be surprisingly effective when employed against unshielded foes – not to mention curiously stylish. Over longer distances, however, its lack of scope and modest magazine capacity renders the Magnum largely ineffective. It is also rather slow to reload, a fact you should take into consideration before opting to use it against large groups of enemies. It is, however, quite useful for placing exact headshots.

OFFICIAL DESIGNATION	M6C MAGNUM SIDEARM
PROJECTILE TYPE	12.7MM SEMI, ARMOR PIERCING
DUAL-WIELD	YES
DAMAGE	MEDIUM
RANGE	CLOSE
ACCURACY	MEDIUM
RATE OF FIRE	MEDIUM
AUTOFIRE CAPABILITY	MANUAL
MAGAZINE CAPACITY	12 BULLETS
AMMUNITION (ADDITIONAL)	48 (4 MAGAZINES)
RELOAD SPEED	SLOW
MELEE ATTACK	AVERAGE
SCOPE	NO

SMG

OFFICIAL DESIGNATION	M7/CASELESS SUB MACHINE GUN
PROJECTILE TYPE	5MM
DUAL-WIELD	YES
DAMAGE	LOW
RANGE	CLOSE
ACCURACY	LOW
RATE OF FIRE	HIGH
AUTOFIRE CAPABILITY	CONTINUOUS FIRE
MAGAZINE CAPACITY	60 BULLETS
AMMUNITION (ADDITIONAL)	180 (3 MAGAZINES)
RELOAD SPEED	SLOW
MELEE ATTACK	AVERAGE
SCOPE	NO

The SMG's strength is its high rate of fire. While individual shots are not enormously damaging, its full automatic mode has led to it being dubbed the "bullet hose" by users in the UNSC. When dual-wielded, it allows the Master Chief to drown targets in a veritable torrent of projectiles.

The SMG has a number of shortcomings. Its accuracy is strictly limited unless used at close range. Furthermore, full automatic fire leads to enormous recoil, forcing the SMG's muzzle steadily upward. You will need to compensate for this effect by constantly adjusting your aim. Finally, its phenomenal capacity for filling the air with lead means that its magazine can be depleted in what will seem like a heartbeat. If there's no cover available to hide behind while reloading in your current area, you may be better served by another weapon.

BATTLE RIFLE

OFFICIAL DESIGNATION	BR55 RIFLE
PROJECTILE TYPE	9.5MM
DUAL-WIELD	NO
DAMAGE	MEDIUM
RANGE	MEDIUM (WITH SCOPE: HIGH)
ACCURACY	MEDIUM (WITH SCOPE: HIGH)
RATE OF FIRE	MEDIUM
AUTOFIRE CAPABILITY	SHORT BURSTS
MAGAZINE CAPACITY	36 BULLETS
AMMUNITION (ADDITIONAL)	108 (3 MAGAZINES)
RELOAD SPEED	SLOW
MELEE ATTACK	SLOW
SCOPE	2X

Replacing the MA5B Assault Rifle found in Halo: Combat Evolved, the Battle Rifle was built with high reliability and ease of use in mind. With every pull of its trigger the BR55 fires a burst of three bullets. It is a precise, clinical tool when used by a well-trained soldier. If the SMG could be described as a brutish cudgel, the Battle Rifle is more akin to a scalpel in the right hands.

The BR55's optical scope has a 2x zoom facility, which allows the Master Chief to make accurate hits – even headshots – over greater distances than you might at first suspect. Under most circumstances, the Battle Rifle's short bursts, long range and average damage make it a great all-round weapon, although it is less effective in close quarters. That said, if you equip a Shotgun as your secondary weapon, you can safely claim to be equipped for most eventualities.

SHOTGUN

OFFICIAL DESIGNATION	M90 SHOTGUN
PROJECTILE TYPE	8-GAUGE MAGNUM (3.5")
DUAL-WIELD	NO
DAMAGE	HIGH
RANGE	VERY CLOSE
ACCURACY	LOW
RATE OF FIRE	LOW
AUTOFIRE CAPABILITY	MANUAL
MAGAZINE CAPACITY	12 BULLETS
AMMUNITION (ADDITIONAL)	36 (3 MAGAZINES)
RELOAD SPEED	VERY SLOW
MELEE ATTACK	FAST
SCOPE	NO

A weapon design that has barely changed since first conceived, the Shotgun is a close-range firearm that can stop any creature, Human or Covenant, in its tracks. Deadly at short distances, it is a weapon that even Elites should fear: it can overload some shields in a single shot. With it, you can make aggressive charges towards foes, punching through flesh and armor before they have the opportunity to return fire. It can also be, in turn, a great means of defense. When pinned down under cover – or having ducked behind a corner to allow the Master Chief's shields time to recharge – any Covenant soldier with the temerity to rush your position should meet with a venomous rebuke from your M90.

Alas, due to the high spread of its projectiles, the Shotgun is practically useless over medium and long distances. It should always be complemented by a secondary weapon that addresses this most salient of weaknesses. Additionally, the M90 is reloaded one cartridge at a time. During furious combat exchanges, it will feel as if you could grow a beard in the time it takes to load it up – and that's just for female Halo 2 players. Every opportunity that you get, hide and perform a manual reload. Note that you can interrupt the process of loading the Shotgun by firing at any time. You can then, as you might expect, use the remaining cartridges.

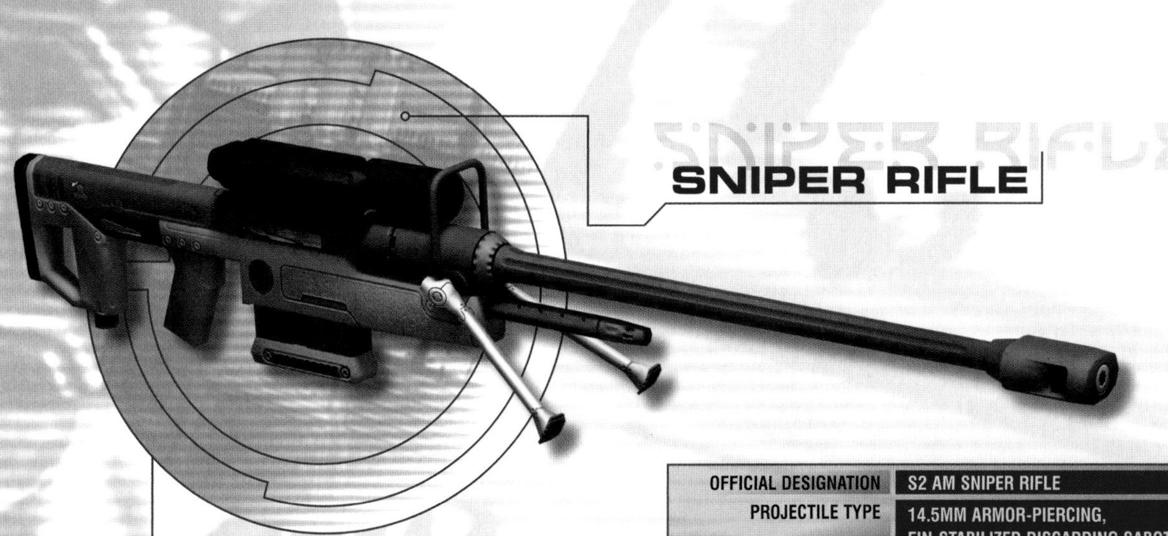

SNIPER RIFLE

OFFICIAL DESIGNATION	S2 AM SNIPER RIFLE
PROJECTILE TYPE	14.5MM ARMOR-PIERCING, FIN-STABILIZED DISCARDING SABOT
DUAL-WIELD	NO
DAMAGE	VERY HIGH
RANGE	VERY LONG (WITH SCOPE)
ACCURACY	VERY HIGH (WITH SCOPE)
RATE OF FIRE	LOW
AUTOFIRE CAPABILITY	MANUAL
MAGAZINE CAPACITY	4 BULLETS
AMMUNITION (ADDITIONAL)	20 (5 MAGAZINES)
RELOAD SPEED	SLOW
MELEE ATTACK	AVERAGE
SCOPE	5X, 10X

The Sniper Rifle is equipped with a scope that offers two levels of magnification: 5x and 10x. A lethal armament when equipped by a patient marksman, it enables you to pick off enemy forces from afar with impunity – unless, of course, your opponents have their own snipers. You should always, with the exception of Hunters, try to make headshots: these will inflict the maximum possible damage. Even the mightiest Elite can be dispatched with one or two such impacts. The sheer velocity of the 14.5mm rounds will pierce their energy shields.

Ammunition for the Sniper Rifle is rare: you should conserve it carefully, making every shot count. It is also a slow weapon to reload, so always try to have at least two bullets available at all times. During multiplayer matches, it takes a great deal of skill to keep an enemy in your sights at 10x zoom. Try finding a spot that will require your opponents to approach you directly. Finally, you should always have a good secondary weapon to equip if discovered, as the Sniper Rifle is not a wise choice at close range.

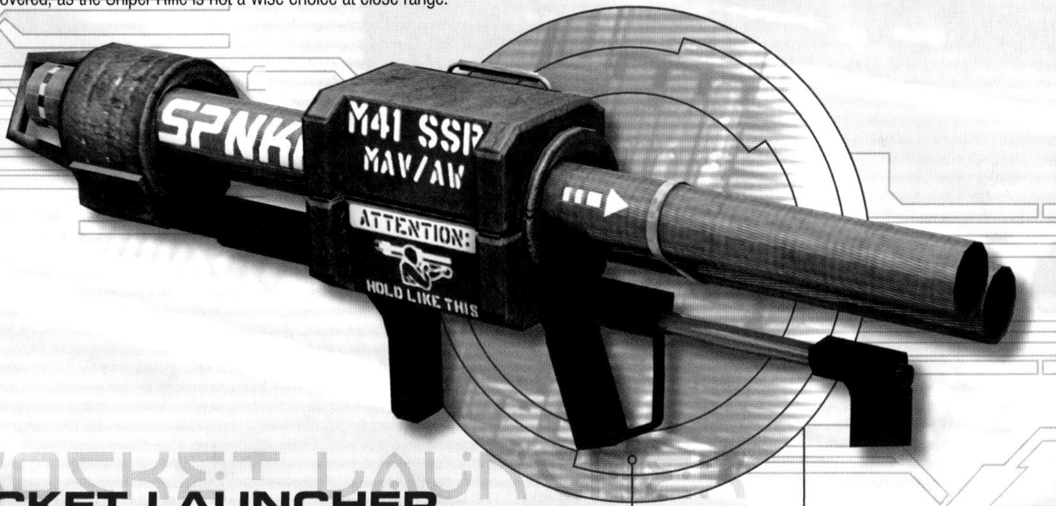

ROCKET LAUNCHER

OFFICIAL DESIGNATION	M41 SSR MAV/AW
PROJECTILES	102MM SHAPED-CHARGE, HIGH-EXPLOSIVE TRACKING ROCKETS
DUAL-WIELD	NO
DAMAGE	VERY HIGH
RANGE	LONG
ACCURACY	HIGH (CHARGED: HOMING)
RATE OF FIRE	LOW
AUTOFIRE CAPABILITY	MANUAL
MAGAZINE CAPACITY	2 ROCKETS
AMMUNITION (ADDITIONAL)	6 (3 MAGAZINES)
RELOAD SPEED	SLOW
MELEE ATTACK	SLOW
SCOPE	2X

The portable Rocket Launcher fires explosive missiles that can be fired with a homing capacity. Its basic point-and-launch functionality remains the same, though: just direct it and pull the trigger. Its rockets are slow and noisy; they give a distinct audio cue that will warn all nearby enemies of the incoming danger. As a rule of thumb, it's best to aim the SPNKr – as it is also known – at the feet of infantry targets or, where relevant, a nearby wall. Its rockets have a large blast radius and can be devastating when used against groups of assailants or, when brandished carelessly, the Master Chief himself. It is also, of course, an anti-vehicular weapon of great potency.

The Rocket Launcher has a homing feature. If you are targeting an enemy vehicle and your reticle is red, you can hold R to lock on. Once the trigger is depressed and held, a second crosshair will appear. Match it with the first crosshair, then release the trigger to fire a homing rocket.

If you want to cancel the targeting process, press B to switch to another weapon.

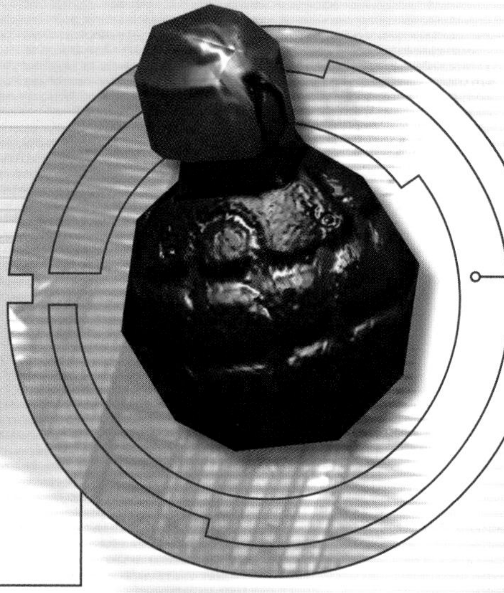

FRAG GRENADE

OFFICIAL DESIGNATION	M9 HE-DP FRAGMENTATION GRENADE
DAMAGE	HIGH
RANGE	LONG
AMMUNITION (ADDITIONAL)	4 GRENADES

As well as the titular effect of launching lethal high-speed shards when deployed, the Frag Grenade is also packed with high explosives. It is an anti-personnel weapon that can introduce chaos and carnage to even the most well-drilled group of infantry, and is also effective against vehicles. When thrown, its timer begins on first impact with a surface; detonation follows shortly afterwards. This feature makes it ideal for disrupting (or eliminating) well-armed or entrenched enemies from a position of relative safety. If you aim it at a wall, you can judge its bounce to drop it in the desired spot. It takes practice, but is a technique you should hone as soon as possible.

The Frag Grenade isn't as effective against shielded or especially hardy foes as it ideally could be – think Elites, Brutes and Hunters – so you should use a couple when facing strong enemies. A good tactic is to soften up a few assailants with a grenade, then follow up with a burst of automatic fire. It can also be deployed to facilitate a hasty retreat. Try throwing one at the ground while backpedaling or before turning to run. Following enemies will either be in for a nasty surprise or, alternatively, simply deterred from giving chase. This can afford you the luxury of a moment to, figuratively, catch your breath – and, of course, recharge your shields.

TURRETS

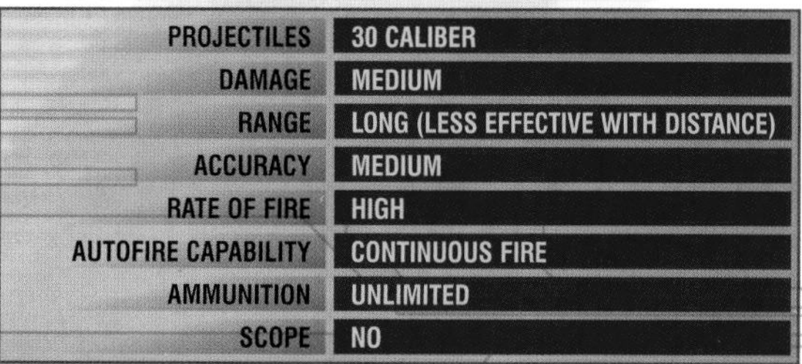

PROJECTILES	30 CALIBER
DAMAGE	MEDIUM
RANGE	LONG (LESS EFFECTIVE WITH DISTANCE)
ACCURACY	MEDIUM
RATE OF FIRE	HIGH
AUTOFIRE CAPABILITY	CONTINUOUS FIRE
AMMUNITION	UNLIMITED
SCOPE	NO

Manning a turret is not entirely dissimilar to using a vehicle: press ⓧ to take control, and repeat to relinquish it. There are two human and two Covenant turrets. The human turrets are high-powered machine guns found in two sizes – portable and fixed. Their two Covenant equivalents fire scorching blasts of superheated plasma. (The latter can also be found equipped with energy shields that protect their operator – see page 31 for more details.)

These gun emplacements are mounted in various positions throughout the Campaign game and appear in a number of multiplayer maps. While using one you are extremely exposed to enemy fire: you immediately become a target that all good commanders will order neutralized with haste. With a fixed field of fire, the effectiveness of a turret depends on the direction that your enemies are approaching from. Still, with unlimited ammunition at your disposal, they are very handy for thinning out an advancing force, and will even cause the drivers of vehicles no small amount of anguish.

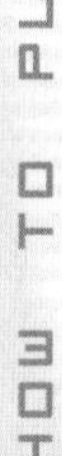

Covenant Weapons

Covenant weapons are, technologically at least, far more advanced than those used by their human foes. Since the events of Halo: Combat Evolved, they have introduced new armaments to their frontline troops. If the Master Chief is to triumph, he must learn to use their varied characteristics to his advantage – and so, therefore, must you.

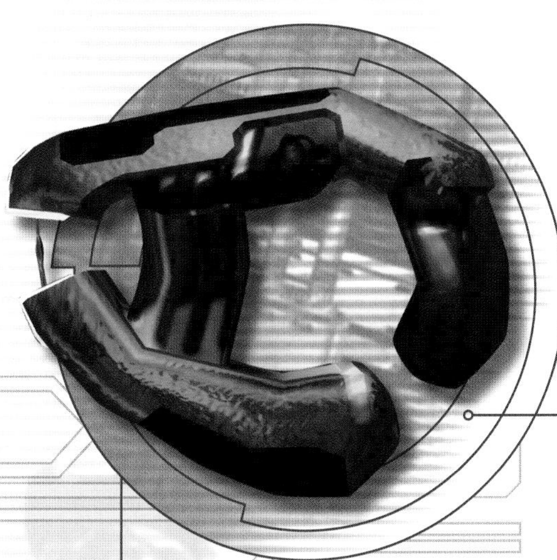

PLASMA PISTOL

AMMUNITION	SUPERHEATED PLASMA
DUAL-WIELD	YES
DAMAGE	LOW
RANGE	CLOSE
ACCURACY	MEDIUM (CHARGED: HOMING)
RATE OF FIRE	LOW (CHARGED SHOTS), MEDIUM (RAPID SINGLE SHOTS)
AUTOFIRE CAPABILITY	MANUAL
ENERGY PER ROUND	0.5% (CHARGED: 15%)
AMMUNITION (MAX.)	100%
OVERHEATING	AVERAGE
MELEE ATTACK	FAST
SCOPE	NO

As a rule, the Plasma Pistol is equipped by lower-ranking Covenant. Its basic form of fire is rather inefficient against large groups or stronger foes, even in a dual-wield configuration. Attempts to imitate automatic fire by pulling the trigger quickly will soon lead to it overheating. Why then, you might wonder, should you choose to use it at all?

The short answer is: charged shots. The Plasma Pistol's secondary fire mode is one of the most unique weapons in Halo 2. Keep the trigger depressed, and a large ball of plasma will form at the muzzle of the pistol. Point it at a shielded foe, then release to fire. This plasma ball has a limited homing capability and will, on contact, completely eliminate an enemy's shields – even Overshields (see page 172). Be warned: this process depletes the Plasma Pistol's battery by a massive 15%; moreover, the resultant projectile is rather slow. Still, when equipped with a UNSC weapon and Plasma Pistol, the Master Chief can slaughter individual Elites in little more time than it takes to dispatch a couple of common Grunts.

PLASMA RIFLE

AMMUNITION	SUPERHEATED PLASMA
DUAL-WIELD	YES
DAMAGE	MEDIUM
RANGE	CLOSE
ACCURACY	MEDIUM
RATE OF FIRE	HIGH
AUTOFIRE CAPABILITY	CONTINUOUS FIRE
ENERGY PER ROUND	0.5%
AMMUNITION (MAX)	100%
OVERHEATING	AFTER APPROXIMATELY 6% TO 7%
MELEE ATTACK	FAST
SCOPE	NO

The Plasma Rifle is another staple of Covenant troops, and is mainly brandished by Elites. It fires blue-white plasma at high velocity and can be fired automatically. It is inclined to overheat rapidly, however, and is limited by a built-in failsafe system that kicks in once its temperature reaches a certain level. As with all hand-held plasma weapons, you should always give it time to cool when necessary. Short, successive bursts of fire tend to work best, particularly against the energy shields of Jackals and Elites. When its battery is exhausted (or, optimally, when simply low), the Plasma Rifle should be replaced.

Brutes have their own version of this weapon: the Brute Plasma Rifle. Red in color and typified by a higher discharge rate, this variation is even more prone to overheating. Using its continuous rapid fire mode will activate its failsafe cooling module after expending a mere four percent of its battery.

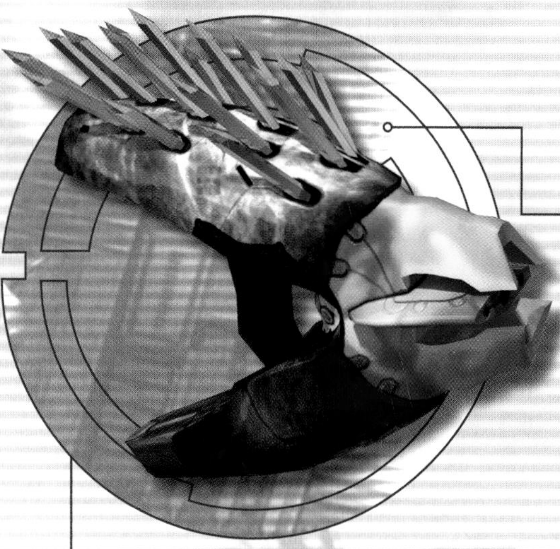

NEEDLER

AMMUNITION	CRYSTALLINE PROJECTILES
DUAL-WIELD	YES
DAMAGE	LOW TO HIGH
RANGE	LONG
ACCURACY	HOMING
RATE OF FIRE	HIGH
AUTOFIRE CAPABILITY	AUTOMATIC
MAGAZINE CAPACITY	30 NEEDLES
AMMUNITION (ADDITIONAL)	90 (3 MAGAZINES)
RELOAD SPEED	AVERAGE
MELEE ATTACK	FAST
SCOPE	NO

Many players did not realize the true function of the Needler in Halo: Combat Evolved until they attempted the Legendary skill setting. On the default Normal level, the Needler always appeared somehow underpowered: occasionally useful, yes, but invariably eclipsed by better options. Legendary veterans, though, christened it the "Elite Killer": a weapon specifically suited to dispatching the Master Chief's most intelligent assailants. For Halo 2, the Needler has been upgraded. It is now a far more effective weapon in general combat.

The Needler fires crystalline projectiles that home in on targets over long ranges and can bounce from obstacles – so even enemies behind cover can be hit in certain instances. These needles are imbedded on impact and, following a short pause, detonate in an oft-deadly explosion of shards. If there are at least eight needles in a target, the explosion can be as deadly as a grenade. This applies to the unfortunate pin-cushion in question, his nearby allies and, if you're not careful, the Master Chief and Marines as well. Dual-wielding two Needlers makes you a fearsome opponent, but don't overestimate its power: before its deadly missiles hit home and explode, your opponents are perfectly capable of returning fire. Some may also find that rapidly discharging Needler rounds limits their view of the battlefield.

CARBINE

AMMUNITION	ENERGY PROJECTILES
DUAL-WIELD	NO
DAMAGE	MEDIUM (WITH SCOPE: HIGH)
RANGE	MEDIUM (WITH SCOPE: HIGH)
ACCURACY	HIGH
RATE OF FIRE	LOW
AUTOFIRE CAPABILITY	MANUAL
MAGAZINE CAPACITY	18 PROJECTILES
AMMUNITION (ADDITIONAL)	72 (4 MAGAZINES)
RELOAD SPEED	AVERAGE
MELEE ATTACK	AVERAGE
SCOPE	2X

Compared with other examples of the Covenant's armory, the Carbine is somewhat unusual: its energy projectiles are fast and damaging, but its single-shot design seems strangely old-fashioned. Don't misgauge its strength. When used by a professional, the Carbine is an accurate weapon redolent of a cross between the Sniper Rifle and Battle Rifle.

With a 2x zoom facility, it's possible to make lethal headshots from afar. The Carbine's only real shortcomings are that your position is betrayed by a yellow trail with each shot, and that its rate of fire is rather slow. When you get your hands on one, be sure to take advantage of it.

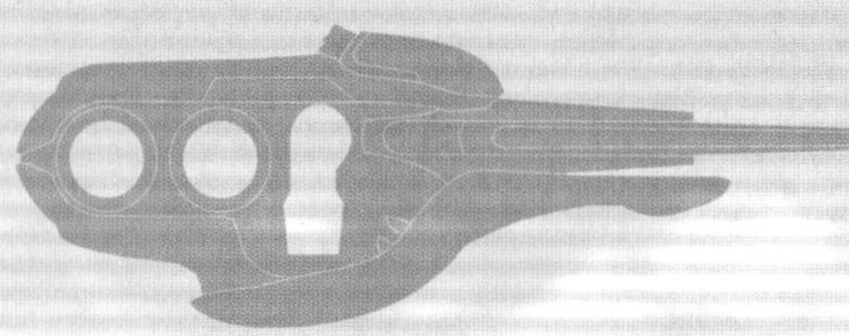

BEAM RIFLE

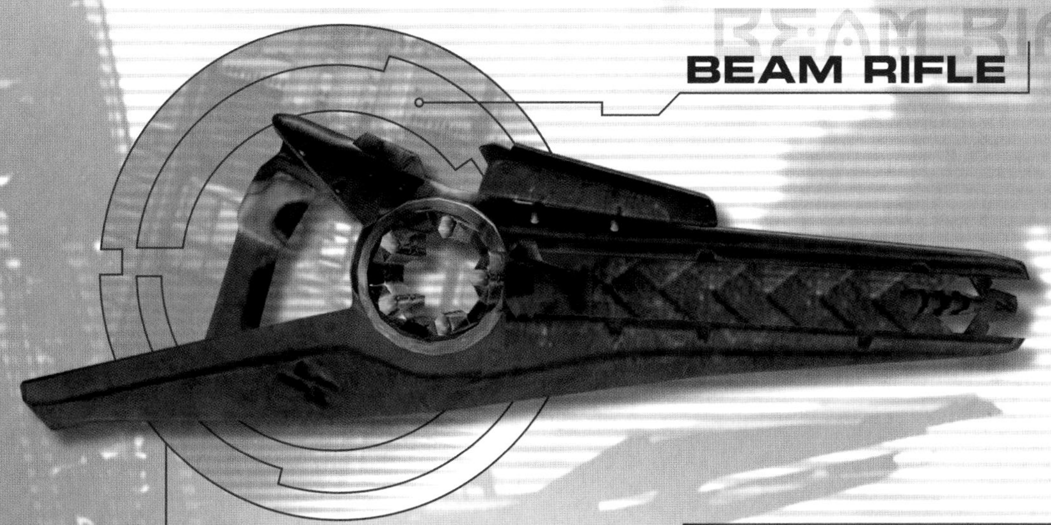

The Beam Rifle is the Covenant equivalent of the Sniper Rifle, with identical zoom capabilities and similar stopping power. Once again, it is best utilized to deliver headshots. The difference between the two is their ammunition type – in this case, an accelerated particle beam. The Beam Rifle has an integral battery that is limited to around twenty shots; like other Covenant weapons, it overheats with repeated fire.

Similarly, its weaknesses are identical to those of the Sniper Rifle. Principally, it is not a close-quarters weapon. Secondly, your position will be revealed by the tell-tale trail that accompanies each shot.

AMMUNITION	ACCELERATED PARTICLE BEAM
DUAL-WIELD	NO
DAMAGE	VERY HIGH
RANGE	VERY LONG (WITH SCOPE)
ACCURACY	VERY HIGH (WITH SCOPE)
RATE OF FIRE	LOW
AUTOFIRE CAPABILITY	MANUAL
ENERGY PER ROUND	5 TO 6%
AMMUNITION (MAX)	100%
OVERHEATING	AFTER TWO SHOTS IN QUICK SUCCESSION
MELEE ATTACK	MEDIUM
SCOPE	5X, 10X

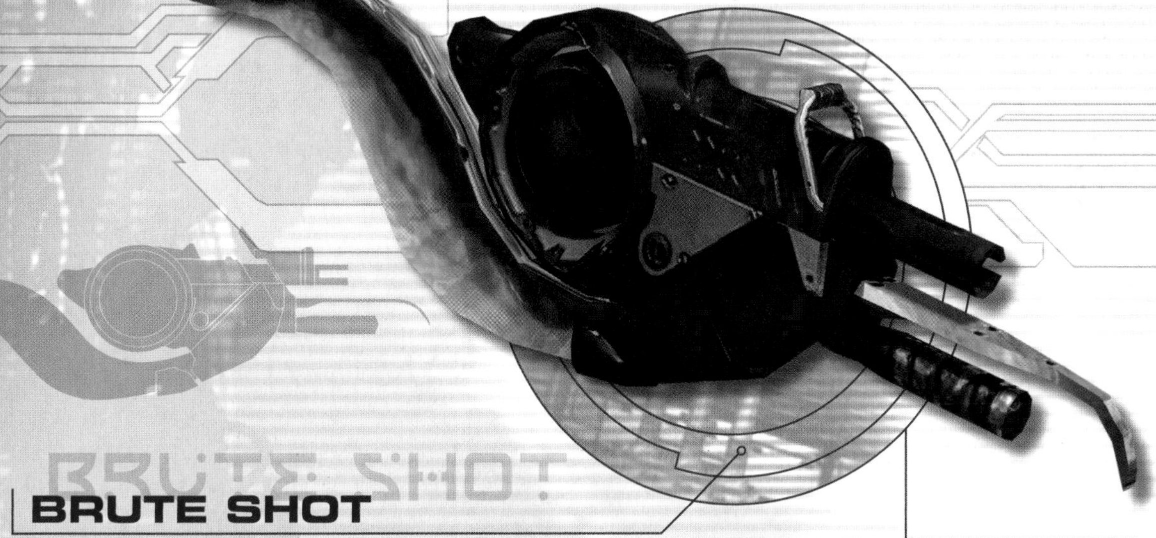

BRUTE SHOT

AMMUNITION	GRENADES
DUAL-WIELD	NO
DAMAGE	HIGH
RANGE	LONG
ACCURACY	MEDIUM
RATE OF FIRE	MEDIUM
AUTOFIRE CAPABILITY	MANUAL
MAGAZINE CAPACITY	4 GRENADES
AMMUNITION (ADDITIONAL)	12
RELOAD SPEED	SLOW
MELEE ATTACK	SLOW
SCOPE	NO

High-ranking Brutes generally favor the Brute Shot, a grenade launcher that allows them to pepper targets with high explosives. It will take a little time to judge the trajectory of each launch correctly. As the grenades lose height over distance, it can be frustratingly imprecise on first use. When you first find one, take the time to practice: once you pass a Checkpoint, try to hone your skills before using Revert to Last Checkpoint in the Pause Menu to resume.

The grenades fired by the Brute Shot explode immediately on contact with vehicles or soldiers. When they hit inanimate objects or architecture, though, they will bounce before detonating. Brutes use this feature to flush hidden targets from cover, a tactic you would do well to imitate. Lastly, the Brute Shot is equipped with a large blade for melee attacks. There is a right and a wrong end. Avoid the latter!

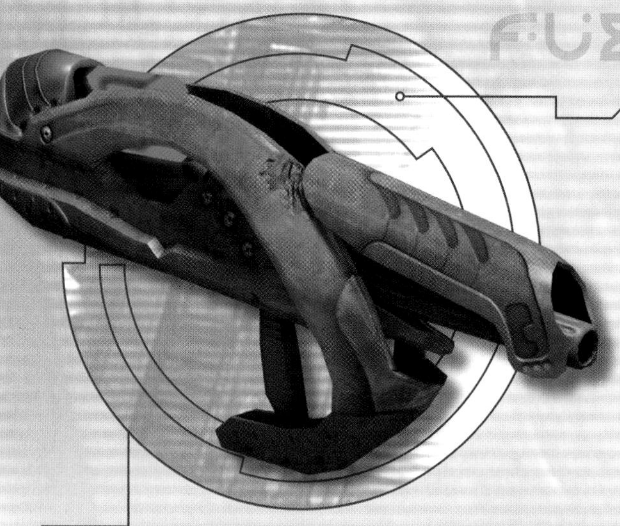

FUEL ROD CANNON

AMMUNITION	EXPLOSIVE ENERGY PROJECTILES
DUAL-WIELD	NO
DAMAGE	VERY HIGH
RANGE	FAR
ACCURACY	LOW
RATE OF FIRE	MEDIUM
AUTOFIRE CAPABILITY	MANUAL
MAGAZINE CAPACITY	5 EXPLOSIVE BULLETS
AMMUNITION (MAX.)	25 (5 MAGAZINES)
RELOAD SPEED	MEDIUM
MELEE ATTACK	SLOW
SCOPE	NO

The Fuel Rod Cannon is a cumbersome and unwieldy device that, when equipped, obscures your field of view. It fires energy projectiles on a deteriorating arc: remember to aim slightly higher than usual to hit distant targets. You should take the time to become accustomed to the ballistic trajectory that shots follow, and how they sink under the influence of gravity. You can use this characteristic to your advantage, hitting far targets that are on the other side of obstacles. Its green projectiles explode on impact, bathing the unfortunate souls at ground zero in an explosive wave. Even vehicles can't withstand a sustained barrage from the Fuel Rod Cannon.

Useful for bombarding distant enemy emplacements, this weapon should be fired with care. As with the Rocket Launcher, it's easy to damage yourself with ill-considered close-range shots or by hitting nearby scenery.

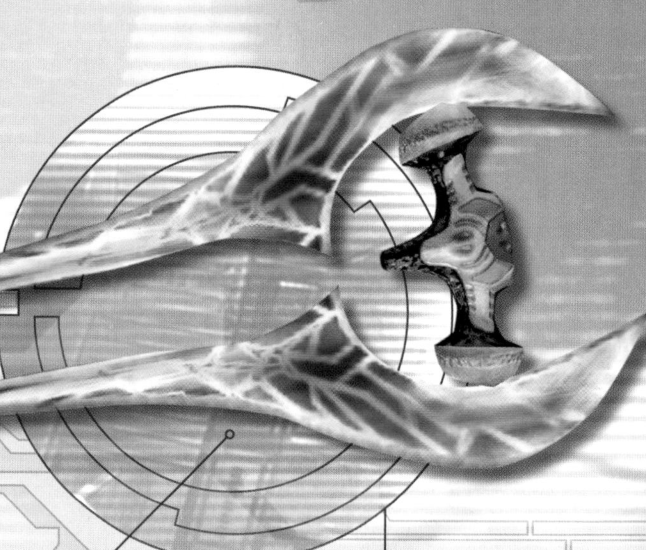

ENERGY SWORD

DAMAGE	HIGH
RANGE	CLOSE COMBAT
MELEE ATTACK	FAST

Senior Elites use this traditional weapon with pride in battle; its use by their lower orders or other Covenant is strictly forbidden. When utilized in close combat, the Energy Sword can slice through shields and armor with consummate ease. The trick, of course, is to get close enough to do so. Most opponents will be wise enough to fire and move backwards as you charge; at anything other than short distances, this is almost suicidal. That's why this weapon is very useful against the Flood.

The energy of this weapon is limited in Campaign mode: it begins at 100% and will decrease when used. Every deadly hit will reduce its power stocks by around 10%. The sword will disintegrate when its energy level reaches zero.

The Plasma Sword has a special attack that might surprise inexperienced opponents during multiplayer matches. After training your crosshair on your adversary for a moment, it will become red. When this happens, press R to execute a ferocious lunge.

PLASMA GRENADE

DAMAGE	HIGH
RANGE	LONG
AMMUNITION (MAX)	4 GRENADES

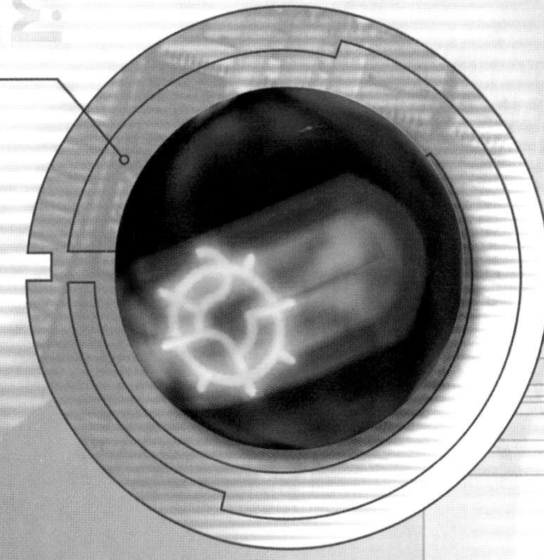

Don't make the mistake of assuming that Frag Grenades and Plasma Grenades are interchangeable: they both have very distinct characteristics. In the hands of a raw recruit, the Plasma Grenade is a dangerous weapon. When thrown by a master, however, they can be almost consistently lethal. This is due to their curious (and conditional) adhesive properties. If a Plasma Grenade hits a wall or generic piece of furniture, it will drop to the floor and explode after a short time. Should it hit a biological creature or vehicle, it will be irrevocably stuck until it explodes. Should you tag enemies with one of these, some may panic – and, ideally, run into their allies and envelop them in the ensuing explosion.

Of course, this works in reverse: if tagged, the Master Chief is history, although you might want to enjoy the satisfaction of taking the thrower with you if you can. A Plasma Grenade on the floor is much less dangerous. Its blast radius is not huge and can easily be avoided due to the delay before it explodes – if, that is, you actually see it land. If your opponents are throwing grenades, it's always a good idea to keep moving.

PLASMA CANNON

AMMUNITION	SUPERHEATED PLASMA
DAMAGE	MEDIUM
RANGE	LONG
ACCURACY	MEDIUM
RATE OF FIRE	HIGH
AUTOFIRE CAPABILITY	CONTINUOUS FIRE
AMMUNITION	UNLIMITED
SCOPE	NO

The Plasma Cannon is the Covenant version of the human Turret-MG. It has a high refire rate and – as Halo: Combat Evolved aficionados will attest – is a force to be feared. Usually operated by Grunts, the gunner is easily dispatched by a well aimed shot to the head. There are also Plasma Cannons that are equipped with shields. Reminiscent of those carried by Jackals, these energy-based barriers are impervious to UNSC bullets. You'll need to use Covenant plasma weaponry or grenades to destroy them.

The Weapons of the Forerunner

SENTINEL BEAM

AMMUNITION	UNKNOWN
DUAL-WIELD	NO
DAMAGE	MEDIUM
RANGE	LOW
ACCURACY	MEDIUM
RATE OF FIRE	CONTINUOUS
AUTOFIRE CAPABILITY	CONTINUOUS FIRE
ENERGY PER ROUND	1%
AMMUNITION (MAX)	100%
OVERHEATING	AFTER 19%
MELEE ATTACK	SLOW
SCOPE	NO

Precious little is known about this appropriated Forerunner technology. First encountered when used by the Sentinels on Installation 04, short bursts of it cause little damage, but sustained beam assaults are withering. The Sentinel Beam is best used by maintaining contact with a target until it expires or is destroyed. Once its power source is depleted, the weapon should be discarded. It is highly effective when used to strip shields – like those of, say, an Elite.

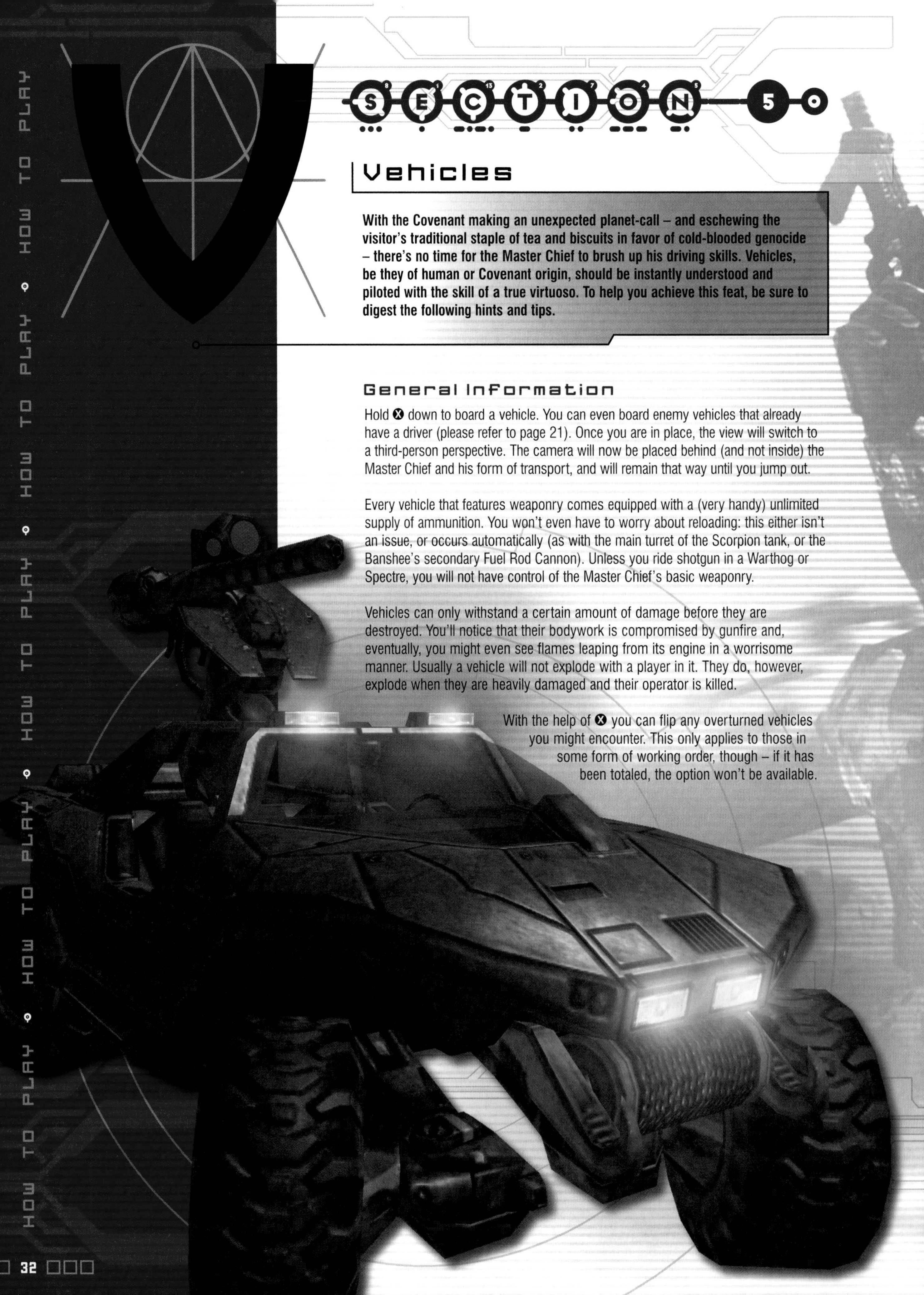

Vehicles

With the Covenant making an unexpected planet-call – and eschewing the visitor's traditional staple of tea and biscuits in favor of cold-blooded genocide – there's no time for the Master Chief to brush up his driving skills. Vehicles, be they of human or Covenant origin, should be instantly understood and piloted with the skill of a true virtuoso. To help you achieve this feat, be sure to digest the following hints and tips.

General Information

Hold ⓧ down to board a vehicle. You can even board enemy vehicles that already have a driver (please refer to page 21). Once you are in place, the view will switch to a third-person perspective. The camera will now be placed behind (and not inside) the Master Chief and his form of transport, and will remain that way until you jump out.

Every vehicle that features weaponry comes equipped with a (very handy) unlimited supply of ammunition. You won't even have to worry about reloading: this either isn't an issue, or occurs automatically (as with the main turret of the Scorpion tank, or the Banshee's secondary Fuel Rod Cannon). Unless you ride shotgun in a Warthog or Spectre, you will not have control of the Master Chief's basic weaponry.

Vehicles can only withstand a certain amount of damage before they are destroyed. You'll notice that their bodywork is compromised by gunfire and, eventually, you might even see flames leaping from its engine in a worrisome manner. Usually a vehicle will not explode with a player in it. They do, however, explode when they are heavily damaged and their operator is killed.

With the help of ⓧ you can flip any overturned vehicles you might encounter. This only applies to those in some form of working order, though – if it has been totaled, the option won't be available.

UNSC Transportation

Granted, when compared to Covenant tanks and attack craft – with their amazing antigravity systems – these human means of transportation might seem a little... well, archaic. They are, however, great fun to drive – and, if you have the skill, they can punch well beyond their weight.

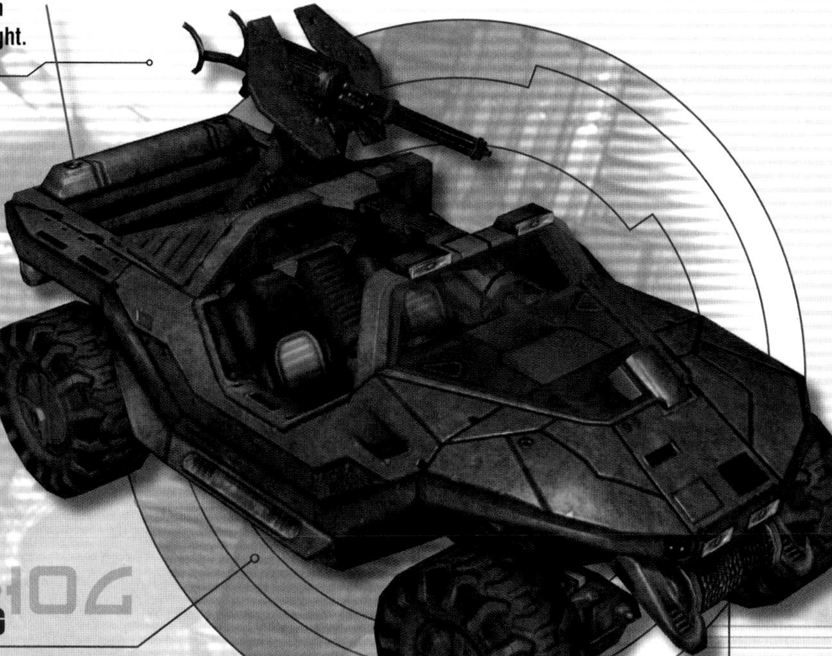

WARTHOG

VEHICLE TYPE	WEAPONRY
M12 WARTHOG LRV[1]	M41 LAAG[2]
M12G1 WARTHOG LAAV[3]	M68 GAUSS CANNON

1: LRV = light reconnaissance vehicle 2: LAAG = light anti-aircraft gun 3: LAAV = light anti-armor vehicle

Information: Informally (and affectionately) known simply as the Warthog, these light reconnaissance vehicles are a mainstay of UNSC deployments. Suitable for all terrains, it's surprisingly maneuverable for a means of conveyance that weighs in excess of three tons. In Halo 2 you will encounter two models.

The **M12 Warthog LRV** is armed with a three-barreled, 12.7mm machine gun known as the M41 LAAG. Capable of firing from 450 to 550 bullets per minute, it also has notable penetration power. This turret has been devastatingly effective in countless deployments against other vehicles and, in particular, against infantry.

The M68 Gauss Cannon of the **M12G1 Warthog LAAV** fires 25mm projectiles. Its asynchronous linear induction motor produces a bipolar magnetic field to fire the projectiles at hyper-sonic velocity. It can penetrate armor and can even stop tanks, but its low rate of fire makes it largely unsuitable for sorties against large groups of enemy infantry. It does work quite well against single Covenant soldiers, though.

The Warthog can – and ideally should – hold a crew of three: the driver, an armed passenger, and an operator for its fixed gun. You can enter all three positions: the driver's seat on the left, ride shotgun on the right, and grab the gunner's spot at the rear. Once you are in the Warthog you will be nicely protected – unless, of course, you are playing on the Heroic or Legendary skill levels...

Driver: You cannot use weapons while behind the wheel of the Warthog. Controlling it will take a little practice, but Halo veterans will rejoice at the news that they are now much easier to drive. Press the left thumbstick up to accelerate (your direction is indicated by a helpful blue marker) and down to brake or reverse; the right thumbstick controls both your steering and view angle. You can brake with Ⓐ, while L will allow you to use the emergency brake to perform power slides at high speed. Honk the horn with R to signal to Marines that they should hop aboard.

	CONTROLLING THE WARTHOG (DRIVER)
L	ACCELERATE, BRAKE/REVERSE
R	VIEW/STEER
Ⓐ	BRAKE
R	HORN
L	E-BRAKE

Passenger: Riding shotgun, you can shoot with your own weapons. Aim with the right thumbstick. As usual, you fire with R and swap available firearms by pressing Ⓨ.

Gunner: You control the ordnance mounted on the back of the vehicle. Use the right thumbstick to pivot the weapon in the desired direction and R to fire. The M41 LAAG has full automatic fire, but the Gauss Cannon fires single rounds.

Tips:

- The Warthog is, even without a complement of gunners, a deadly weapon: just run over your enemies.

- If you are finding it difficult to drive the Warthog, take the time to practice on a Custom Game in multiplayer mode. Naturally, you should be sure to pick a level that actually features one – Zanzibar should suffice. Whether you need to refine your skills or not, it's just nice to get the opportunity to drive a Warthog without the air being alive with gunfire.

- In multiplayer mode, you can steal vehicles from other teams. For example, if someone is pinning down your colleagues with a Warthog machine gun, you could sneak up, jump behind the wheel and drive it away. Feel free to experiment.

SCORPION

Information: The sturdy M808B Scorpion MBT (MBT: Main Battle Tank) is an armored track vehicle for use during planetary combat. Its prime function is to provide anti-vehicular support – the destruction of light and heavy vehicles -- but it can lay waste to infantry. The Scorpion is equipped with two weapons systems:

- Primary: 90mm high velocity shell (large, single projectile cannon), anti-vehicle
- Secondary: 7.62mm AP-T (Armor Piercing Tracer), anti-personnel

Its special ceramic-titanium armor renders the Scorpion almost invulnerable to the effects of light to medium-heavy weapons. The driver is well protected in the center of the vehicle.

Crew and Controls: While controlling the Scorpion you will also act as its gunner. You can enter the vehicle when the onscreen prompt to press Ⓧ appears. The left thumbstick controls your acceleration. The right thumbstick allows you to turn the camera and pitch it up and down. The Scorpion automatically turns to the direction the camera is pointing when you accelerate.

CONTROLLING THE SCORPION (DRIVER)	
Ⓛ	MOVE VEHICLE
Ⓡ	MOVE ANGLE OF VIEW/TURRET
R	FIRE MAIN CANNON
L	FIRE MACHINE GUN

Press R to fire the main cannon. It takes a short time for the automatic reload system to prepare the next shell, so pick your shots carefully. L fires your secondary weapon, a machine gun. It has continuous fire, and should be used against infantry and light vehicles. Both weapons are stocked with an infinite supply of ammunition, so don't be shy to employ either trigger.

Tips:

- The Scorpion may be slow, but it's an inexorable force in most situations. The only real weakness of this adamantine weapons platform is that it has a blind spot surrounding it: if enemies are too close to the tank, you won't be able to get a clear shot. As the Scorpion is very slow, it is quite difficult to run enemies over. You need a considerable amount of speed to make a kill – and that's one thing that this tank doesn't have…

- In the Campaign, Marines can sometimes hitch a ride on the sides of the Scorpion. As with passengers riding shotgun in the Warthog, they can employ their own weapons and engage nearby infantry. This allows you to deal with more pressing issues. Be mindful that they have little or no cover: an incoming Fuel Rod Cannon blast, for example, can be fatal for your allies. Protect your passengers by moving at all times, or by taking cover when facing a larger force.

- You'll need powerful armaments to eliminate an enemy-controlled Scorpion: either an equivalent vehicle or a Rocket Launcher, for example. There is another option, though. Either make a mad dash towards it or, better still, sneak up on your armored adversary. Now jump on the tank and attack the driver with melee attacks. As soon as you've broken the hatch, you could also plant a grenade inside the tank. The only option your opponent has is to leave the vehicle and defend himself in person.

PELICAN

The Pelican is a UNSC dropship used to deliver and extract combat units. It is also used to deliver vehicles. You won't have the opportunity to pilot this craft yourself, but you will find yourself in the passenger compartment from time to time. You'll also learn to appreciate its sporadic visits. When it arrives it's either picking you up, or making an important delivery.

Covenant vehicles are designed for rapid conquest of enemy territory. Powered by Boosted Gravity Propulsion Drives they are, like-for-like, blessed with greater maneuverability than their UNSC counterparts.

GHOST

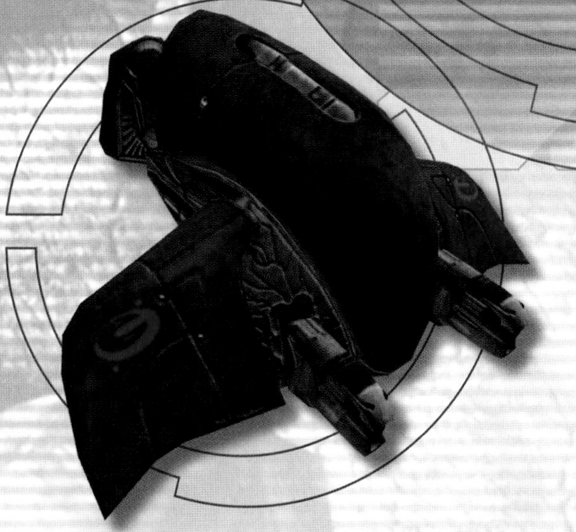

CONTROLLING THE GHOST	
L	MOVE VEHICLE FORWARDS/BACKWARDS, STRAFE LEFT OR RIGHT
R	ADJUST ELEVATION OF FIRE, STEER LEFT AND RIGHT
R	FIRE WEAPONS
L	BOOST
A	AIRBRAKE

Information: The Ghost is a light vehicle deployed for speedy reconnaissance of enemy territory, or to provide fire support for infantry or larger vehicles during combat. It hovers on a fixed elevation just above the ground and, in the hands of an able pilot, is capable of incredible speeds and daredevil jumps over certain low pieces of scenery. It's not the most hardy craft you'll find on the battlefield, but you can cause no end of chaos with its Twin Plasma Cannon. The Ghost can redirect power from its weapons to its engines to provide a short-term boost of speed, but doing so will disable its weaponry. You can enter a Ghost from just behind its wings.

Crew and Controls: Controlling the Ghost is similar to moving the Master Chief in principle, if not exactly in practice: the difference is the greater momentum that its weight and speed entail. Move the vehicle forward, backward and strafe left and right with the left thumbstick. The horizontal axis of the right thumbstick turns the craft and its vertical axis allows you fire, to a limited extent, at enemies either above or below your position. The Ghost's onboard weapons will always point in the direction it is facing. Using A will allow you – with some practice and a nice feel for timing – to do some pretty stunts, because the airbrake lifts the front end of the vehicle slightly.

Tips:

- The Ghost is the fastest vehicle in Halo 2. It's an ideal means of transportation when you need to cross large distances in a hurry.

- From the rear, the driver of a Ghost is largely unprotected; its bonnet and wings offer limited cover at the front of the vehicle. It's also easy to hijack a Ghost if its pilot is foolish enough to slow down.

- The Ghost's primary strengths are its speed and agility. It's not a great choice if you're facing an armored vehicle like a Scorpion, but it's an effective anti-infantry weapon.

- Its Dual Plasma Cannons operate immaculately during continuous fire – unlike hand-held Covenant plasma weaponry, they will not overheat. Don't forget that you can fire above and below your position. An accomplished Ghost driver can even take out an incautiously-piloted Banshee.

BANSHEE

Information: The Banshee is the only vehicle in Halo 2 to offer you the (almost) boundless freedom of flight. It's a flexible craft during air-to-air battles, but the Covenant generally use it to bombard ground troops. The Banshee has two weapons, both of which are fired in the direction you are facing. The primary mode of attack is a Twin Plasma Cannon. Your secondary option is a Fuel Rod Cannon. Both have an infinite supply of ammunition, although the Fuel Rod Cannon – read an overview on page 30 – has a slow fire rate. You can hop into a Banshee via the opening at its rear.

CONTROLLING THE BANSHEE	
L↑	ACCELERATE
L↓	DECELERATE, LIMITED HOVER ABILITY
←L→	MOVE TO THE LEFT/RIGHT
R	CHANGE VIEW/DIRECTION, STEER TO THE LEFT, RIGHT, UP AND DOWN
R	FIRE TWIN PLASMA CANNON
L	BOOST
B	FIRE FUEL ROD CANNON
A+L↑	LOOP
A+←L→	BARREL ROLL/TWIST TO THE LEFT OR RIGHT

Crew and controls: The driver lies in a cockpit which closes to offer limited protection from enemy fire. Don't rely on the Banshee's weak armor, though – you really should dodge incoming attacks. Press A and L down to perform a loop, or press A and push L to the left or right to make a barrel roll.

The Banshee moves at all times: it cannot actually hover in a precise spot. The only way to stay in one general position is to press L downwards, but the craft will begin to sink towards the ground. As with the Ghost, this revised Banshee can briefly sacrifice its weapons in favor of a quick burst of speed if you press L. Both weapons and the tricks possible with A will be unavailable while using this function.

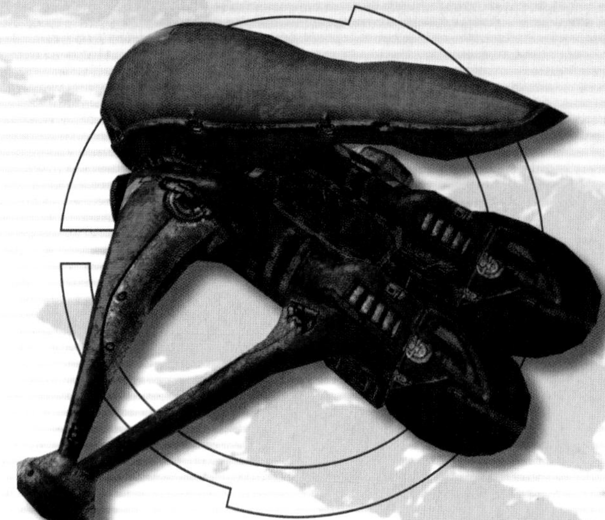

Tips:

- The sheer maneuverability of the Banshee makes it unique. It is reasonably fast, but cannot withstand much damage before it explodes. Weapons with a high fire rate are a threat, as are Scorpion cannons and Rocket Launchers when wielded by dead-eyed adversaries.

- Don't make frontal attacks: you're vulnerable to return fire when you do, and the Banshee really doesn't have the armor to support such foolhardy sorties. Try to catch enemies by surprise, and vary your flight pattern. The Banshee is also a great ranged weapon. Subjecting your enemies to a bombardment from your Fuel Rod Cannon may not be the most exhilarating method of attack, but it works.

- You can exit the Banshee at any time, but be sure not to press X while hundreds of feet above the ground!

WRAITH

CONTROLLING THE WRAITH	
L (stick)	MOVE VEHICLE FORWARD/BACKWARD, STRAFE LEFT/RIGHT
R (stick)	CHANGE VIEW, STEER TO THE LEFT/RIGHT
R	FIRE WEAPON
L	BOOST

Information: The Wraith is the Covenant's battle tank. Its heavy armor makes it an extremely difficult target to destroy, but this toughness comes at a price: the enormous weight supported by its Boosted Gravity Propulsion Drive makes it very slow. A Wraith is armed with a plasma mortar of great destructive power. It also has two auto-firing plasma cannons mounted on each wing, which the player can't control – they'll shoot automatically at any enemy in range. You'll find the entrance on the top of the tank.

Crew and Controls: As with the Scorpion, a Wraith pilot controls both movement and its cannon, but it differs in that it cannot transport infantry. Generally, controlling a Wraith is akin to driving a morbidly obese Ghost – it's very slow indeed. You can move forward, backward and strafe with L (stick). R (stick) adjusts the tank's direction and alters the elevation of its main cannon. Each blast from the latter is slow but fantastically powerful on impact. As with the Scorpion's cannon, you will have to wait for a few moments between shots.

When you need to hurry to a specific position, press L for a very brief speed increase. The Wraith's propulsion system will need several seconds to recharge before you can use it again.

Tips:

- Two small automatic weapons on the Wraith's hood offer additional protection against nearby infantry. If, however, you manage to evade these and jump on the vehicle, you can assault the driver with melee attacks.

- The boost capability of the Wraith is handy for running pedestrians over.

- As soon as you've destroyed the cover of the driver's cabin, you can throw a grenade inside. Be sure to jump off immediately to avoid being caught in the resultant explosion.

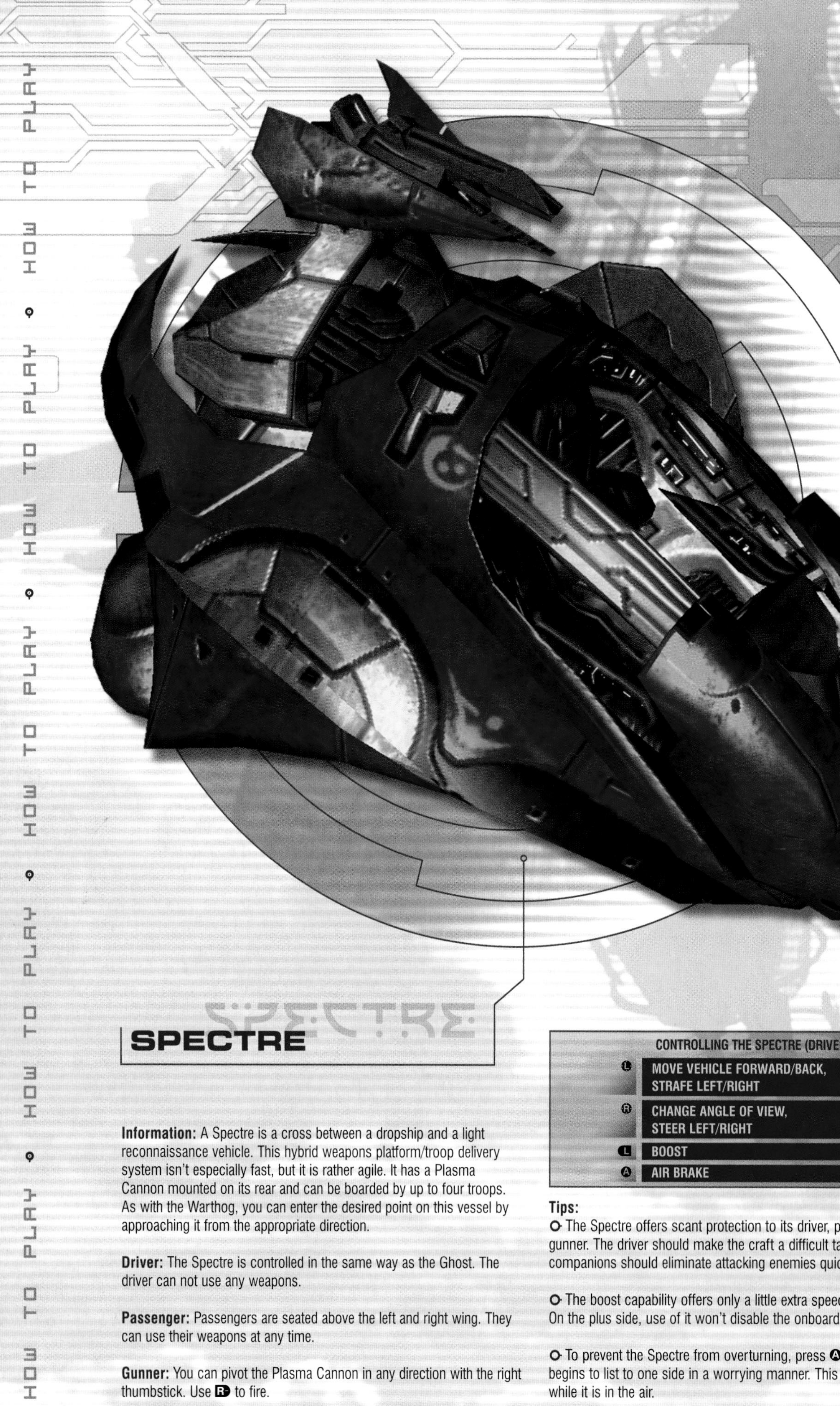

SPECTRE

Information: A Spectre is a cross between a dropship and a light reconnaissance vehicle. This hybrid weapons platform/troop delivery system isn't especially fast, but it is rather agile. It has a Plasma Cannon mounted on its rear and can be boarded by up to four troops. As with the Warthog, you can enter the desired point on this vessel by approaching it from the appropriate direction.

Driver: The Spectre is controlled in the same way as the Ghost. The driver can not use any weapons.

Passenger: Passengers are seated above the left and right wing. They can use their weapons at any time.

Gunner: You can pivot the Plasma Cannon in any direction with the right thumbstick. Use R to fire.

CONTROLLING THE SPECTRE (DRIVER)	
L	MOVE VEHICLE FORWARD/BACK, STRAFE LEFT/RIGHT
R	CHANGE ANGLE OF VIEW, STEER LEFT/RIGHT
L	BOOST
A	AIR BRAKE

Tips:

- The Spectre offers scant protection to its driver, passengers and gunner. The driver should make the craft a difficult target at all times. His companions should eliminate attacking enemies quickly and efficiently.

- The boost capability offers only a little extra speed when activated. On the plus side, use of it won't disable the onboard cannon.

- To prevent the Spectre from overturning, press A when the vehicle begins to list to one side in a worrying manner. This way, you stabilize it while it is in the air.

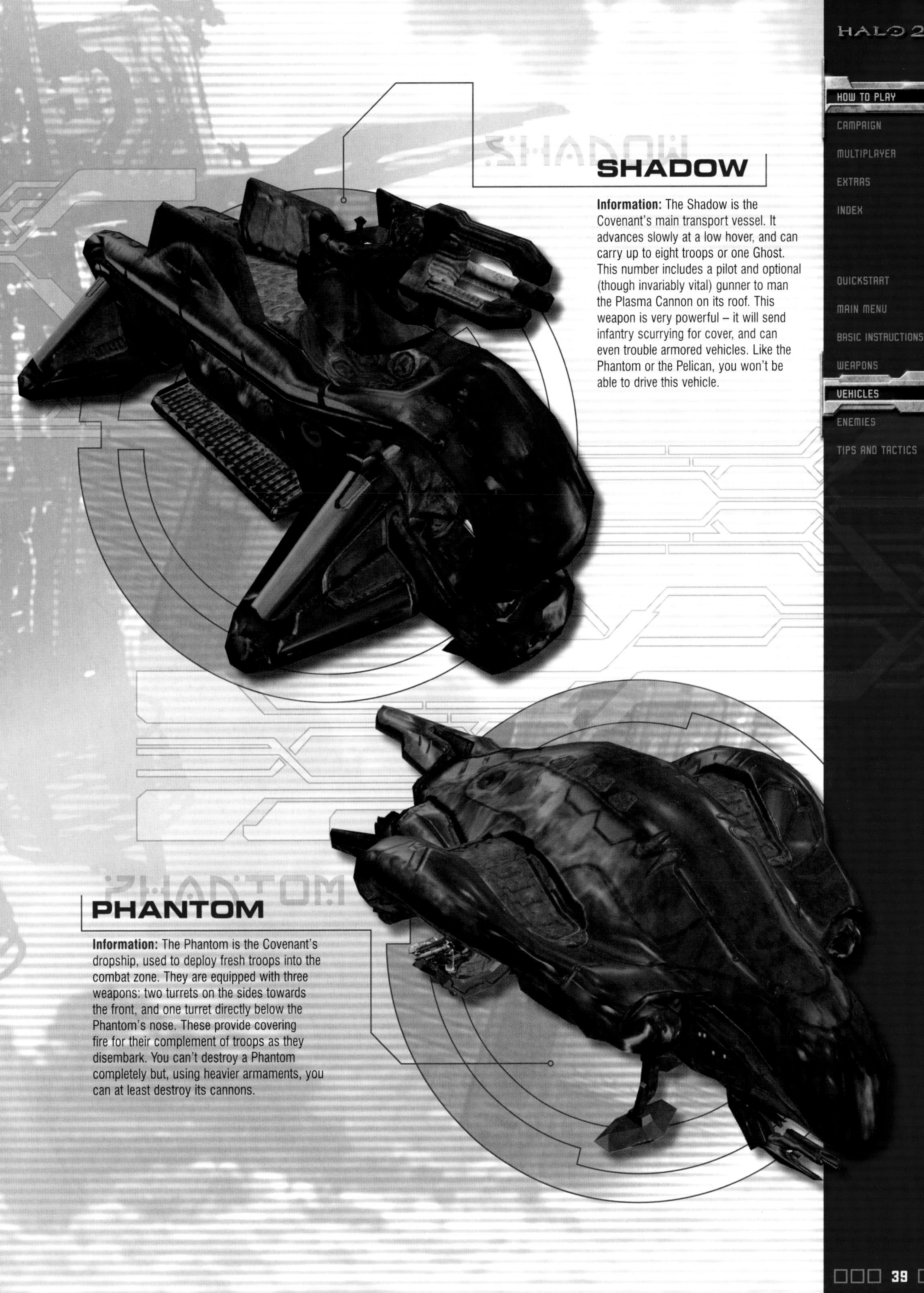

SHADOW

Information: The Shadow is the Covenant's main transport vessel. It advances slowly at a low hover, and can carry up to eight troops or one Ghost. This number includes a pilot and optional (though invariably vital) gunner to man the Plasma Cannon on its roof. This weapon is very powerful – it will send infantry scurrying for cover, and can even trouble armored vehicles. Like the Phantom or the Pelican, you won't be able to drive this vehicle.

PHANTOM

Information: The Phantom is the Covenant's dropship, used to deploy fresh troops into the combat zone. They are equipped with three weapons: two turrets on the sides towards the front, and one turret directly below the Phantom's nose. These provide covering fire for their complement of troops as they disembark. You can't destroy a Phantom completely but, using heavier armaments, you can at least destroy its cannons.

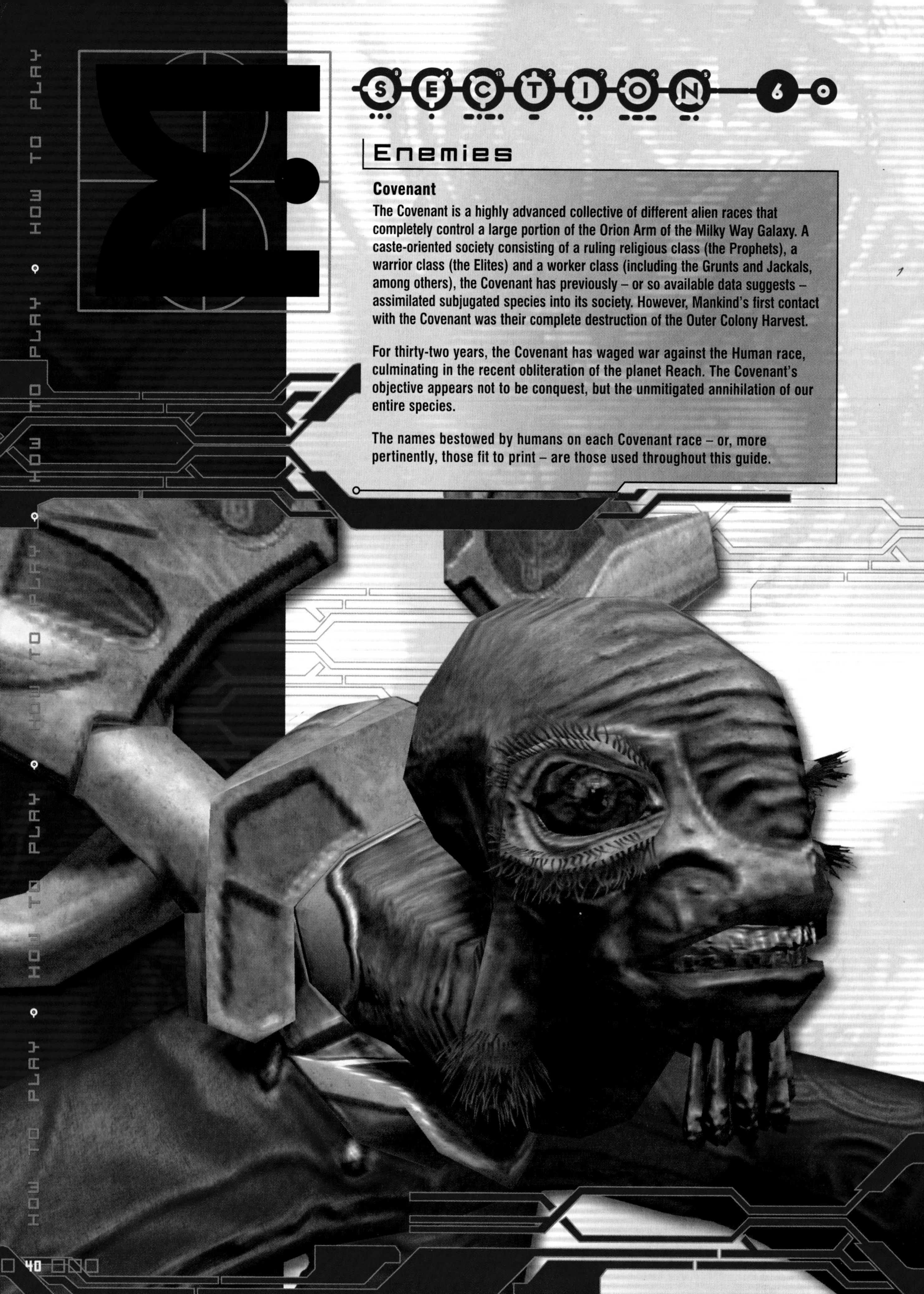

SECTION 6

Enemies

Covenant

The Covenant is a highly advanced collective of different alien races that completely control a large portion of the Orion Arm of the Milky Way Galaxy. A caste-oriented society consisting of a ruling religious class (the Prophets), a warrior class (the Elites) and a worker class (including the Grunts and Jackals, among others), the Covenant has previously – or so available data suggests – assimilated subjugated species into its society. However, Mankind's first contact with the Covenant was their complete destruction of the Outer Colony Harvest.

For thirty-two years, the Covenant has waged war against the Human race, culminating in the recent obliteration of the planet Reach. The Covenant's objective appears not to be conquest, but the unmitigated annihilation of our entire species.

The names bestowed by humans on each Covenant race – or, more pertinently, those fit to print – are those used throughout this guide.

GRUNT

Grunts are the lowliest beings in the Covenant hierarchy. Relying on giant rebreather packs to provide them with a methane atmosphere, these creatures are prone to frequent lapses in vigilance when not strictly policed by a nearby Elite commander. Lacking the protection of strong armor or shield technology, they are particularly vulnerable to ballistic weaponry.

Essentially cannon fodder – yet dangerous when attacking in groups, particularly on higher difficulty levels – Grunts can be dispatched with a few body shots, a solitary bullet to the head or a forceful melee attack. As you progress through Halo 2, you will encounter different varieties of Grunts. Red Major Grunts, for example, can sustain greater damage than their yellow Minor Grunt equivalents.

COVENANT NAME	UNGGOY
PREFERRED WEAPONS	PLASMA PISTOL, NEEDLER, PLASMA GRENADE
TYPES	MINOR GRUNTS (YELLOW), MAJOR GRUNTS (RED), GUNNER (GREEN), SPECOPS (BLACK)

TIPS

- The use of fixed gun emplacements is a Grunt specialty. Using one, this otherwise weak enemy can lay waste to an attacking force unless quickly terminated. You should remove their threat immediately. A shot to the head will suffice, but bear in mind that other Grunts may take a slain comrade's place.

- Be mindful that many Grunts will use Plasma Grenades. In Halo: Combat Evolved, they would often announce the imminent use of an explosive with a warning to their allies. Lately, though, it appears that Grunts have discovered the value of discretion.

- Grunts are usually led by at least one Elite. If their leaders are killed during a battle, they will often flee, with groups scattering in arbitrary directions. Take advantage of this while you can – with time, even the most cowardly Grunt will regain a degree of composure.

- If a Grunt is asleep on duty, it feels safe and secure. You can safely assume that more of its kind are not far away and are probably accompanied by stronger Covenant species. You should kill sleeping Grunts with a silent melee attack.

JACKALS

Jackals, like Grunts, are members of the Covenant worker class. The differing abilities of both species means that they complement each other well during battles, and will often be found together. The speed, equipment and comparatively greater ferocity of the Jackals make them more dangerous foes than Grunts. Their most common varieties carry a portable energy shield that is impervious to all ballistic fire (or, to be more specific, those without an incendiary payload – their shields are no match for well-placed missiles).

Some Jackals carry a Beam Rifle. These snipers can fire with deadly precision over great distances, but they do not carry energy shields. This is a good thing – you can take this type of Jackal down with a few shots.

TIPS

- Grenades – even the sticky Plasma Grenade – will bounce from a Jackal's shields. When confronted by a pack of these awkward antagonists, try to throw your explosive in an arc that will land it just behind them.

- With the exception of the rocket, Jackal shields are impervious to Marine firearms. Covenant plasma weaponry is a different matter entirely. A charged Plasma Pistol shot or a Plasma Rifle will work very well indeed.

- Without a shield, a Jackal is physically weak and can be killed with a few shots at most or a melee attack. The latter is always a useful technique at close quarters: shield or no shield, the frail Jackal is no match for a rifle butt to the head.

- The Jackal's shield has a small but noticeable embrasure that its user fires through. You can (and should) exploit this opening with a well-placed shot.

COVENANT NAME	KIG-YAR
PREFERRED WEAPONS	PLASMA PISTOL, BEAM RIFLE
TYPES	MINOR JACKAL (GREEN SHIELD), MAJOR JACKAL (ORANGE SHIELD), SNIPER (NO SHIELD)

ELITES

COVENANT NAME	SANGHEILI
PREFERRED WEAPONS	PLASMA RIFLE, PLASMA GRENADE, ENERGY SWORD
TYPES	MINOR ELITE (BLUE), MAJOR ELITE (RED), STEALTH ELITE (GREY), SPECOPS (BLACK), RANGER (JETPACK), ZEALOT (GOLDEN), HONOR GUARD

The Elites are a proud warrior race, subservient only to the Prophets they traditionally protect with formidable, Energy Sword-wielding Honor Guards. Masters of combat, they can use a wide variety of weapons. Even the most lowly, subordinate Elite can be a mighty adversary.

With their enormous strength and quick reflexes, Elites are physically superior to humans in every respect; they are also cunning tacticians, keen shots and clinically brutal in close-range melee encounters. Their stylized battle armor is very tough, and their entire bodies are covered with energy shields that can regenerate in a short period of time. It would not be wildly erroneous to compare this race (and its capabilities) with the SPARTAN-II super-soldiers – of which, the Master Chief is the only known survivor.

Elites are deployed in all roles: they are foot soldiers, commanders, drivers and pilots. There are many different types. All are dangerous. Some carry Energy Swords, some are equipped with stealth equipment, and others use rocket packs and specialist plated battle suits that allow them to fight even in the vacuum of space. The Elite should never be underestimated.

TIPS

- The color of its armor will indicate the rank of an Elite. In our parlance, they are promoted in accordance with the number of humans they have killed. Once you encounter each type and memorize the color scheme, you will know to approach the higher echelons of the Elite hierarchy with caution.

- Elites are highly intelligent, and demonstrate it with a good combination of offensive and defensive strategies. When their shields are depleted, they will attempt to find cover to allow them time to replenish. For this reason, wounding an Elite is never enough: you should continue to fire until you see it fall.

- Charged Plasma Pistol shots can dispel an Elite's shield immediately. Other weapons take more time, particular human firearms. When its shield is depleted, an Elite will often utter an angry cry.

- You can easily penetrate an Elite's shield with a Sniper Rifle. Always attempt to make a headshot: these inflict the most damage and will lead to a greater number of fatalities.

- The Elite is an accomplished melee fighter. When you inflict a physical blow, don't be surprised to reel as it reciprocates in kind. To avoid these assaults, step back to evade the counterattack, then move closer to hit it again. If an Elite is unaware of your presence, a blow to the back of its head will be a killing strike.

DRONES

The Drones, like the Brutes (see page 46), are a Covenant species that were not found in Halo: Combat Evolved. These sentient insects are about the size of a Grunt and have little apparent intelligence or personality, but they do have hard shells and the ability to fly. Drones are fast airborne marksmen, and their agility makes them difficult to hit.

Used in conjunction with other Covenant forces, Drones make aerial assaults that are hard to withstand. Not only does their presence reduce available cover, they are a sufficient danger in their own right when working as a group. They can coordinate attacks with frightening efficiency. As with Grunts, isolated Drones are easy to deal with.

COVENANT NAME	YANME'E
PREFERRED WEAPONS	PLASMA PISTOL, NEEDLER
TYPES	--

TIPS

- Drones do not have shields and are easily damaged – if, that is, you can keep them in your sights. Their agility can make them awkward opponents to contend with, especially when there are ground-based foes closing in on your position.

- Information suggests that this species survives (and, indeed, is most comfortable) in outer space. Gravity greatly reduces the effectiveness of their wings; Drones need to rest by landing on walls and the ground. This is a strategic shortcoming that you should exploit whenever you can.

- When fighting Drones, clever use of cover is a necessity. A wall or roof – and optimally, both – can reduce the angles from which they can attack. Automatic weapons should be your first choice when fighting groups of Drones. The Needler, with its homing ammunition, is always a good option.

HUNTERS

Hunters are heavily-armored collectives of worm-like organisms united under a common consciousness. They always attack in pairs. New intelligence suggests that these creatures mate early and form lifelong partnerships. This explains why a Hunter becomes so enraged when its mate is slain – it will roar, charge towards the enemy responsible, attack inanimate objects and may even vent its frustrations on the lower orders of its Covenant allies. These living tanks are deployed as shock troops, their speed and incredible strength scattering opposing forces like ninepins.

Hunters wear practically impenetrable armor made from an unknown substance. These suits include an integrated Fuel Rod Cannon, a mortar-style plasma weapon that can mean trouble for even a mighty Scorpion tank. Hunters use this weapon at long to middle ranges, but will switch to melee attacks at close quarters.

COVENANT NAME	LEKGOLO
PREFERRED WEAPONS	FUEL ROD CANNON
TYPES	--

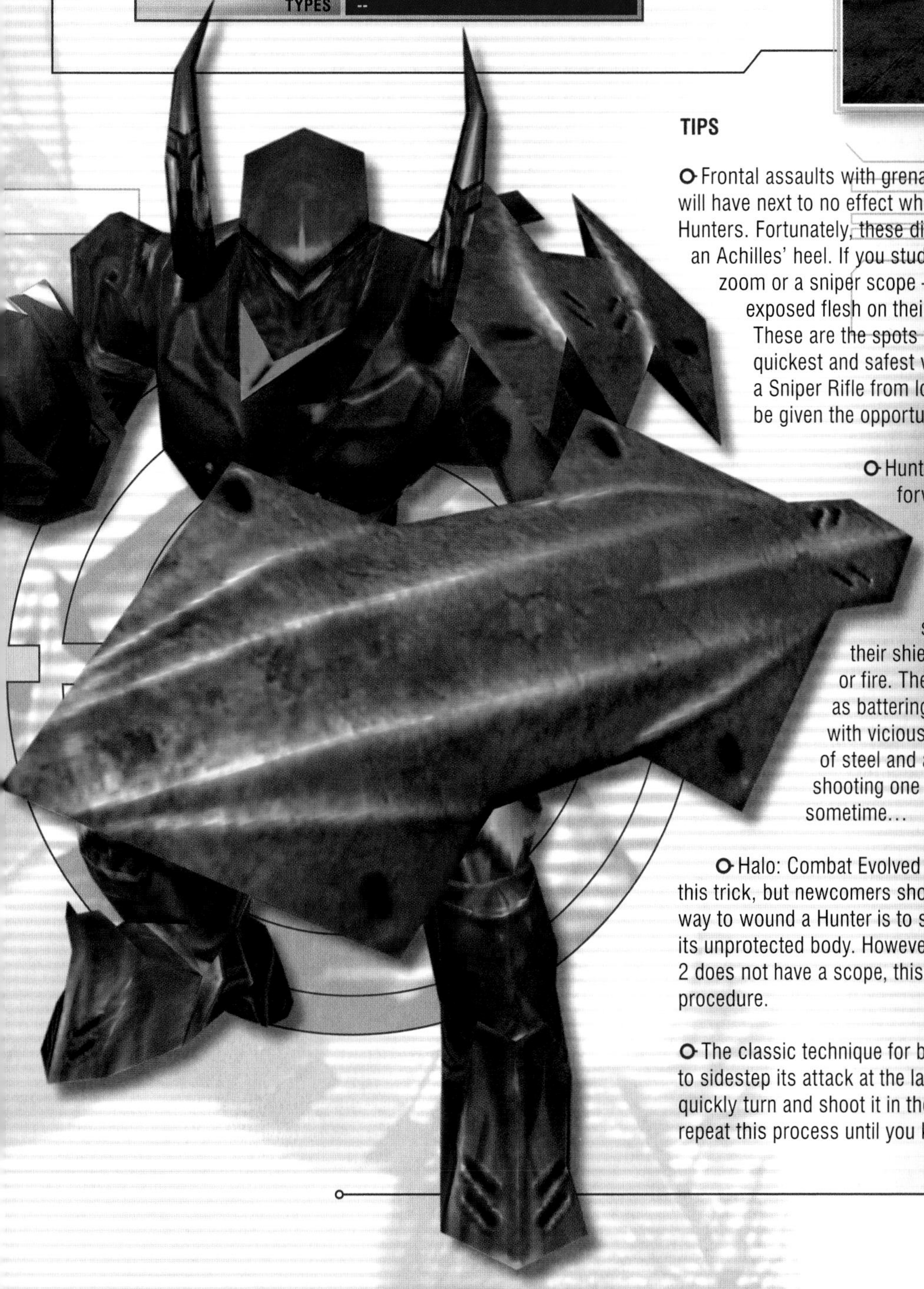

TIPS

- Frontal assaults with grenades, rifles or melee attacks will have next to no effect when employed against Hunters. Fortunately, these disconcerting beasts do have an Achilles' heel. If you study one closely – use your zoom or a sniper scope – you'll see that there is exposed flesh on their back, stomach and face. These are the spots you should aim for. The quickest and safest way to kill a Hunter is with a Sniper Rifle from long distance. You will rarely be given the opportunity to do so, though.

- Hunters tend to tilt their heads forward to protect their exposed faces as they run, so you should not – as a rule – aim for this area. Their stomachs are, similarly, protected by their shields as they either charge or fire. They also use their shields as battering rams, breaking bones with vicious ease. If you're got nerves of steel and a suicidal disposition, try shooting one in the belly with a Shotgun sometime…

- Halo: Combat Evolved veterans will already know this trick, but newcomers should pay attention. A good way to wound a Hunter is to sneak behind it and fire at its unprotected body. However, as the Magnum in Halo 2 does not have a scope, this is now a far more tricky procedure.

- The classic technique for besting a charging Hunter is to sidestep its attack at the last available moment, then quickly turn and shoot it in the back. You will need to repeat this process until you kill it.

BRUTES

Up until this point, humanity had no contact with these fur-covered giants. It transpires that a longstanding rivalry between Elites and Brutes has only been suppressed with great difficulty. Recent events have caused a power shift in the Covenant, with the Brutes now accorded with a key role in the fight against humanity – and by decree of the Prophets, no less.

Brutes possess enormous strength, great stamina and powerful weapons that differ from the standard Covenant armaments. The abilities of the Brutes might, on first encounter, seem reminiscent of the Elites, but their behavior on battlefield lacks more than a little refinement. Notable for their raw aggression, strength and cruelty, these beasts do not use shield technology. Worryingly, they appear not to need it.

COVENANT NAME	JIRALHANAE
PREFERRED WEAPONS	BRUTE PLASMA PISTOL, BRUTE SHOT
TYPES	MINOR BRUTE, MAJOR BRUTE, BRUTE CAPTAIN, HONOR GUARD

TIPS

- The special weapon of the Brutes is the Brute Shot, a grenade launcher with a blade attachment for effective melee attacks. It's dangerous from afar and can be deadly at close range.
- The last surviving Brute of any given group will go berserk: it will discard its weapons and attempt to simply bludgeon its enemies to the ground with the sheer force of its body mass.
- Brutes don't have any firearm-specific weaknesses. Your best weapon against them is a mixture of force and ferocity – but even headshots and sticky Plasma Grenades are barely enough to curtail their existence.

PROPHETS

COVENANT NAME	PROPHETS
PREFERRED WEAPONS	UNKNOWN
TYPES	UNKNOWN

Cofounders of the Covenant, the Prophets appear to exert complete control over religious and political affairs, leaving the task of actual conquest to Elites and the subordinate races. Precious little is known about these mysterious rulers. They appear to be physically weak and use a form of anti-gravity system to hover. They are protected by the mighty Elite Honor Guards.

The latest intelligence indicates that there is a triumvirate of Covenant leaders. They are known as the Prophet of Truth, Prophet of Mercy and the Prophet of Regret.

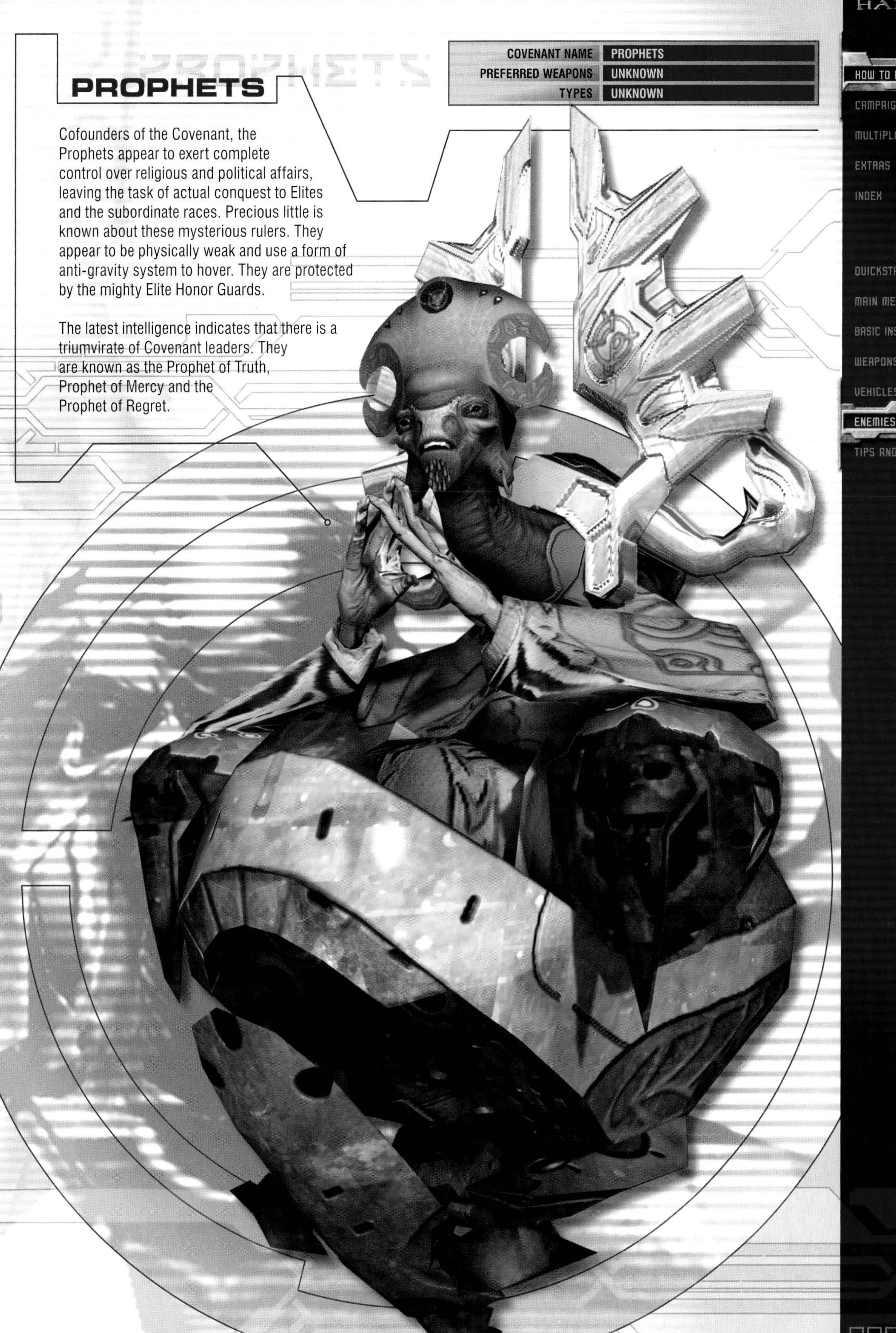

Tips and Tactics

Many Halo: Combat Evolved players have admitted that they didn't discover or properly appreciate many techniques and tactics until they had played it through for a second or third time. Halo 2, with its greater depth and masses of content, is an even harder game to master. The following tips and tricks will help you become a better, more knowledgeable player from the moment you begin your very first Campaign.

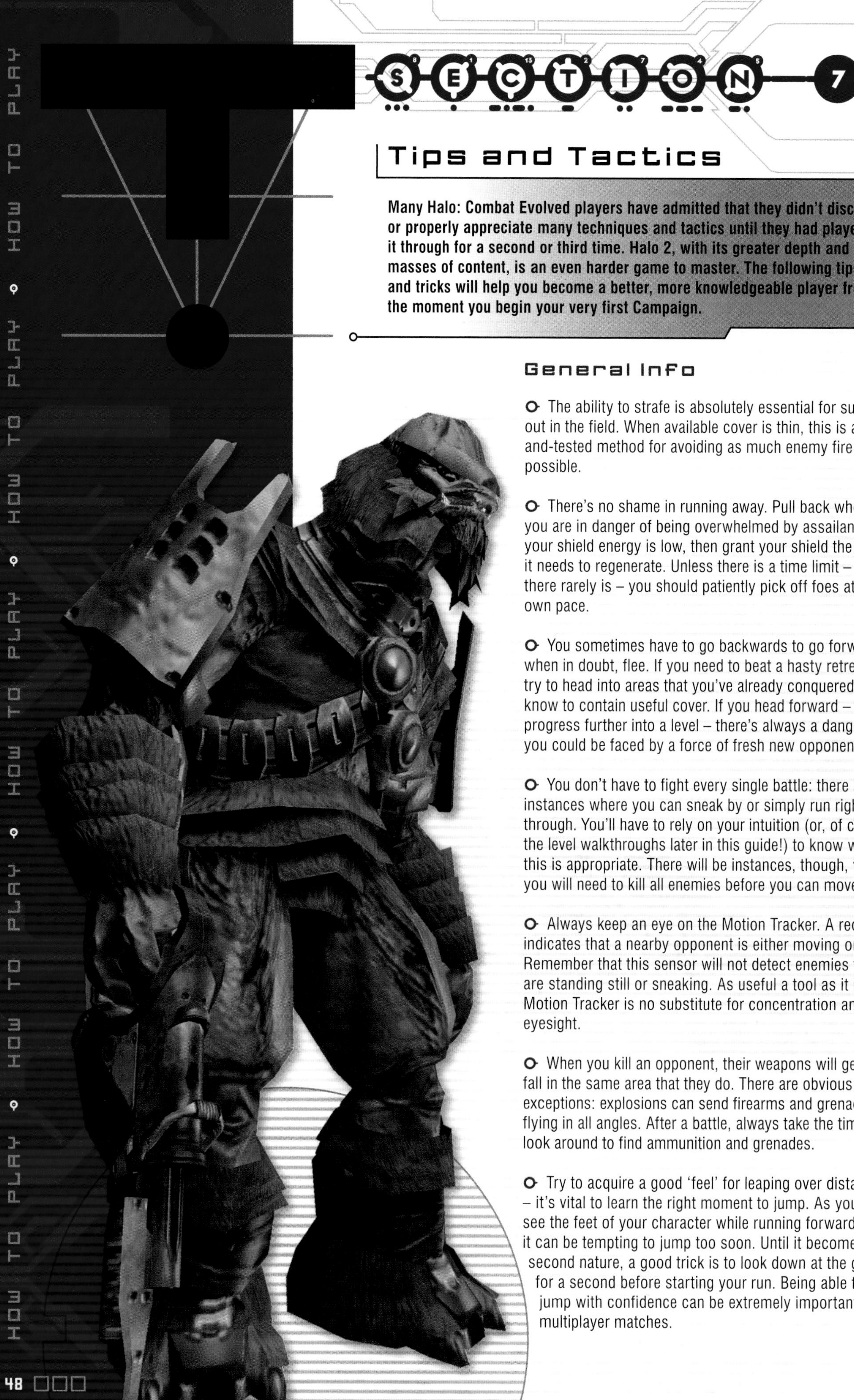

General Info

- The ability to strafe is absolutely essential for surviving out in the field. When available cover is thin, this is a tried-and-tested method for avoiding as much enemy fire as possible.

- There's no shame in running away. Pull back when you are in danger of being overwhelmed by assailants and your shield energy is low, then grant your shield the time it needs to regenerate. Unless there is a time limit – and there rarely is – you should patiently pick off foes at your own pace.

- You sometimes have to go backwards to go forwards: when in doubt, flee. If you need to beat a hasty retreat, try to head into areas that you've already conquered or know to contain useful cover. If you head forward – that is, progress further into a level – there's always a danger that you could be faced by a force of fresh new opponents.

- You don't have to fight every single battle: there are instances where you can sneak by or simply run right through. You'll have to rely on your intuition (or, of course, the level walkthroughs later in this guide!) to know when this is appropriate. There will be instances, though, where you will need to kill all enemies before you can move on...

- Always keep an eye on the Motion Tracker. A red dot indicates that a nearby opponent is either moving or firing. Remember that this sensor will not detect enemies that are standing still or sneaking. As useful a tool as it is, the Motion Tracker is no substitute for concentration and keen eyesight.

- When you kill an opponent, their weapons will generally fall in the same area that they do. There are obvious exceptions: explosions can send firearms and grenades flying in all angles. After a battle, always take the time to look around to find ammunition and grenades.

- Try to acquire a good 'feel' for leaping over distances – it's vital to learn the right moment to jump. As you can't see the feet of your character while running forward, it can be tempting to jump too soon. Until it becomes second nature, a good trick is to look down at the ground for a second before starting your run. Being able to jump with confidence can be extremely important for multiplayer matches.

- If you duck at the very highest point of a jump – remember to keep the thumbstick held forward – you can gain a tiny additional bit of height. This can be used to climb onto a few hard-to-reach places.

- Turn off your stereo, close doors and windows, silence family members and listen carefully. A large part of becoming a skilled player – both in multiplayer and Campaign modes – is being able to notice audio cues, then reacting accordingly. From the hiss of an armed Plasma Grenade to the sound of onrushing feet on a metal floor, Halo 2's sound effects are not mere audio furniture: they're clues, and should be heeded.

- Doors generally open as you approach. If there's a red light on one, it's locked – and how fortunate it is that the Covenant use an easily-distinguishable color code! Enemy forces will occasionally enter an area via these 'closed' openings, and it is sometimes possible to dive inside if you're quick. It's rarely necessary to do so, though – it's always a dead end, and may be an awkwardly indefensible position.

- If you start Halo 2 on a high difficulty level and encounter major problems later on in the game, you won't have to restart from the very beginning. Just go to the Select Level option and restart the last stage you unlocked on a lower difficulty setting. Be warned: you won't be able to resume your old game if you do this. Conversely, those feeling brave and boisterous can raise the challenge at any point in the same manner.

- Use Checkpoints to experiment: you can practice throwing grenades, try crazy stuff, even kill yourself, because you can (or will) always return to the last Checkpoint you passed. There are no penalties for dying or reverting to your last saved position (via the Pause Menu) on dozens, even thousands of occasions.

- The controller setting Look Sensitivity is quite useful. You should probably leave it alone from the start, because the default configuration is best to begin with. As you become more experienced, though, you might want to try out higher settings. The faster you can turn your character to react to a threat, the higher your chances of survival are. But it's vitally important to stay in total control – this setting should never be too high. This is especially important for multiplayer matches.

Enemy Forces

Even the lowliest recruit can take down a Grunt – a quick burst of rifle fire or a well-aimed headshot will suffice. Besting a Covenant Elite, by contrast, is an entirely different proposition. Like the Master Chief, these are almost always protected by energy shields. You can only inflict genuine damage after removing that barrier...

Consider your opponents' field of vision. When you can see an enemy's face, you can almost guarantee that he can also see you. If you've been discovered, there's little point in hiding: all nearby Covenant will enter a state of heightened awareness.

Try to predict your opponents' next move. If you're firing at an Elite, it's likely to strafe to the left or right. Depending on the distance between you and it and the weapon in hand, you may have to fire not at where it is, but where it will be.

Taking occasional pot-shots at an Elite is absolutely pointless (unless, that is, you're using a Rocket Launcher). To beat it, you must first disable its shield. If you're successful, you'll notice that flashes appear over its body. It's now genuinely vulnerable to your shots. If you wait too long before finishing it off – if it dives behind cover and out of your reach, for example – its shields will regenerate.

Some weapons are more powerful when used against certain foes than others. The opposite is also true: firearms can be weaker or even practically worthless when employed against some enemy types (Fig. 1).

01

Pay attention to the Covenant color code: Red Elites, for instance, will be tougher than their blue equivalents – and especially so on higher skill settings.

When you throw a grenade at a group of opponents, their immediate reaction will be to jump out of harm's way. This kind of reflex could cause them to, for instance, inadvertently throw themselves into an abyss. Take note of opportunities that your environment can offer at all times. Sometimes, it's better to be a master tactician than an expert marksman...

Try to aim for the head of your opponent, as hits have a much greater impact there. Keep in mind that opponents like Elites will sometimes duck to escape your shots (Fig. 2).

02

- Try to target and kill individual opponents: firing indiscriminately into a group is rarely a productive method of attack. With every enemy you dispatch, you reduce the potential firepower of an attack group. Simply wounding them is not enough, although it's occasionally wise to force an especially aggressive warrior to retreat. If you keep a cool head at all times and methodically whittle away your foes, intimidated survivors may pull back or – in the case of Grunts when their allies and, in particular, Elite commanders are killed – lose discipline and flee.

- Choose your opponent wisely. If you play easier difficulty levels, enemies like Grunts usually do not pose a lethal threat. Sometimes it's better to ignore them and concentrate your fire on a dangerous opponent like an Elite. However, on higher difficulty levels and later on in the game, you should reconsider your methods. Even Grunts are dangerous foes, and it will be suicidal to take on a high-ranking Elite while other enemies are around to give it covering fire.

- Cover is vital. If you leave yourself open to attacks from all sides, your chances of survival can be slim. On lower difficulty settings, it's possible – and great fun – to charge into a group of Covenant and instigate a wild firefight. Scattering or distracting your enemies with a grenade is a great way to begin a charge.

- Melee attacks are more powerful than you may initially realize. It can be easier over short to middle distances to simply run over and end the confrontation with a resounding thud or two. There are exceptions, though. Some enemies are very hardy and, in a toe-to-toe exchange of blows, can best the Master Chief with ease – like Hunters or Brutes. As a wise old soldier might say: don't enter an ass-kicking contest against a giant porcupine. It's also unwise to rush into the middle of a group of enemies to hit one of them over the head. There are far more artful ways to commit suicide in Halo 2… (Fig. 3).

- The most effective attack is a solid blow to the back of an opponent's head. Whenever you get the opportunity to sneak up from behind and hit the enemy, just take your chance. If you're wearing Active Camo you should definitely exploit your temporary invisibility to wreak some silent havoc.

- Always use a melee attack to dispatch sleeping foes. Once a member of the Covenant force raises the alarm, all enemies in the area will awake. Do you really want to be attacked by the Grunts you left behind?

- You will encounter situations where two different parties will be fighting. You should try to help your allies – although this isn't always strictly necessary – but if both groups are not fond of SPARTAN-117 it will pay to hold back. Be clever: either wait to engage the weakened eventual victors, or make well-placed shots to manipulate the flow of the battle. You can choose to curtail their quarrel by intervening with a searing rebuttal… but, in a pinch, a grenade or two will often suffice.

03

Using Weapons

- Don't forget that you can hurt or even kill yourself with certain weapons. A Rocket Launcher hitting an obstacle or nearby victim can make even a mighty SPARTAN-II look very foolish and, moreover, very dead; a close-range grenade explosion can have similarly fatal consequences for the Master Chief.

- You don't have to stop running to pick up a weapon from the ground. If you hold the Ⓧ down at the right moment, you can pick up a firearm while running over it. If you're pinned down and short on ammunition, this trick can mean the difference between life and death.

- You cannot pick up a battery-powered weapon if you hold the same weapon with a higher battery level in your hand. Therefore, if an onscreen prompt says that you can collect one, just pick it up immediately (unless you are in the middle of a firefight, that is).

- Always keep track of how much ammunition the Master Chief has left in his weapons. Use breaks in combat or hide behind cover to reload. If you're regularly finding that the Master Chief is automatically reloading during combat, you're not paying attention. Try to have a full clip whenever possible.

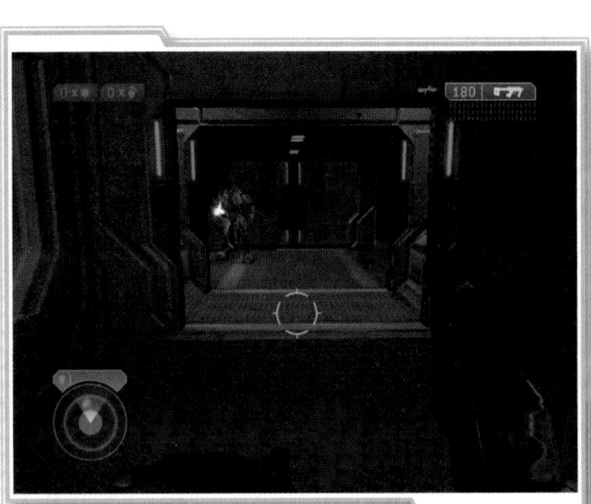

04

- Automatic reloading invariably, and with due irony, occurs when you have a dangerous target directly in front of you. If you're holding a Shotgun or overheated Plasma Rifle, you won't have time to wait if you have a Brute or Elite leaping for your throat. Switch to your secondary weapon or, if you can, execute melee attacks. Ideally, you'll perform the switch before you run out of bullets or the plasma weapon begins to boil... (Fig. 4).

- Don't forget that you can interrupt the long reloading process of the Shotgun by simply pulling the trigger. You can then use the shells that were loaded up until that point.

- Learn to use the right weapon at the right time. The Rocket Launcher, for example, is quite a formidable weapon but rather inappropriate over short distances. Likewise, a Sniper Rifle might be a precise and deadly instrument when used from afar, but it would take a player with ice in their veins to use it with any success against a Covenant charge.

- Try to carry primary and secondary weapons that broaden your attacking horizons. When outdoors, it might be a good idea to have ranged and close-quarters firearms. If you're running towards a distant enemy, you could use the Battle Rifle over medium distance first, then switch and continue your attack with the Shotgun at close range.

- When dual-wielding weapons, try not to use them simultaneously. It may, granted, look cool and pack a powerful punch, but having to reload two SMGs at the same time or wait for two Plasma Rifles to cool at once leaves you horribly vulnerable. Consider using the weapons consecutively: as one SMG is reloaded, switch to the other. Reloading takes a longer period of time to complete when dual-wielding.

- The charged weapons of the Covenant are more effective against shields than projectile weapons. You could use a Plasma Pistol to destroy a Jackal's shield, then change to the Magnum to deliver a decisive shot. If you hold a human and a Covenant weapon in either hand, you can use them in sequence to great effect. You will, however, have to do without grenades... (Fig. 5).

05

- A charged Plasma Pistol shot can overload an energy shield with just one hit. Use it against an Elite before switching to a secondary weapon (or using your other dual-wielded weapon) to take it out for good (Fig. 6).

06

- Use your grenades efficiently. Try to predict how and where they will bounce before you throw them. Frag Grenades can be thrown into seemingly inaccessible places if you use the surrounding architecture to your advantage.

- Choose the right grenade for the right situation. An adhesive Plasma Grenade will take out most opponents, but it's less effective if you can't make it stick. They also take a while to explode: it's not judicious to throw one at an onrushing Hunter or enraged Elite...

- Grenades are an absolute necessity when fighting against larger groups. Simply throwing one can turn your enemies' attention – and, ergo, their aim – briefly away from your position. Once it explodes, use the ensuing disorder to your advantage.

- While you might harbor dreams of finding more ammunition for an empty weapon, it's inexpedient to limit your combat power by carrying empty firearms around. Unless you can be almost positive that you will find a supply of ammo, it's better to simply drop it and grab another weapon. If you're using plasma-based guns, try to swap them for less depleted replacements when the opportunity arises.

- Read the dedicated sections on firearms (see page 22) and enemies (from page 40) to learn more about the advantages and disadvantages of specific weapons, and how they pertain to the strengths and weaknesses of your enemies.

Vehicles

- In brief: use them whenever available. Note that although you can now hijack vehicles, so can certain opponents – but only when you're driving slowly. Keep the pedal to the metal if you're trying to demote an Elite Commander to the rank of roadkill… (Fig. 7).

07

- The driver is well protected inside a Scorpion tank or a Wraith. Skilled players will be glad to hear that you can jump onto the vehicle and smash open the hatch up by repeatedly hitting Ⓑ. Watch the onscreen display: it will indicate when you are able to throw a grenade into the vehicle using Ⓛ (Fig. 8).

08

- You can run enemies over while you're driving a vehicle, be it a Warthog, Ghost or even a well-piloted Banshee. Most enemies will dive for cover in an intelligent manner, waiting until the last moment to give you no time to turn. You can outwit them by swerving and sliding the Warthog on approach to use its widest extent as a battering ram.

- If your vehicle has additional seats or a turret, always take the time to collect a few nearby allies if they are available. The extra firepower is extremely handy. To collect passengers, simply drive over to them and stop your vehicle. You can even attract their attention by honking your horn…

Allies

- In several missions you'll be accompanied by allied forces. These colleagues seem to be quite useful at first, but you shouldn't overestimate their ability. More often than not, they will be overwhelmed by superior Covenant forces. Some people might view human soldiers as a diversion at best; others will labor long and hard to preserve the lives of as many as possible. Neither way is right or wrong: it's entirely your choice. If your targeting reticule is trained on an ally it will turn green; it will be red when pointed at an enemy.

- They may not eliminate significant amounts of enemies, but human troops always create a diversion. This can give you a priceless opportunity to sneak up on Covenant forces.

- Your colleagues are most important when you get your hands on a vehicle like the Warthog. As you can't drive and shoot at the same time, you'll need someone to man the turret. You can, if you wish, take the turret and leave the driving to someone else... (Fig. 9).

09

- It was morally dubious – even in a virtual environment – but certain Halo: Combat Evolved players would sometimes kill human soldiers in order to steal their weapons. This isn't necessary in Halo 2, as you can now swap firearms with your allies if you wish. Stand in front of one that is carrying the weapon you require, then press and hold Ⓧ. Your ally must have a different weapon for the swap to take place. It's also not possible to give him an empty weapon in exchange. Additionally, Marines will not accept an Energy Sword or Brute Shot.

HOW TO USE THE WALKTHROUGH

The following information serves as a brief introduction to the various elements that you will find in the walkthrough. You should read this before embarking on the Campaign mode.

A Maps

At the beginning of each mission you will find a map for the whole area. Study each one carefully and use them to negotiate each level. The numbers on the map correspond to the numbers in the headlines of the text.

You'll find collectable items – firearms, grenades and Energy Swords – marked on each map. The icons tell you what kind of weapon you'll find. The enemy icons give you a general idea which adversaries you will encounter in specific locales. If you see a label for "Grunts", for example, you can rest assured that you will meet lots of Grunts in that area.

Letters mark the connections between maps. If you reach an "A", look for "A" on the next map to continue from there. If you need an explanation of the different icons used on the maps, you can find the legend on the foldout cover of this guide.

B Headlines

Headlines usually begin with a number. Look for this number on the map to find the location that the text pertains to.

C Information

The text of the guide tells you about the situations you'll encounter in the game: what you have to do, what you can do, and what you definitely shouldn't do. Use this information to find out what your objective in a specific situation is, and which enemies you will encounter on your way to victory.

D Index Tab

The index tab on the right margin of each double-page spread will help you to find your way around this guide. Use it to rapidly pinpoint the information you require.

E Difficulty Level

Generally, the information in the walkthrough relates to Halo 2's Normal mode, but significant differences you might face on higher difficulty levels are specifically noted. You will encounter tougher enemies when playing on Heroic or Legendary, and some groups of enemies may be larger, in different locations, or both.

F Multiplayer

On the multiplayer maps, large letters with arrows link to corresponding screenshots of the area in question. These views will help you find your bearings when you first begin playing Halo 2's multiplayer mode. Other elements include the default position for weapons and the positions of Hills for King of the Hill, the bomb for "Neutral Bomb Assault", and Territories for the selfsame game type.

Outskirts MAP

A

Hotel Zanzibar

Sniper Alley

Landing Zone

70

Midship
Don't let its luxury fool you – the Pious Inquisitor is one of the fastest ships in the Covenant fleet.
F

210

MISSION 2

Cairo Station

Defend the station's MAC gun from Covenant boarders

MISSION BRIEFING:

Master Chief, defend this station! Repel the alien boarders! Find the Covenant point of entry and push them back to their boarding craft!

1 You Need a Weapon!

Go downstairs and take a look at the weapon lockers on the wall (Fig. 1). Grab one of the Battle Rifles and two SMGs to dual-wield (see page 17). You'll drop the second SMG automatically when performing a melee attack or when swapping from primary to secondary weapon. You can practice firing and aiming your new weapons now if you wish. The invasion of the … as soon as you follow the hallway and … creation R-01.

C

Note how the S… when fired constantly, and learn how to … adjusting your aim and rate of fire. Do… afterwards. If you have sufficient space for another magazine in your inventory, you'll pick them up automatically as soon as you run over a loaded weapon. You'll find general tips on fighting in the How To Play Chapter from page 48, and useful information on weapon usage from page 22 onward.

01

2 "Home Field Advantage"

Mission Objective: Repel the Covenant boarders

Get behind the makeshift barrier and duck (press the left thumbstick in until you hear a click, then hold it there). As soon as the bulkhead opens, yellow Grunts and blue Elites will rush into the hall (Fig. 2). Take your double SMGs and fire on them as they enter. Elites can withstand quite a bit of damage, so you should follow them with constant fire. Remove a finger from one trigger or the other occasionally so both SMGs won't be automatically reloaded at the same time. Should that happen, swap to the Battle Rifle: breaks in your assault are not advisable right now! Somewhat later, enemies will appear on the balcony above the bulkhead.

You'll find many Plasma Pistols and Plasma Rifles after this battle – you can learn more about these weapons on page 27. Swap them with your current firearms and try them out if you like. On higher difficulty levels a com… human and alien weapons is advisable, … ight on with SMGs and the Battle … en you're ready, grab your favored … through the bulkhead. Stick to the … venant in the hallway (Fig. 3). Now … n the right and enter Security R-01 thro… marked with green lights.

E

D

02

03

TIP

It is worth noting that Sergeant Johnson is invulnerable and makes a great ally – you can literally hide and he will use his turret to take down the Covenant invaders.

TIP

Watch the floor – red markings will almost always show you the direction of rooms that you should visit next. Commons Red is an exception, though. The direct way is barred, so you'll have to take a small detour through Security R-01. There are also red flashing lights over the doorways that you are supposed to go through.

3 Security R-01

The staircase at the other end of the room will lead you down to the inside courtyard (area Commons R-01). If you want to evade the enemies positioned there, jump through the opening on the left side. There is even a turret there for keeping the Covenant force in check (Fig. 4). If you want to utilize this gun emplacement, you can take the controls with ⊗. Find out more on how to use a turret on page 26.

Use the cover offered by plant tubs and other obstacles in the hall downstairs. There is less danger of being attacked on all sides when moving through a corridor. Your next goal is to reach Hangar A-01. To get there, walk through the last bulkhead on the left side and then continue upstairs.

04

TIP

The only enemies you definitely have to kill on Cairo Station are the intruders in the hangars and in the Firing Control Room. It's always safer to approach each area slowly – try to take care of everything on your way in a careful and considered manner.

65

CAMPAIGN

The opening cinematic sequence takes place in High Charity, the Holy City of the Covenant. You'll see the Supreme Commander of the Fleet of Particular Justice on trial, and learn how this Elite is held responsible for the destruction of Halo by the Master Chief. Following this, the action will switch to Cairo Station, a space station in Earth orbit, where the arch-enemy of the Covenant is having his new equipment checked.

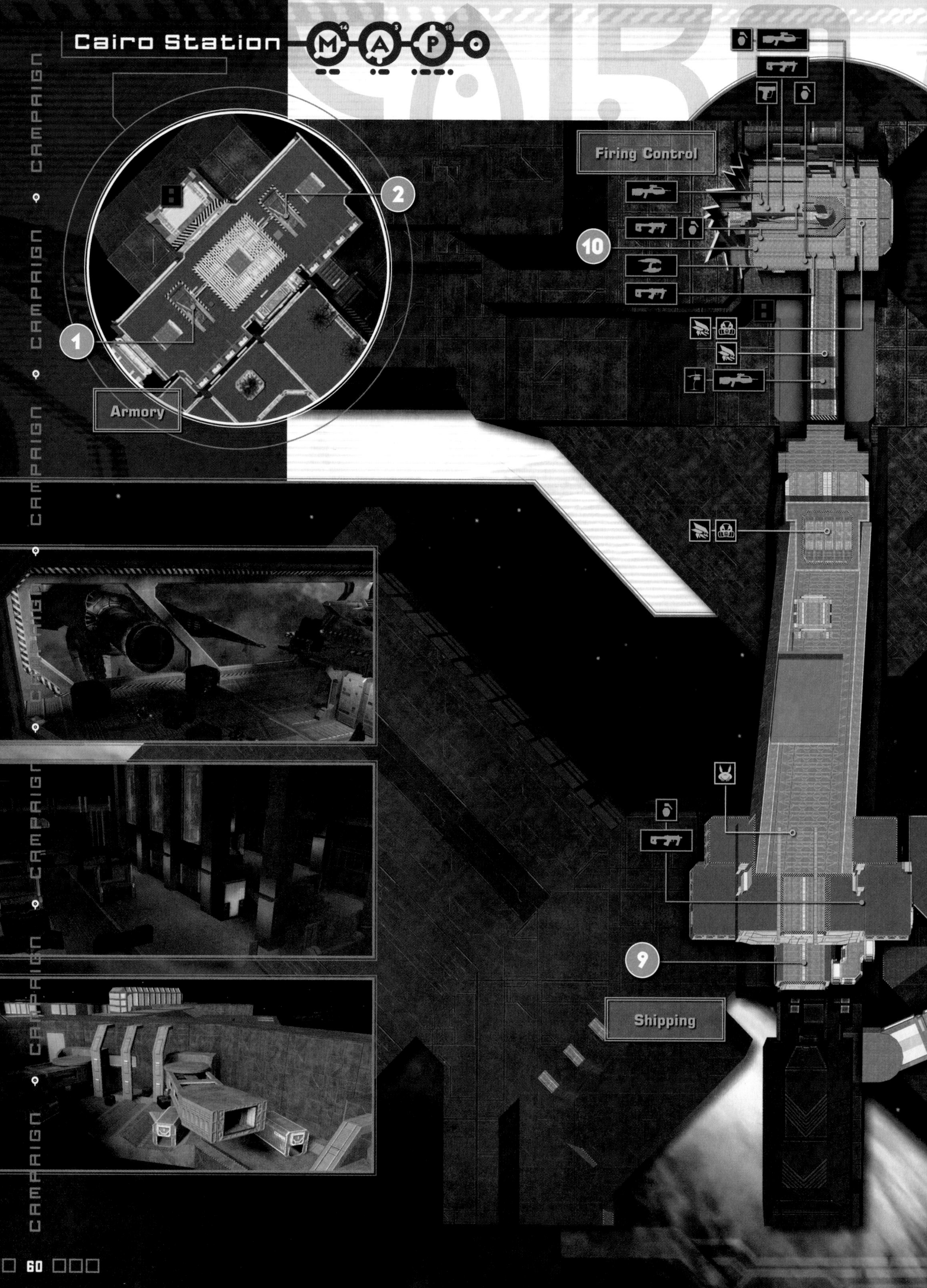

Armory
1
2
Firing Control
10
9
Shipping
CAMPAIGN

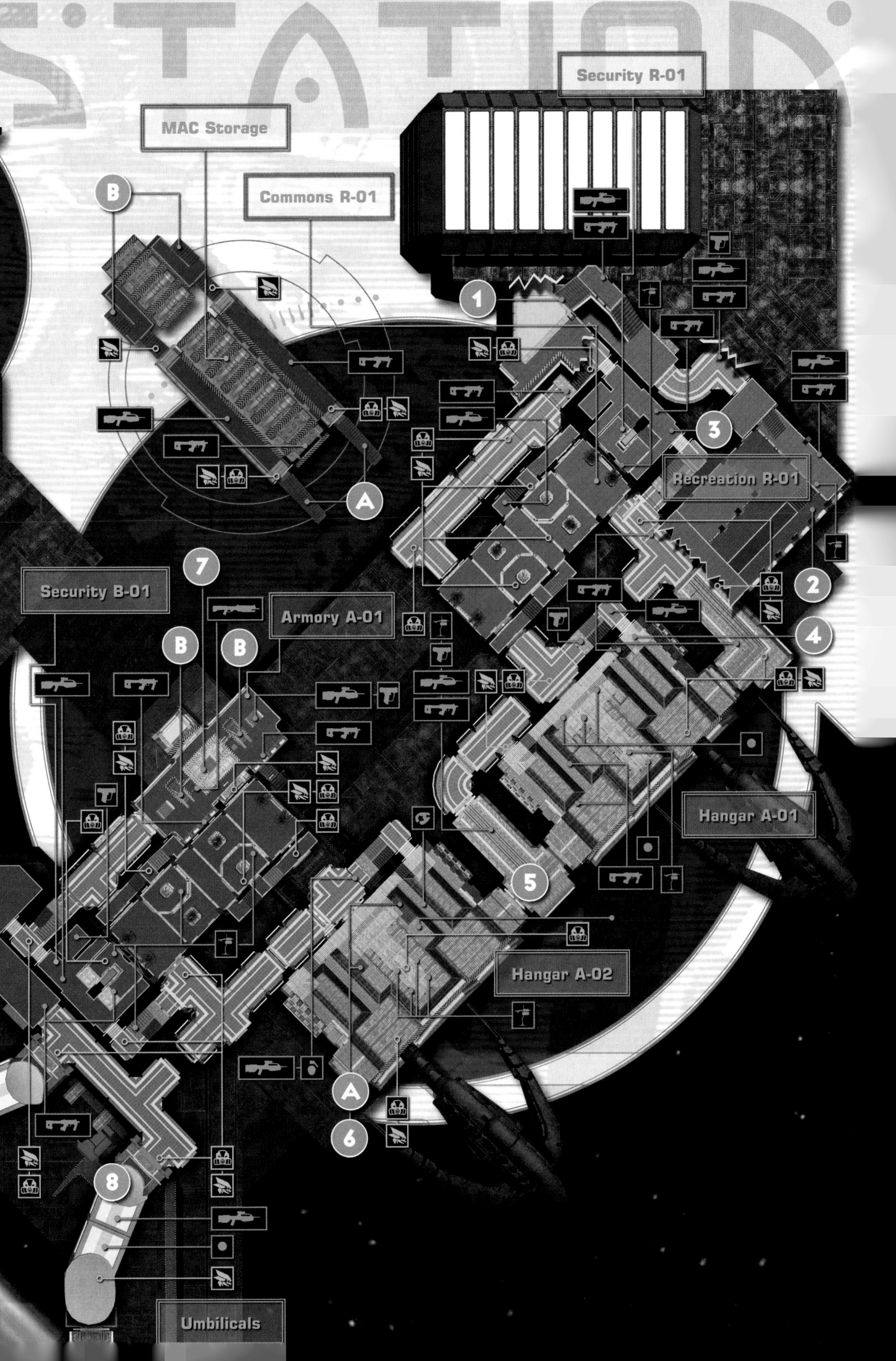
STATION
Security R-01
MAC Storage
Commons R-01
Recreation R-01
Security B-01
Armory A-01
Hangar A-01
Hangar A-02
Umbilicals
A
B
1
2
3
4
5
6
7
8

MISSION 1

Armory

Suit up, prepare for battle

MISSION BRIEFING:

Master Chief, follow the instructions of the Gunnery Sergeant. Get your battle suit checked and tested. When you've finished that, accompany Sergeant Johnson to the bridge of the station.

1 "One Size Fits All"

When testing the Targeting device (Fig. 1) you'll have to move the right thumbstick as directed to touch the lights with your crosshair. If you would prefer to play with inverted aiming, you can press your right thumbstick down to touch the upper light with your crosshair and up to reach the lower light. Halo 2 will note your preference and will automatically activate the Look Inversion option. Of course, you can also play without inverted aiming, or change this setting at any point by entering the Pause Menu. Choose Controller Settings then adjust Look Inversion to suit you. See page 9 for more advice.

As soon as the Gunnery Sergeant moves to the Zapper, you'll have the opportunity to get used to the controls. You don't have access to any weapons right now, but feel free to practice basic movement. You can find detailed instructions on how to control the Master Chief from page 10 onward.

01

2 Energy Shield Test

As soon as you're ready, get into the next machine (Fig. 2). Hold ⊗ down when ordered to start the shield test. Watch your shield energy display on the bottom-left of the screen. Remember: an empty (or low) shield indicator is a reminder that you really, really need to find some cover from enemy fire to allow it time to recharge.

After the test, Sergeant Major A.J. Johnson will arrive to collect you. Follow him to the elevator and into the train. Get off when the train stops and enjoy the long movie sequence. It'll end soon enough with the appearance of a Covenant fleet above Earth. With this, your defense of Cairo Station begins...

02

MISSION 20

Cairo Station

Defend the station's MAC gun from Covenant boarders

MISSION BRIEFING:

Master Chief, defend this station! Repel the alien boarders! Find the Covenant point of entry and push them back to their boarding craft!

1 You Need a Weapon!

Go downstairs and take a look at the weapon lockers on the wall (Fig. 1). Grab one of the Battle Rifles and two SMGs to dual-wield (see page 17). You'll drop the second SMG automatically when performing a melee attack or when swapping from primary to secondary weapon. You can practice firing and aiming your new weapons now if you wish. The invasion of the Covenant will start as soon as you follow the hallway and first step into the hall Recreation R-01.

Note how the SMGs will move upwards when fired constantly, and learn how to minimize this effect by adjusting your aim and rate of fire. Don't forget to reload afterwards. If you have sufficient space for another magazine in your inventory, you'll pick them up automatically as soon as you run over a loaded weapon. You'll find general tips on fighting in the How To Play Chapter from page 48, and useful information on weapon usage from page 22 onward.

01

2 "Home Field Advantage"

Mission Objective: Repel the Covenant boarders

Get behind the makeshift barrier and duck (press the left thumbstick in until you hear a click, then hold it there). As soon as the bulkhead opens, yellow Grunts and blue Elites will rush into the hall (Fig. 2). Take your double SMGs and fire on them as they enter. Elites can withstand quite a bit of damage, so you should follow them with constant fire. Remove a finger from one trigger or the other occasionally so both SMGs won't be automatically reloaded at the same time. Should that happen, swap to the Battle Rifle: breaks in your assault are not advisable right now! Somewhat later, enemies will appear on the balcony above the bulkhead.

02

You'll find many Plasma Pistols and Plasma Rifles after this battle – you can learn more about these weapons on page 27. Swap them with your current firearms and try them out if you like. On higher difficulty levels a combination of human and alien weapons is advisable, but you can opt to fight on with SMGs and the Battle Rifle if you prefer. When you're ready, grab your favored armaments and walk through the bulkhead. Stick to the right and fight the Covenant in the hallway (Fig. 3). Now go up to the stairs on the right and enter Security R-01 through the door marked with green lights.

03

TIP

It is worth noting that Sergeant Johnson is invulnerable and makes a great ally – you can literally hide and he will use his turret to take down the Covenant invaders.

TIP

Watch the floor – red markings will almost always show you the direction of rooms that you should visit next. Commons Red is an exception, though. The direct way is barred, so you'll have to take a small detour through Security R-01. There are also red flashing lights over the doorways that you are supposed to go through.

3 Security R-01

The staircase at the other end of the room will lead you down to the inside courtyard (area Commons R-01). If you want to evade the enemies positioned there, jump through the opening on the left side. There is even a turret there for keeping the Covenant force in check (Fig. 4). If you want to utilize this gun emplacement, you can take the controls with ⓧ. Find out more on how to use a turret on page 26.

04

Use the cover offered by plant tubs and other obstacles in the hall downstairs. There is less danger of being attacked on all sides when moving through a corridor. Your next goal is to reach Hangar A-01. To get there, walk through the last bulkhead on the left side and then continue upstairs.

TIP

The only enemies you definitely have to kill on Cairo Station are the intruders in the hangars and in the Firing Control Room. It's always safer to approach each area slowly – try to take care of everything on your way in a careful and considered manner.

4 Hangar Bay A-01

Turn to the right as soon as you enter the hangar – you'll find grenades on the ramp. You can learn how to use them on page 26. A nearby soldier fires a turret at the invaders down in the hall (Fig. 5). You could support him with your Battle Rifle, hurl grenades at the Covenant, or jump down and engage them in close combat. On higher difficulty levels you will have to survive without him – there are many such changes whenever you play on the Heroic or Legendary skill settings.

As soon as the Marines start talking about the Malta, do yourself a favor and look out of the window if you don't want to miss the explosion of the neighboring space station. You should also keep an eye on the door behind the Pelican (Fig. 6). It will eventually open, allowing access to the second hangar, but several more Grunts and Elites will immediately rush through it. Throw grenades to disrupt their entrance before they can get inside.

TIP

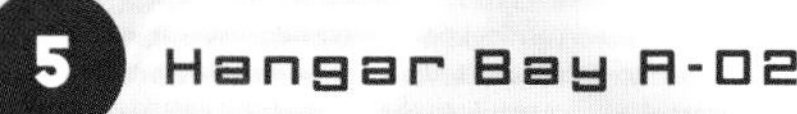

Jump on the boxes to get back to the upper level and replenish your supply of Frag Grenades. Always take the time to collect grenades and try to keep your stocks at maximum whenever possible. You should habitually search battlefields for unused Plasma Grenades.

5 Hangar Bay A-02

Use the Scope of the Battle Rifle to take out the Grunts using the Turrets on the upper level (Fig. 7). Alternatively, you can also get to the upper level via the bulkhead on the right side. You'll find more Frag Grenades on your way.

The Covenant in the hall put up fierce resistance. Using a Plasma Rifle or the charged shot of a Plasma Pistol will allow you to crack the stationary energy shields (Fig. 8) for a moment, and will also temporarily disable the full-body energy shields of the Elites. Combine a plasma weapon with a SMG in your other hand to fight as efficiently as possible. Additionally, the use of grenades against intruders is never wrong. As the Covenant invaders boarding here will always land on the same spot, it's a great idea to throw a grenade there at opportune moments.

05

06

07

08

MISSION BRIEFING:

The Covenant has hidden a bomb on the station! Master Chief, find the bomb! You'll have to locate the detonator to allow Cortana to disarm it.

09

6 "Priority Shift"

Mission Objective: Find the Covenant Bomb

After you've stopped the invasion in the hangar, the Athens will explode outside. The doors to MAC Storage will now open. Go to the stairs in the floor of the hangar and follow them downwards (Fig. 9). Attack the Covenant you find there with grenades and fire as you approach them. After that, grey Elites with Stealth devices will enter through the door on the other side. Don't worry – you can see them quite well over a short distance. Throw a Plasma Grenade at the Elite as soon as the door opens. Leave the cellar through the door the Elites came through and head in the direction of the Armory.

10

7 Armory & Commons B-01

You won't be able to prevent the Elites from shooting the Gunnery Sergeant. He'll drop a Shotgun that you can collect, if you like. At close range, it's a great weapon for killing Elites with relative ease. There are also weapon dispensers on the wall of the armory. You should now cross through the blue inner courtyard (Commons Blue) and leave the Security area on the balcony. Kill the Grunts stationed in the Turrets (Fig. 10), then head through the corridors.

11

Use the plant tubs to jump up to the above turret (Fig. 11). You can reach it if you hold down the left thumbstick button at the highest point of your jump to gain a little extra height. If you find this too difficult, you can instead take the easy way and use the staircase on the left side. The exit to Tram Station B-01 is on the right side of the Security area. Unsurprisingly, there's a battle going on there. Fight your way through the Tram Station to the last Umbilical.

TIP

Even though Cortana is insistent that you should hurry up, there's no reason to feel unduly pressured. There is no actual time limit here, so you can dispatch Covenant forces at your leisure.

12

8 "Authorized Personnel Only"

Jetpack-wearing Elite Rangers (Fig. 12) will be waiting for you at the exit of the second Umbilical. Jump out. Your goal, the door to the Portside Shipping area, is at five o'clock – behind you and a little to the right. Turn around and follow the station wall to the left. Should you encounter stiff opposition from your flying adversaries, you can take cover inside the containers.

9 Shipping

In the Shipping hall, a bunch of Drones will fly towards you from the elevator shaft. If you want to enjoy a little more fighting experience, the platforms on the side offer some cover from aerial attacks (Fig. 13). Do not forget to take the Frag Grenades from the corpse on the right side. The exit is at the bottom of the elevator shaft. It will open as soon as you've fought some of the Drones, and Grunts and Elites will appear from the airlock. You can take them out from the top before you jump down the diagonal shaft. If the elevator has been activated, and is on its way upwards, press one of the control panels to switch the elevator to a downward heading.

As soon as you've made it outside, you'll be attacked on the moveable bridge (which is actually a part of the station's MAC gun) by Rangers. Your goal is the elevator door on the far left side (Fig. 14). The elevator will take you to the Firing Control area. The door with the red lights in the elevator will remain closed – the exit opens on the other side.

13

14

10 "Return to Sender"

Many Elites are guarding the bomb in Fire Control (Fig. 15). Your priority here is to first take down the Grunts with your Scope. Now take the Plasma Rifle and the SMG lying on the floor. Get yourself to the left side under the cover of the machine, then try to entice the Covenant to attack you individually. There are extra SMGs and Battle Rifles located on the walls underneath the middle section. If no-one is following you any more, attack the enemies on the left side – the resistance will be lower. Fire on each Elite with the Plasma Rifle until it overheats to disable their energy shields, then use the SMG to dispatch them. Alternatively, you could use just one weapon and try to stick a Plasma Grenade to the Elite's body. As soon as you've defeated every single enemy, you've saved the station.

15

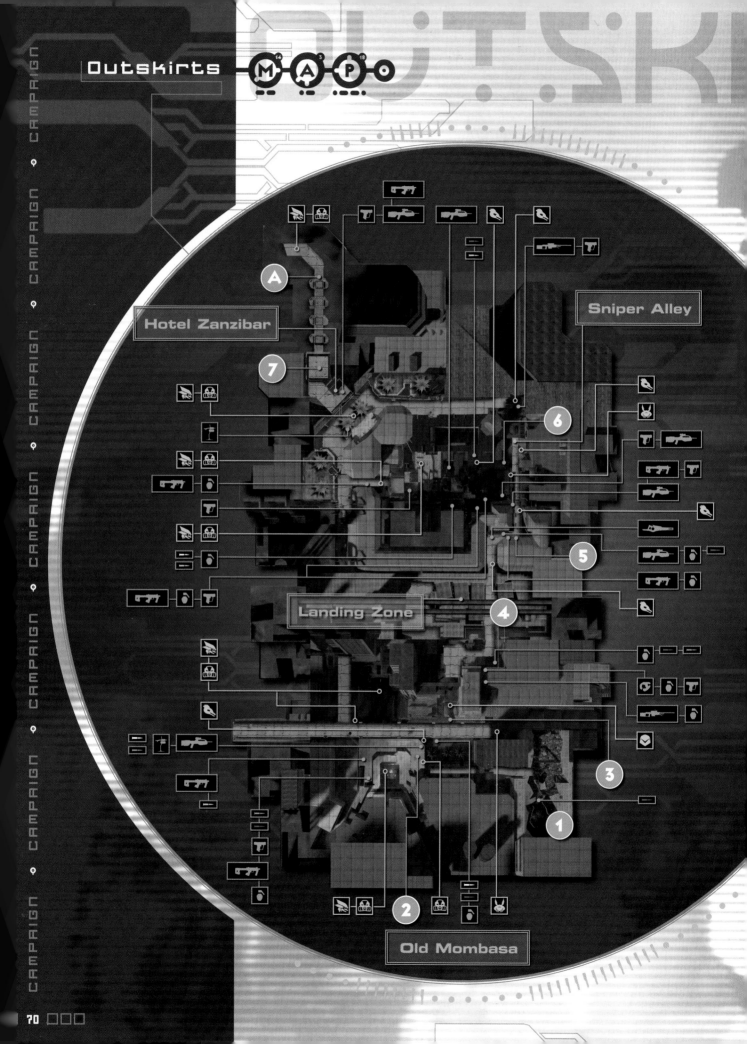

Outskirts MAP

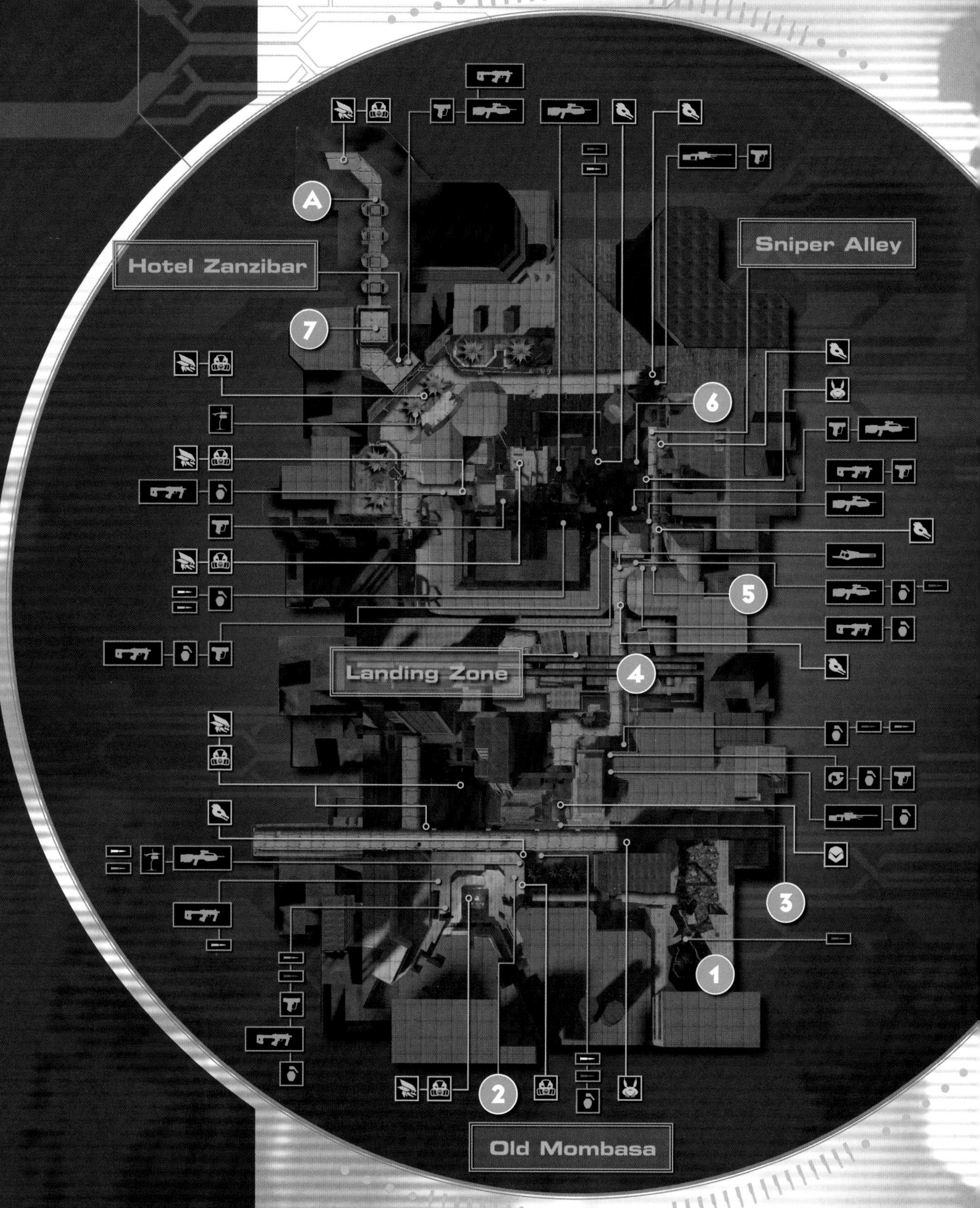

Hotel Zanzibar

Sniper Alley

Landing Zone

Old Mombasa

A

7

6

5

4

3

2

1

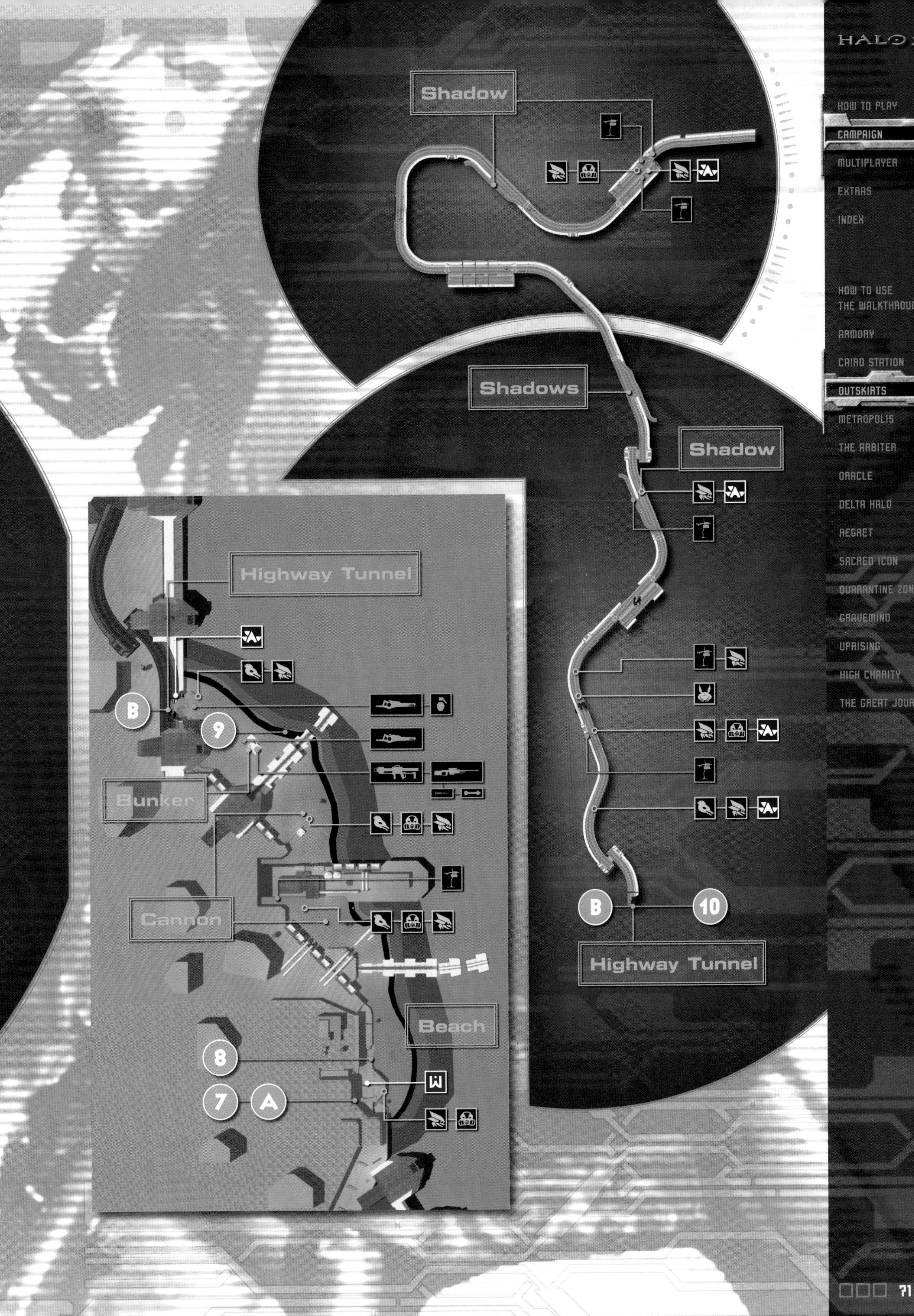
Shadow
Shadows
Shadow
B
10
Highway Tunnel
Highway Tunnel
B
9
Bunker
Cannon
Beach
8
7
A
W

MISSION 30

Outskirts

Rally scattered Marines and clear hostile contacts from the old city

MISSION BRIEFING:

Master Chief, secure the landing zone. Conquer the building and defend it against attackers until a Pelican can reach you. Clear the landing zone and start searching for the Marines from the second downed Pelican.

1 "They'll Regret That Too"

You'll begin this level with an SMG and a Battle Rifle. You can swap one of your guns with Sergeant Johnson and take his Sniper Rifle if you want. You can read more about swapping equipment with allies on page 55. The Sniper Rifle is perfect for fighting over large distances. Turn to page 25 to acquaint yourself with the characteristics of this powerful weapon.

As you leave the landing zone, a Grunt will come towards you. Kill it before it can alert its colleagues (they're near to the building on the other side of the courtyard). You have to take down all the Covenant in this area – and that includes the shield-bearing Jackals. Dispatch them with plasma weapons or with massive constant fire. You could also use the Sniper Rifle. The best way of doing things is to flank to the right while your Marines draw their attention, allowing you to shoot the Jackals in the back.

There's an Elite and other aliens in the atrium of the ruin. Jump onto the truck on the street to get to the upper level of the building (Fig. 1). Using this route means that you won't have to use the stairway in the indoor courtyard. You might also want to check out the weapons and ammunition supply by the steps (Fig. 2) in the western part of the building.

01

02

2 Hold Your Position!

Mission Objective: Defend the Marines until help arrives

After you've defeated the local Covenant force, you'll get a new Mission Objective. The Marines here will support you to the best of their abilities. They'll distract the enemy at very least, and may even achieve some kills, but you're not responsible for their survival. You could even finish the mission on your own (although Sergeant Johnson will always survive). From this point, several groups of enemies will appear and you'll have to dispatch them all. Many of these will be spotted and announced by Johnson and the Marines. Listen carefully: these audio cues can help you target your foes quickly and efficiently.

"Here they come. Up high.": An Elite appears on the roof on the other side (Fig. 3). The rest come through the two smaller lanes under it. (On higher difficulty levels, Jackal snipers appear on the rooftops and can kill you with a single shot.)

"More on the street. Left side.": Grunts and Elites appear on the crossing on the left side.

"New contact!" or **"Across the street, down low.":** Grunts and Elites will emerge from the two small alleys.

"We got Jackals in the courtyard.": Jackals and at least one Elite appear in the alley leading to the landing zone.

"Buggers heading over the rooftops.": A swarm of Drones appears over one of the buildings in the line of sight of the turret (Fig. 4).

Try to disrupt and destroy enemies emerging from the alleys by using well-timed grenades. You can manage most of the attacks from the canopy. After several waves, an enemy Phantom makes an appearance. Take cover under the canopy or in the atrium to avoid incoming fire from the dropship. It will deploy troops in the middle of the square. Greet them with grenades if you can (Fig. 5). After that, expect another wave of enemies before a Pelican finally appears and announces its intention to land.

03

04

05

3 Hunters!

Now you just have to get through the gate. Two gigantic Hunters will open it for you by breaking through it from the other side. Generally, you can only kill these behemoths by shooting them in the small areas of exposed orange flesh that their armor doesn't cover, particularly on their backs. In this instance, dealing with them should be a lot easier than usual. As soon as the Pelican shows up, get behind the turret and fire on the gate. This way, you can slay the Hunters with a hail of bullets the very moment they enter the square (Fig. 6). Even their mighty shields can't protect them against such a sustained barrage. Should the weapons of the Hunters begin to glow green, leave the turret and run for cover – and quickly!

06

If the turret was destroyed during the battle, you'll have to fight the Hunters up close and personal, man against monster. If this is the case, make sure that Sergeant Johnson has got a Sniper Rifle – his marksmanship can be of great assistance. Try to maneuver the Hunters so that they present their backs to him. (Fig. 7).

07

TIP

If you're in a hurry, there is another way to finish this level: just ignore the Mission Objectives! As soon as the Hunters open the gate, run through to the Landing Zone. Make your way alone to the Hotel Zanzibar, grab a Ghost on the beach behind it, then race to the end of the tunnel. Theoretically, you don't have to kill a single opponent after the Hunters appear to finish the level successfully. This is referred to as "The Path of Shame", as opposed to "The Path of Valor" that you follow by achieving all specified objectives...

4 Landing Zone

Mission Objective: Rendezvous with the Pelican

On the other side of the designated landing zone, Jackals await you – and they have a sniper among their numbers (Fig. 8). You'll find a welcome ammunition supply in a niche, and on the level above it you'll discover a Sniper Rifle. Collect it if you don't already have one, then take out the Jackals on the other side. Never underestimate Jackal snipers – even the Master Chief won't survive two well-aimed shots from a Beam Rifle.

08

5 Sniper Alley

Mission Objective: Find the Marines from second downed Pelican

The so-called "Sniper Alley" is behind the next corner, and you'll soon appreciate the aptness of the name. Peer carefully around the corner and shoot the Jackal standing in the middle of the road with a Beam Rifle. After finishing him off, increase your scope's magnification and shoot the Jackal sniper at the other end of the alley (Fig. 9). Now take out his colleagues on the rooftops and the ground. The Drones are the least of your problems. Always retreat behind the corner to allow your shield time to recharge when necessary. Should you run out of ammunition, you'll find some bullets for the Sniper Rifle and a Beam Rifle here.

Keep an eye on the so-called "space crates" set up by the Covenant (Fig. 10). The function of these devices is still unknown, but you can use them to your advantage. After sustaining a certain amount of damage, they explode – and, in doing so, will injure or even kill nearby Covenant troops. The larger containers, on the other hand, are as solid as rock. They are storage cells for Covenant plasma weapons, and they make good hiding spots for cover. You can also gain a height advantage by standing on one.

09

10

11

12

13

6 Hotel Zanzibar

After passing the arcades, go left into the old town. Expect to encounter more snipers here – dispatch them first. Afterwards, you should equip yourself with weapons more suited to close combat encounters. Your goal is the Hotel Zanzibar, which is besieged by the Covenant at the moment. Use the big green transport crates on the street (Fig. 11) to jump up to the roof. An opening (Fig. 12) allows you to attack your enemies from behind (Fig. 13). Your mission is completed as soon as all Covenant in front of the hotel are dead.

TIP

You can actually climb onto the city rooftops from Sniper Alley. Start jumping from the purple Covenant machine: jump on the protrusion on the wall (Fig. 14), leap from there to the canopy, then jump over to the flat building on the other side of the street.

14

MISSION BRIEFING:

Master Chief, get to the Covenant ship above the Metropolis. Follow the beach until you reach a tunnel. This tunnel links up with the bridge leading into the city. Don't let yourself be detained by the Covenant.

7 The Second Downed Pelican

The dark hotel hallway leads directly to the beach. Your flashlight (©) will only penetrate the gloom to a limited degree. Near the exit, several Elites and Grunts will rush around the corner. After that, a Phantom will require your full attention – it is deploying infantry on the walkway on the other side (Fig. 15). Use the exploding Covenant container to your advantage. When you have dispatched most of the nearby hostiles, a Warthog will arrive.

TIP

Press Ⓛ up to accelerate the Warthog. Steer the vehicle with Ⓡ. A detailed description of each and every vehicle – and how to control them – begins on page 32.

15

8 "A Day at the Beach"

Mission Objective: Destroy the Covenant on the shoreline

Get behind the steering wheel of the Warthog and wait until the former driver has climbed into the passenger seat. Now head off in the direction of the tunnel. You can fight against Covenant forces on the beach as you go, but be wary of the snipers stationed on the floating watchtowers. This mission objective is completed as soon as you've destroyed all enemies at the huge cannons (Fig. 16). However, this is not a mandatory goal, and can be skipped if you wish – you only have to reach the tunnel to end the level. Therefore, you could leave the Warthog entirely and use a Ghost to get there, or even walk. The latter option is not recommended, but entirely possible.

16

9 Highway Tunnel

Take the highway tunnel to the bridge

Between you and the tunnel are many Elites, Ghosts and a Phantom. It's possible to simply race through to the highway tunnel (Fig. 17). If you want to take out a few enemies before doing that, you'll find a Rocket Launcher on top of the bunker. You can use it to destroy the guns on Phantoms, rendering them effectively harmless. The tunnel is very long – you should definitely grab a Ghost or a Warthog.

17

10 "Speed Zone Ahead"

Follow the tunnel to the right until you reach the exit. Occasionally you'll have to drive into a parallel tunnel. The Covenant have constructed makeshift barricades, but you can simply drive by them. If you're piloting a Ghost and a Drone lands on the bonnet and attacks you, jump out of the vehicle to kill the insect before it can inflict serious damage. Alternatively, you could accelerate and collide with a wall to dislodge it.

When you reach a branch in the road, a red light will show you that this exit is barred (Fig. 18). Use the ramp to evade the cannon of the Shadow parked here, but stay on the road. A little later you'll meet a convoy of three Shadows. In a hall not far from the exit, the Covenant will make a last attempt to prevent your escape. All you have to do now is to get through there to reach the bridge – and, by doing so, finish this level.

18

Metropolis

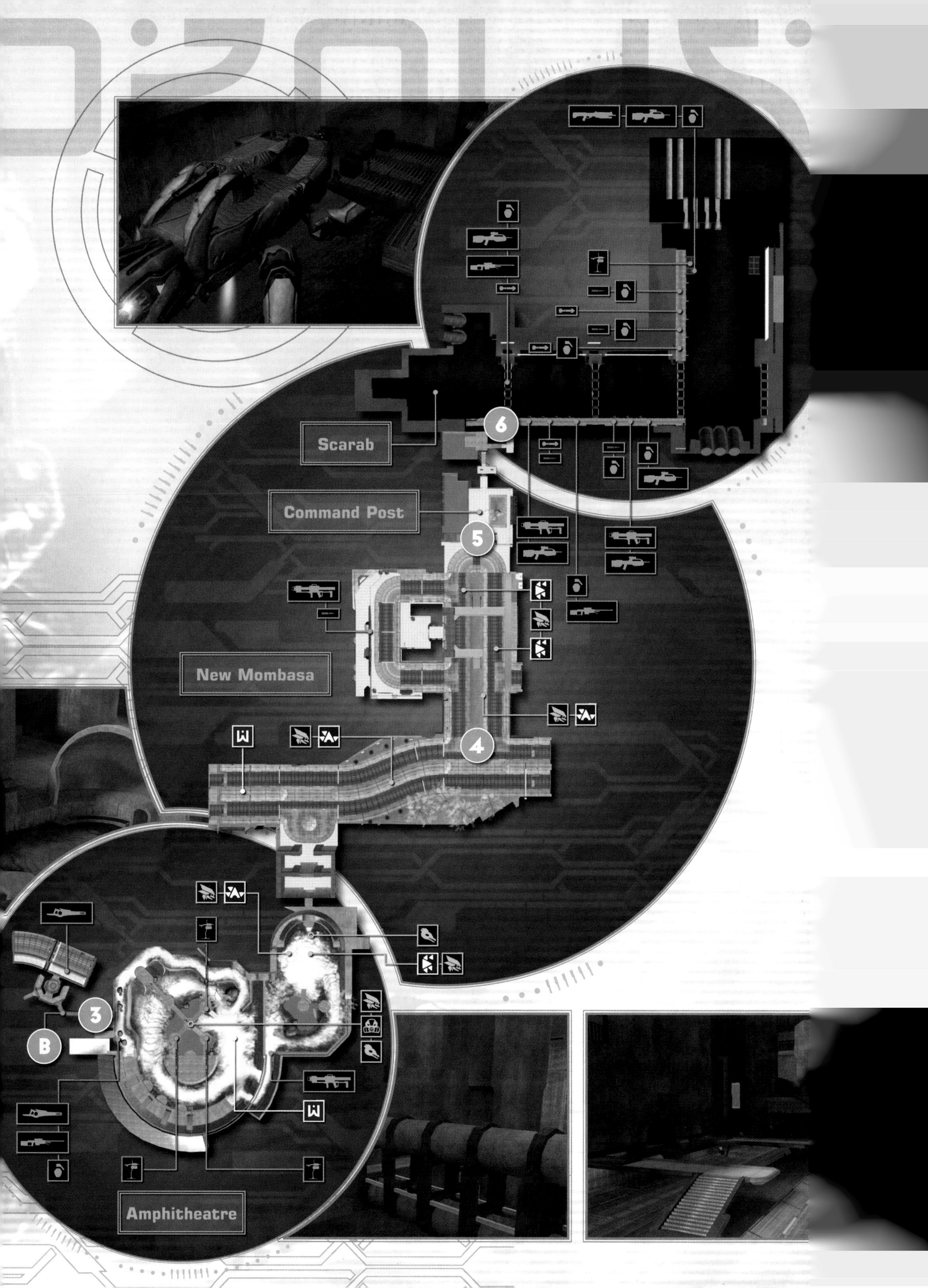

Scarab
Command Post
New Mombasa
Amphitheatre
6
5
4
3
B

MISSION 4

Metropolis

Take the bridge, break the Covenant's grip on the city center

MISSION BRIEFING:

Master Chief, climb into the tank and drive down to the bridge. Advance into the city center through the tunnel and help the Marines stationed there. And finally: destroy that Scarab!

01

02

03

1 "Ladies Like Armor Plating"

Mission Objective: Crush Covenant resistance on the bridge

Climb into the Scorpion. After the two Marines have taken their seats, get rolling. Your comrades will shoot everything within range from their side. Look out for distant movement on the bridge and react as soon as the Ghosts begin to approach you (Fig. 1). One well-aimed hit with the cannon will usually destroy these speedy Covenant vehicles, but it's always worthwhile to bathe them in constant machine gun fire. The engines of a terminally ill Ghost will often explode. Watch out for the characteristic sound these "dying" Ghosts make and remember to keep your distance.

There's a Wraith on the middle of the bridge (Fig. 2). Shots from its mortar cannon are relatively slow and fly in an arc but, as your tank is not blessed with any real degree of acceleration, you should definitely keep one eye on the skies. Hit the Wraith a few times with the Scorpion's cannon to destroy it. Behind the Wraith is a hole in the road. Drive around it – staying to the left is safer. At this point, Phantoms will arrive from behind. Shoot the cannons attached to their undersides. Additionally, Banshees will attack from above, and there are some more Ghosts to deal with. At the toll booth a veritable Covenant armada is waiting for you (Fig. 3). Two Wraiths will emerge from the tunnel – and you'll have to get past them because, typically, the tunnel is where you need to go next. The best strategy when you encounter Wraiths is to keep moving at all times.

TIP

Move the Scorpion with Ⓛ. Turn the tank's cannon with Ⓡ. R fires the cannon, while L fires its machine gun. You'll find a detailed introduction to the Scorpion on page 34.

2 Through the Back Entrance

Mission Objective: Make your way to the surface

A floodgate blocks the road in the tunnel. Get out and continue on foot or, alternatively, with a Ghost or Warthog you could even drive over the ramp on the right side. You can swap your weapon for something better with the Marines down there – you could, for example, grab a Shotgun for close-quarters combat. There's a Beam Rifle on the floodgate (Fig. 4), which is handy for attacking the Covenant further down the tunnel (mainly Elites and Jackal Snipers). Your goal is the exit of the tunnel (Fig. 5). Go through the tubes (take the one on the left side) to reach a park.

04

05

TIP

There are weapons in the Covenant containers. Some are open and you can help yourself to anything you want (Fig. 6).

3 "This Town Ain't Big Enough For Both of Us"

Mission Objective: Regroup with Marine forces in the city center

Take out the enemies in the basin one after the other using a Sniper Rifle or Beam Rifle (Fig. 7). The crew of the Warthog down there would like you to man their cannon, but you should instead take the wheel for yourself and get one of the Marines to be the gunner. Your goal is the passage (Fig. 8) under the right rim of the dome. You could also choose to run through without a vehicle and use the Rocket Launcher lying behind a corner there to fight the Wraith. You might even prefer to board one of the Ghosts. Whatever you opt for, you should go through the arch (Fig. 9) behind the Wraith (under the small dome) and advance into the city center.

06

07

08

09

4 In the City Center

There is a Marine command post in the building at the end of the city. You'll have to destroy the Wraiths on the road, and should destroy the weapons of the attacking Phantom – or, at very least, drive it away with a sustained barrage of fire. You could use a Ghost for that – just dodge the attacks while moving sideways, or instead go and pick up the Rocket Launcher lying in a back road (Fig. 10). A Warthog with a Gauss Cannon will offer support. You could choose to drive it yourself, of course, because this vehicle is another of your many options here. If you are feeling especially brave (or, perhaps, just plain foolhardy), jump on a Wraith and attack the pilot at close range (Fig. 11).

As soon as you've defeated all the Covenant in the city center, the entrance into the building opens – it will be marked with a Waypoint (Fig. 12). A Marine will lead you to your next destination. Should you lose him, just go upstairs and through the glass door.

10

5 "Field Expedient"

Mission Objective: Board and destroy the Scarab

A giant Scarab strides closer and closer to your position, seemingly unstoppable... but then it walks just slightly over the building you're in. Run to the staircase on the left and get back into the building one floor higher. Again, a Marine will guide you, but if you lose him the directions are: up the stairs, through the glass door, right up the next set of stairs and then off to the left. Another glass door leads you outside where you'll be standing almost face-to-face with the Scarab. You'll find many weapons and lots of ammunition as you follow this route, and there are more of both on the bridges. Take everything you need – we recommend the Rocket Launcher and some rockets or a Sniper Rifle. But don't get too greedy. You'll need a suitable close quarters weapon when you eventually board.

11

12

6 Board the Scarab

You have to kill the entire crew of the Scarab. You could jump onto the monstrous vehicle from a bridge at the first possible opportunity, but bear in mind that immediate close combat would be very dangerous. Prepare your attack by firing rockets from the walkway.

Eventually, the Scarab will be trapped and you can jump onto its deck whenever you want to (Fig. 13). The last – and strongest – Elites won't show up on the deck voluntarily. You have to go downstairs to meet them. There is a white Ultra Elite here, and he's equipped with an Energy Sword (Fig. 14). He doesn't initially brandish it, but will draw it if angered – if you can't see him, listen out for the sound. He can kill you with a single swipe, so be careful not to get too close. Take grenades and the Rocket Launcher with you, but remember not to use the latter if you are too close to an opponent. Another option would be to take the Plasma Pistol to neutralize the shields of your assailants, then deliver lethal shots with a different weapon. As soon as the last Covenant falls, a long cutscene will begin. It has a rather special ending...

13

14

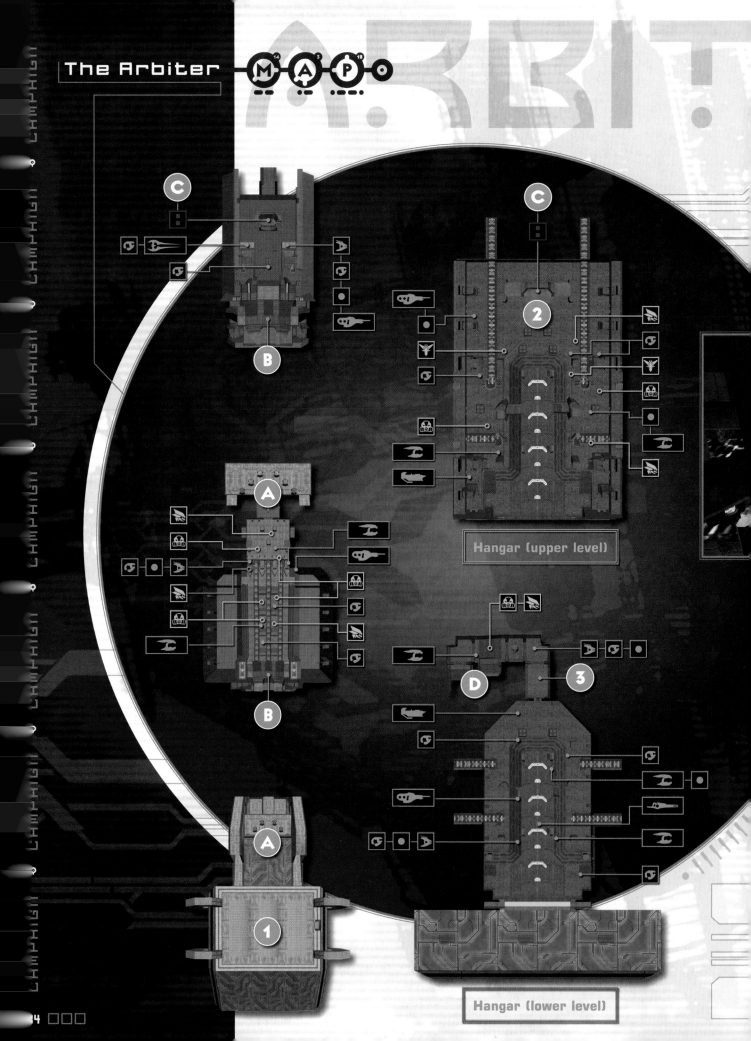

Hangar (upper level)

Hangar (lower level)

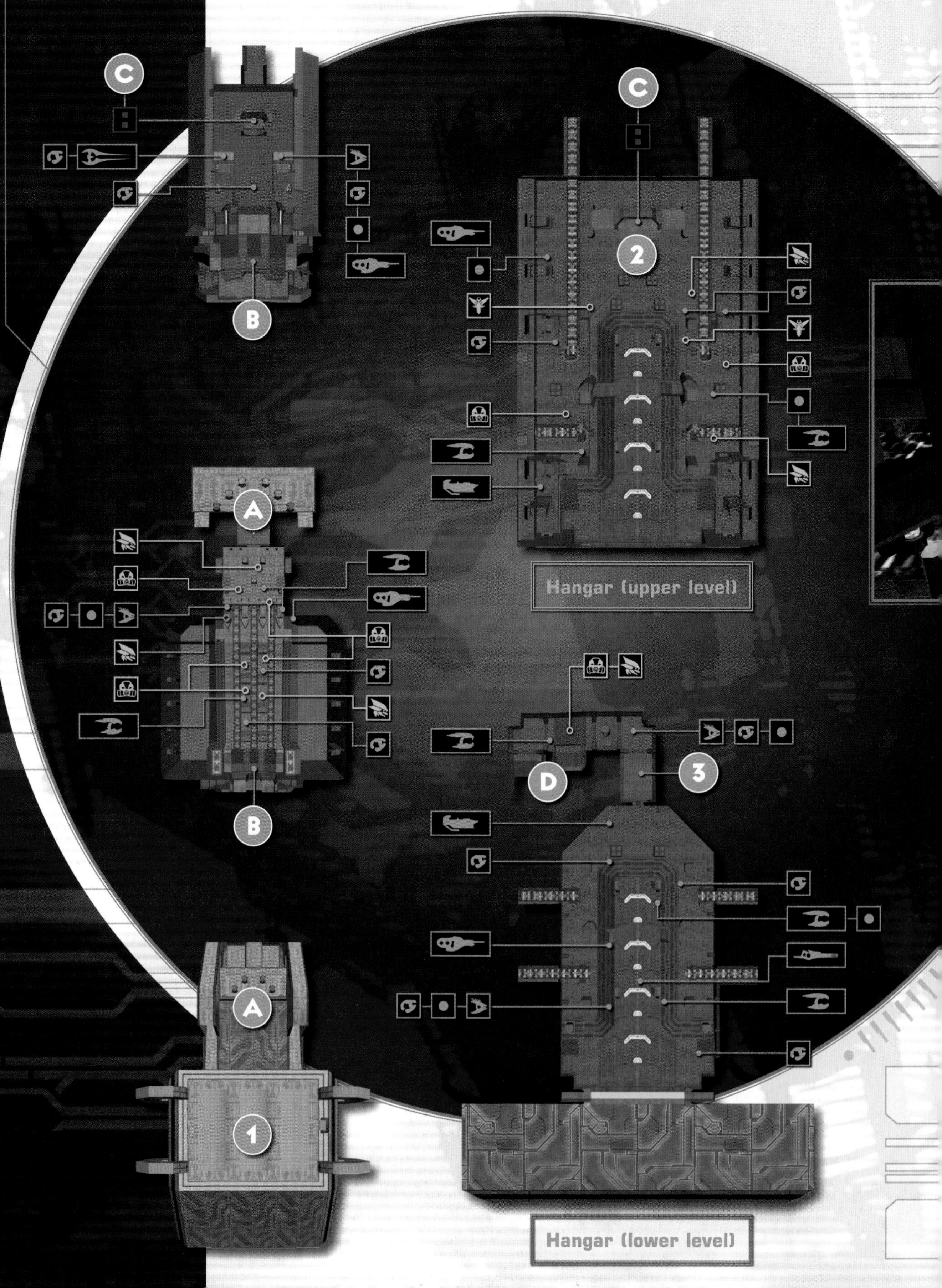

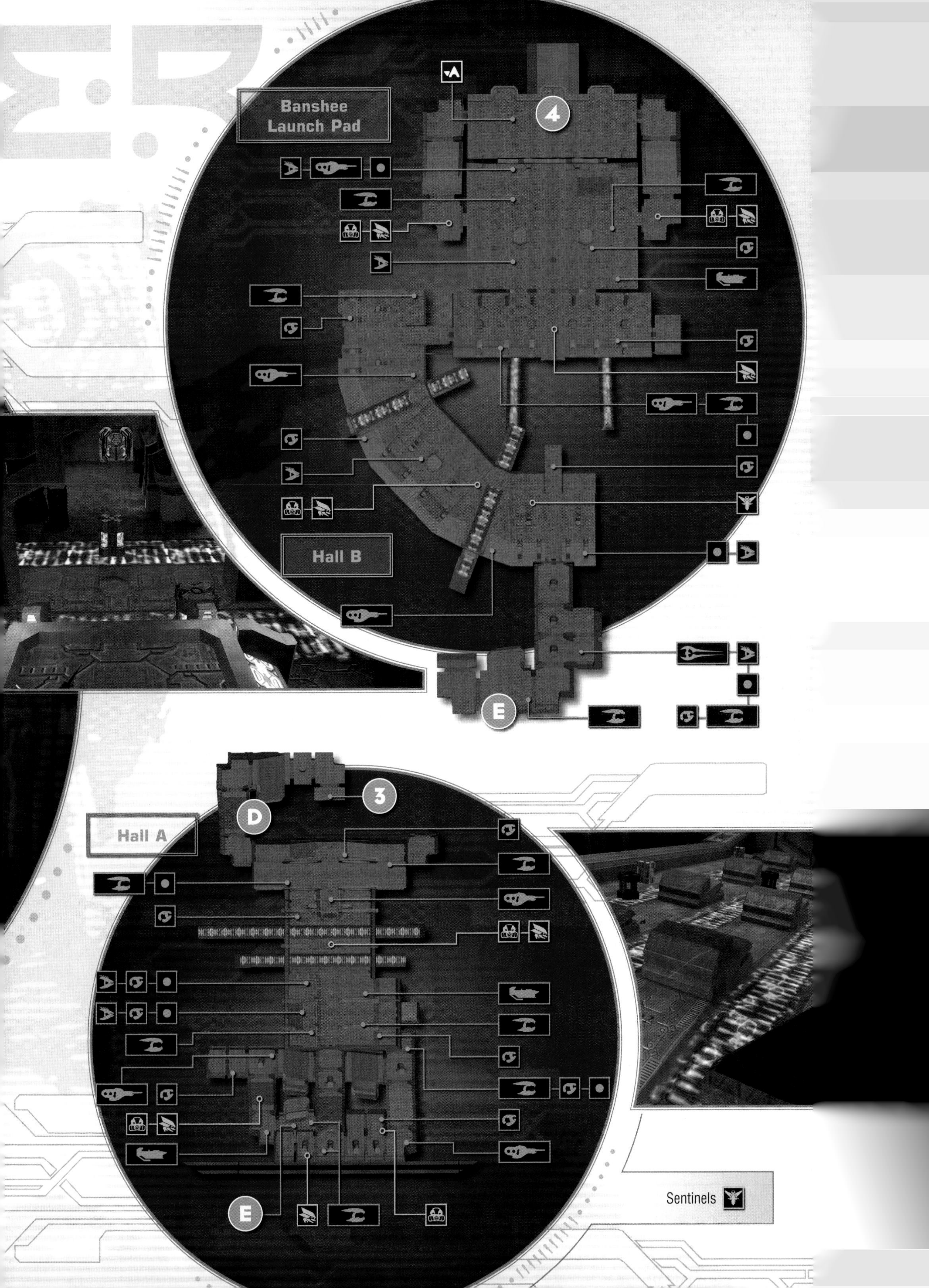
Banshee Launch Pad
4
Hall B
E
3
D
Hall A
E
Sentinels

MISSION 5

The Arbiter

Infiltrate a Forerunner facility, quell the heresy therein

MISSION BRIEFING:

The Heretic Leader must die. You have the element of surprise. Use your Active Camouflage. Act swiftly and with stealth. Quell his heresy, Arbiter – let no blasphemous breath leave his body evermore.

The Blade of the Prophets

We really didn't want to spoil the surprise for you, so the existence of the Arbiter as a playable character has been kept entirely secret until this point. But here we are: you now take the role of the Arbiter! In terms of control, this Covenant warrior is fundamentally identical to the Master Chief – the way you move, shoot and interact with the world around you remains the same. Don't worry: the action will return to the Master Chief in a while. For now, take the opportunity to enjoy the story – not to mention the action – from an alternative perspective.

There is one quite significant difference: the Arbiter is equipped with an Active Camouflage device. Press ◯ to become temporarily invisible. Watch the circle next to the grenades display (Fig. 1) and note that it is depleted at a fairly rapid rate. Once this energy level reaches its lowest extent, the Arbiter will return to full visibility and the circle will begin to fill up again. The Active Camo will be disabled when the Arbiter is attacked or initiates an assault himself. There is one other thing that you should bear in mind: the Arbiter cannot exchange every weapon with certain Covenant allies. A Grunt, for instance, will not take a two-handed firearm.

01

TIP

The most important thing to do in your new role as the Arbiter is to concentrate on who is your friend, and who is your enemy. The members of the Covenant that you have been aggressively slaughtering as the Master Chief are now your allies. You are now supported by SpecOps Elites and SpecOps Grunts (Fig. 2). When aiming your weapon at an ally, the crosshair will turn green; if you're pointing it at an enemy, it will be red. Your allies are also equipped with Active Camo, and will keep it engaged until you alert the enemy.

Your opponents during this level are also Grunts and Elites, but they are Heretics, and are easily distinguished by their bronze color (Fig. 3). Heretic Elites also wear special masks and four "stings" on their back. They prefer to fight with the Carbine or Sentinel Beam. Heretic Grunts are also distinct to behold: they wear blue-white glowing rebreathers on their back. In terms of armaments, they opt for the Needler and Plasma Grenades.

02

03

1 "A Whisper in the Storm"

Mission Objective: Locate the Heretic Leader

Your weapons are the Energy Sword and the Plasma Rifle. You also have four Plasma Grenades. The sword is a powerful weapon, but it'll use around 10% of its energy with every deadly stroke. To find the Heretic Leader, you'll have to go into the very depths of the space station. Run down the ramp with your SpecOps allies. Wait at the airlock outer door until it opens. This is where the fun begins. Press ○ as soon as the inner door opens to engage your Active Camo.

Use your invisibility to get close to the Elite (Fig. 4) and hit him on the head from behind. Now take down the other Heretics in the entrance area. Swap your Plasma Rifle with a Carbine and kill the Heretics on the incline from a safe distance with precise headshots (Fig. 5).

Move up the slope and then walk down again on the other side, and watch out for Heretics lurking behind the low walls. Don't let the conveyor belts carry you into the abyss! Reactivate your Active Camo regularly when advancing into unknown territory – it's also useful for making unseen retreats. On the lower level, you'll find an elevator in the back part of the hall (Fig. 6). More Grunts and Elites will attack you. If any members of your SpecOps team survived, you'll meet them by the elevator. Use the multicolored holo-switch in the elevator to go down (Fig. 7).

04

05

TIP

You can approach this level in an entirely different way, should you so desire. Follow the words of the SpecOps Commander: "Be silent and swift!" Use your Active Camo to proceed and remain unseen through each area. Find places that cover you from prying eyes, wait until your Camo is recharged, then continue running. Using this method, it's possible to get to the elevator without further incident – bar, perhaps, a number of judiciously timed "stealth" kills. You should note, however, that the Arbiter's Active Camo doesn't last as long on higher difficulty levels, rendering this stealth-and-run technique almost useless.

06

07

2 The Hangar

Activate your Camo in the elevator before you reach your destination. Now take cover behind the elevator to take stock of the situation. The spaceship in the hangar is a Seraph. You won't be able to use it. Next to the usual Heretics there are also Sentinels in this hall. Watch out for the bluish glowing containers (Fig. 8): they'll detonate when subjected to sustained fire. This can be very useful when enemies are standing nearby, but deadly should the Arbiter be stood next to one when it explodes. The exit from the hall is on the lower level, opposite the great hangar gate. This door will only open after you've killed all the enemies in the hangar.

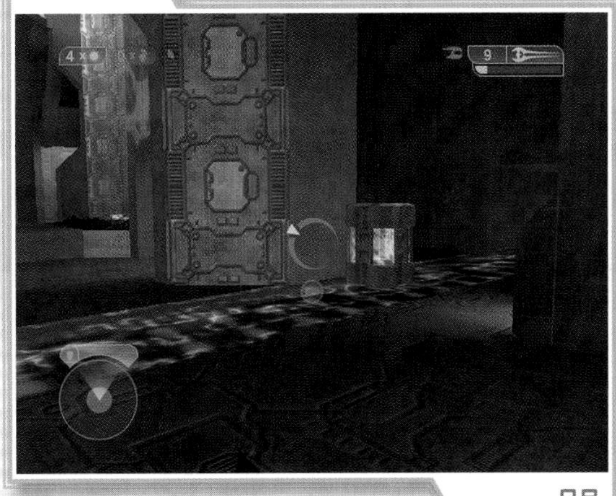

08

As soon as a Heretic sees you, it will notify its comrades. The best thing you can do is to run camouflaged from cover to cover towards the great hangar gate. You'll be ordered to open the gate to allow reinforcements to enter. Use one of the switches on the left or the right next to the gate (Fig. 9). You won't be able to run around outside – the fierce winds will prevent your exit from the hangar.

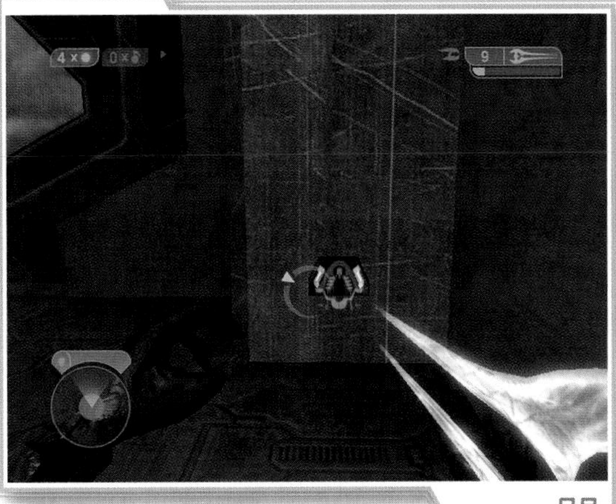

09

As soon as your Phantom enters the hall, it will fire everything it has at your enemies and deploy several SpecOps soldiers to assist you. At the same time, many Heretics will enter the hall, including Grunts carrying Fuel Rod Cannons (read an introduction to this weapon on page 30). The Phantom will soon leave, and the advancing Heretic reinforcements finally open the exit (Fig. 10). Grunts will position Plasma Cannons in front of it. Get a Fuel Rod Cannon if you can grab one and remove this danger as soon as possible.

10

SENTINELS

These flying machines are another Forerunner creation. Using a continuous laser weapon – the Sentinel Beam – they attack foes with a cold, mechanical aptitude. While a graze from the Sentinel Beam will not trouble the Master Chief, continuous contact is very damaging. Multiple Sentinels can strip your shield within seconds – or a heartbeat on higher difficulty levels – and are to be approached carefully.

The Sentinel's anti-gravity systems make them a relatively slow and predictable opponent to target (especially when compared to nimble Covenant Drones). They are more susceptible to plasma than bullets. You should also note that when a Sentinel explodes while sufficiently close to another one, both will be destroyed. Be warned: there are shielded variations of the basic Sentinel that are far harder to destroy.

TIP

- The Sentinel Beam with its continuous fire is a good weapon against this flying menace – as, indeed, are the Needler's homing projectiles. A charged Plasma Pistol shot is generally the quickest way to dispatch them.
- You'll usually encounter groups of Sentinels. However, there are hatches from which these hovering foes can emerge – and they will continue to appear until these openings are destroyed. Doing so should be your top priority.

3 Hunt the Heretic

A corridor leads you away from the hangar (Fig. 11). There will be some Elites and Grunts down here, so watch your Motion Tracker closely. You should rely on the power of grenades and the Energy Sword – or, if you prefer, just improvise with any other available weapon.

After three turns to the left, you'll reach another hall (Hall A on the map). The exit is on the right side. Turn on your Camo and take out a Grunt or two. Now position yourself for reinforcements – they'll arrive shortly via the door across from the point where you entered this area (Fig. 12). You'll now be in another corridor that leads downward in regular slopes to the left. There is another hall at the end of the corridor. Approach solitary Elites from behind on your way and finish them off with a hit on the back of the head. You should also dispatch the Grunts found sleeping in some corners.

In the second hall (Hall B), turn to the left. Start running and press ○. If you're fast enough, you might be able to reach the exit without being noticed. The exit is in a niche on your right side (Fig. 13), shortly before the hall ends. Your goal is mere steps away: you only have to go through a door to finally reach the Heretic Leader. Unfortunately, he's standing on the Banshee launch pad behind a glass screen – and now you definitely will be discovered. One of the doors in the side walls will open. Don't allow the Heretics to detain you for long. Fight your way through them and follow the Heretic Leader.

14

15

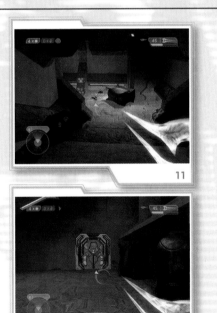

11

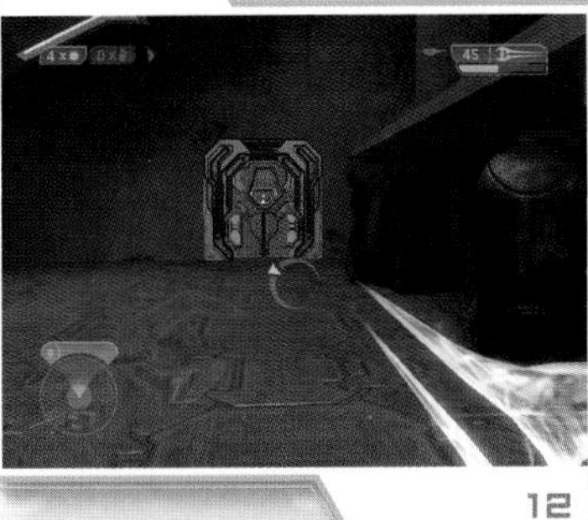

12

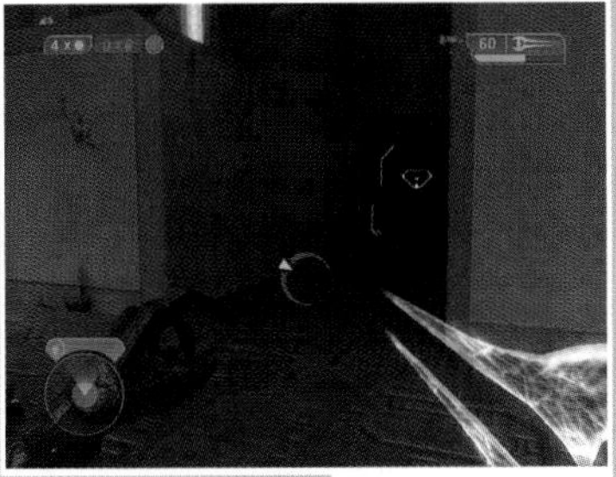

13

4 "To the Hunt"

Mission Objective: Pursue the Heretic Leader

Climb into a Banshee and take off. Look right, to the outer rim of the station (Fig. 14). At the back of the exterior wall – distinguished by blue glowing features – there will be a landing platform (Fig. 15). It's a bit higher than your current altitude. That is where the Heretic Leader has landed his Banshee and fled into the station. As soon as you get close to the platform, you'll receive an order to clear the landing zone. Kill all the Heretics – and watch out for blasts from Fuel Rod Cannons – so you can get inside.

The "official" route is a little more complicated, but a lot more fun. Your Banshee is accompanied by a Phantom (it's marked with a Waypoint). This Phantom assists you in your search for the Heretic Leader. To support it in turn, you'll have to shoot down all the attacking Banshees and destroy the Plasma Cannons on each and every platform and balcony. The search will slowly lead you around the whole station.

TIP

You'll find all the information you need to pilot a Banshee on page 36. The physical state of a Banshee actually has no bearing on its performance. Be it battered or as shiny as the day it left the assembly line, it's actually your own shield level that matters.

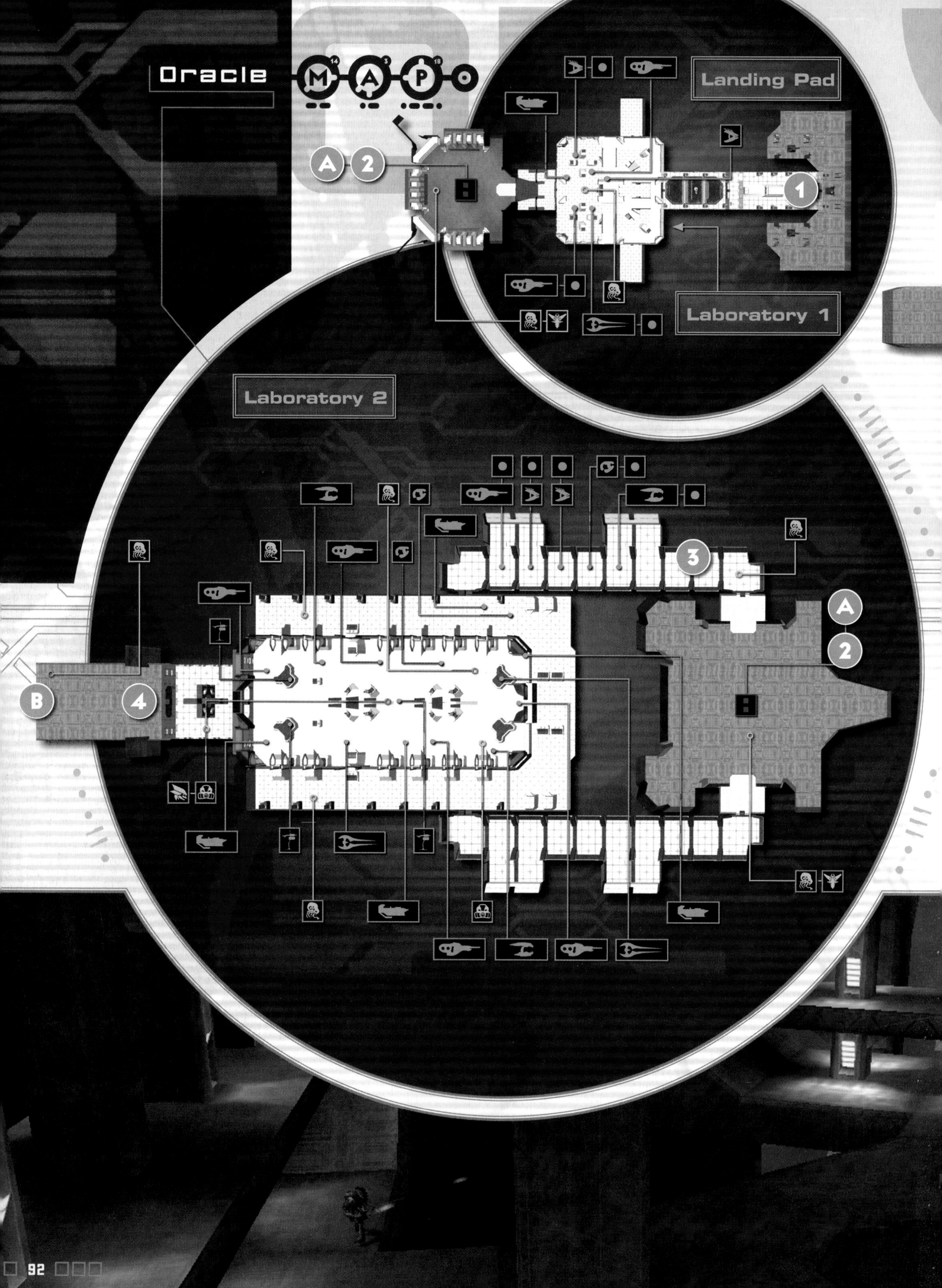
Oracle
M
A
P
Landing Pad
A
2
1
Laboratory 1
Laboratory 2
3
A
2
B
4

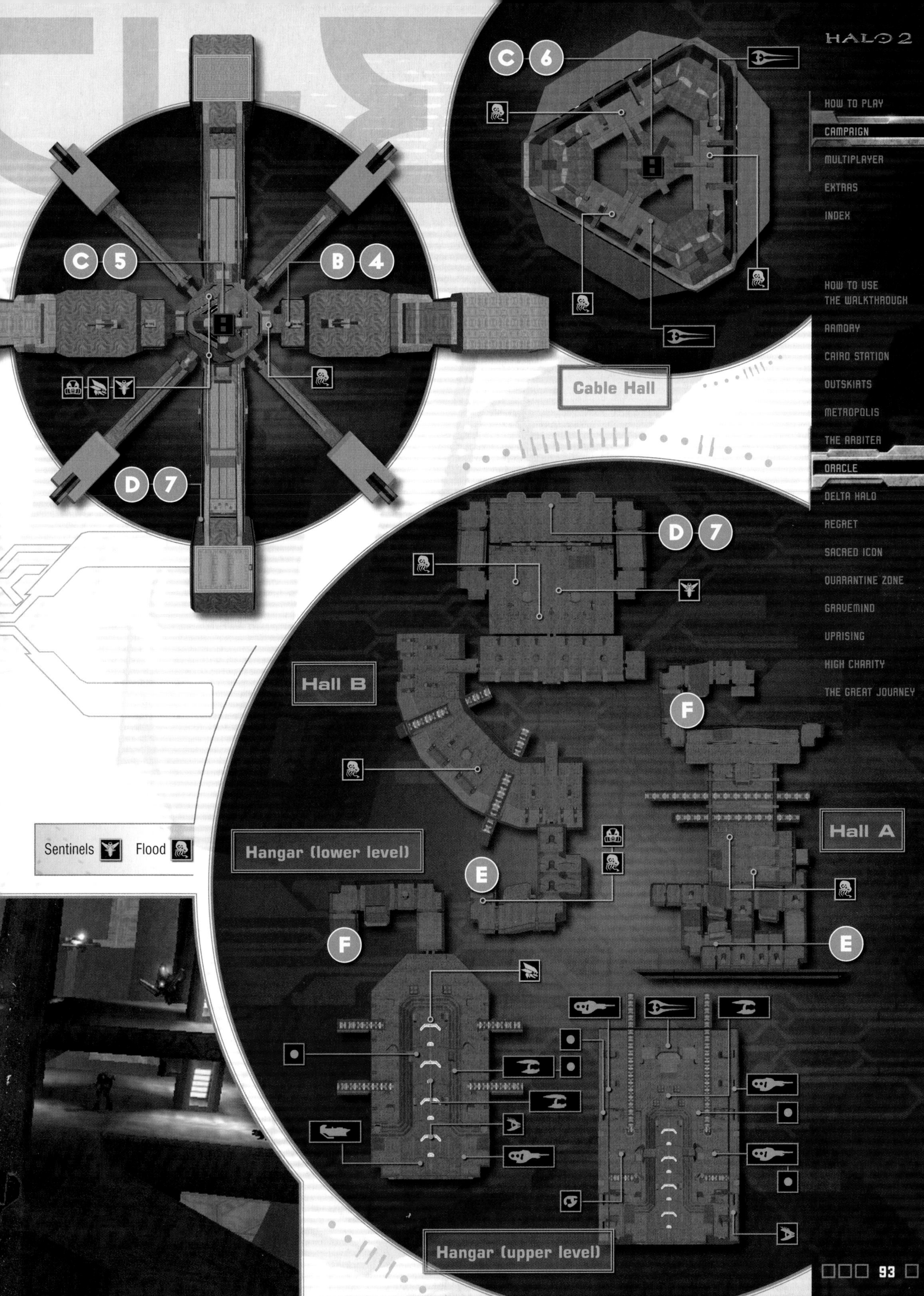
C 6
C 5
B 4
D 7
Cable Hall
D 7
Hall B
F
Hall A
Sentinels
Flood
Hangar (lower level)
E
E
F
Hangar (upper level)

MISSION 6

Oracle

Kill the Heretic Leader. May the will of the Prophets be done

MISSION BRIEFING:

The Heretic Leader is still on the run. Fight your way through the infested labs! Drive him out of his hideout! Pursue him without mercy! Hunt him down and kill him!

01

02

1 "Juggernaut"

Mission Objective: Escape the infested labs

There's a strange ambience in the desolate rooms: it's the silence before the storm. In the first laboratory, jump to the lower level. Shortly afterwards you'll meet the Heretic Leader, but only in the form of a hologram. Use the time you have here to destroy the corpses on the floor (Fig. 1). An Energy Sword is your best weapon for that, and the wisdom of doing so will soon become apparent.

Moments later, the Flood will be upon you (Fig. 2). Countless Infection Forms will rush into the room. These parasites will not only attack all Covenant in the room, but they'll also infect the seemingly "dead" bodies of the Combat Forms, imbuing them with life anew. This is why you were told to completely incapacitate these bodies earlier! You can kill the Infection Forms easily with the Sentinel Beam. You should always walk backwards as you do to avoid being surrounded. You should also shoot at parasites that have attached themselves to your allies. (Only the SpecOps Commander seems to be immune – much like Sergeant Johnson.) When you've defeated every foe, the exit will open. Grab an Energy Sword (there's one on the lower floor) and a Sentinel Beam before leaving the laboratory.

The Flood

Humanity first encountered the Flood on Installation 04, the enormous Forerunner orbital platform that they dubbed "Halo". The basic unit of the Flood is the Infection Form. This terrifying parasitic species infects and then adapts sentient life into a twisted new Flood form. These bodies – all traces of their original personality eliminated, their appearances hideously distorted – become Combat Forms. They are unrelenting, unpitying, unfeeling aggressors of enormous strength. When no longer useful in battle, they become Carrier Forms. These spawn the smaller Infection Form which, going full circle, seeks to assimilate new sentient creatures into this repulsive collective.

As its name suggests, the Flood attacks in endless waves, ruthlessly breaking up resistance with a sheer weight of numbers. Reports from the events on Installation 04 indicate that the Flood is able to use available technology, and even repair and utilize interstellar vehicles. The horrifying possibility that this abomination might escape into the universe at large must be prevented at all costs. The Flood's potential for exponential growth while its "food" exists could lead to the end of all intelligent life.

INFECTION FORM

The Infection Form is the first Flood stage. Individually weak, these vile creatures attack in dozens or even hundreds. When one insinuates itself into a host body, it mutates it into a Combat Form. Their discovery on Halo indicated that the Infection Form can remain dormant for countless millennia until a suitable host awakens it.

A single specimen is no threat to a shielded warrior: it will simply burst on his shield. They so rarely are found alone, though – hence the Flood moniker. As dozens of Infection Forms skitter towards and hit the Master Chief or Arbiter, their shields will sustain incremental damage. Should it be completely depleted, these pernicious foes will penetrate his battle suit. Do not misgauge the danger they represent.

TIPS

- When fighting against the Flood, move backwards and strafe to avoid them.
- Every projectile will burst the Infection Form. As it attacks in large packs, the best choice of firearm is an automatic weapon. Bursts of fire are more effective than single shots or – unless really necessary – full automatic fire. When facing this Flood form alone, try to manage them effectively while expending as little ammunition as is necessary. Use the Sentinel Beam if you can get one: the continuous energy beam is highly effective.
- As a rule, the use of Plasma Grenades against all flood types is inadvisable. As they ruthlessly run towards your position they can close in quickly enough to return your explosive gift. Be especially careful when throwing a Plasma Grenade at distant enemies while surrounded by Infection Forms. You might inadvertently stick it to one of them, which would be very, very stupid indeed.
- The Infection Form is not exclusively concerned with ending the life of player-controlled characters: they will also home in on dead or unconscious Marine and Covenant bodies to corrupt them. Unless you like fighting the aggressive Combat Form, you might want to forestall this eventuality whenever you can.

COMBAT FORM

Your attention should be focused primarily on the Combat Form during all encounters with the Flood. Mutated, zombie-like perversions of the Marines and Covenant Elites that have fallen afoul of the Infection Form, they are fast, tough and agile. Capable of huge leaps towards the Flood's food – which includes, of course, the Master Chief and Arbiter – they are also inclined to striking out with stinging melee attacks.

Combat Forms can employ any weapon that their host body might once have used. They fight without fear of death or injuries: the individual will unthinkingly sacrifice itself to further the cause of the whole. Therefore, former Marines carrying Rocket Launchers are a threat you should neutralize immediately. Combat Forms will also not flinch as they lose limbs. There are many times when you will apparently kill one, only to stare in horror as it stands and rejoins the fray moments later.

TIPS

- Even when you've knocked a Combat Form to the floor, be careful – it may still come back to life. If an Infection Form reaches the body, it will rise to its feet and attack again. Make sure this does not happen. A shot to its head and even severing its remaining limbs might be a good idea – unless your ammo is dangerously low, that is. It's better to be safe than sorry.

- Don't even think about using normal melee attacks against these monsters: it will have no tangible effect and will elicit a quick and dizzying counterattack. The Sniper Rifle is also useless against the Combat Form. As its biological format has been modified beyond recognition, the high-velocity bullets will fly straight through it without causing so much as a murmur.

- For short range exchanges – and the Flood do their best to ensure that every battle always is – the Shotgun is the best human weapon to use against the Combat Form. The Forerunners developed the Sentinel Beam as a means of controlling the Flood. This can be handy for hitting these aberrations from afar.

- The Covenant Energy Sword is very effective against the Combat Form. It will completely destroy the body, leaving nothing behind that could be brought back to life by Infection Forms.

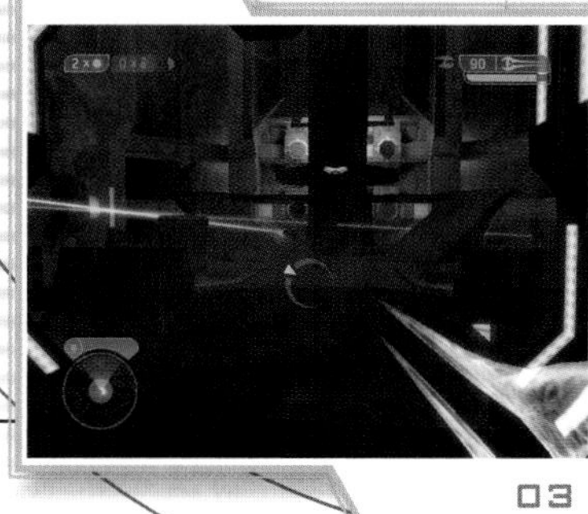
03

2 Take Me Down to Hell

There are several Flood and Sentinels locked in combat on the elevator (Fig. 3). Be careful not to get between their lines of fire. There are Infection Forms inside the specimen capsules on the platform. As the elevator moves downwards at an excruciatingly slow pace, more Combat Forms and Sentinels will come towards you. Fighting the Combat Form will be much easier if you've got an Energy Sword. The attackers will burst after a single hit – and, moreover, it will only take two to three percent of your sword's energy. It's also more efficient in the sense that there will be no bodies remaining for the Infection Forms to reanimate. If you're using another weapon, things won't be that easy: you'll have to keep the attackers in check and destroy their bodies afterwards. The Sentinel Beam is also very effective. It's an excellent anti-Flood weapon, and is lethally precise when used against Sentinels. It's very tempting to simply "spray" the Sentinel Beam, but it's actually more efficacious when used in short, targeted bursts – and it lasts longer that way, too. A good strategy is to let the Sentinels take out as many Flood as they can before you destroy them, as the former are generally easier to dispatch than the latter.

CARRIER FORM

This stage of the Flood cycle of life puts a redundant or damaged Combat Form to further use, its upper body swelling as Infection Forms grow inside it. Cumbersome and grotesquely bloated, it waddles towards targets and initially appears of little threat or consequence.

Do not be deceived. The Carrier Form contains several Infection Forms inside its lumpy, bulbous body chamber. When it reaches a sentient life form it will drop to the ground and rapidly swell. It will subsequently explode, killing or disabling creatures within its vicinity and showering the area with its parasitic payload.

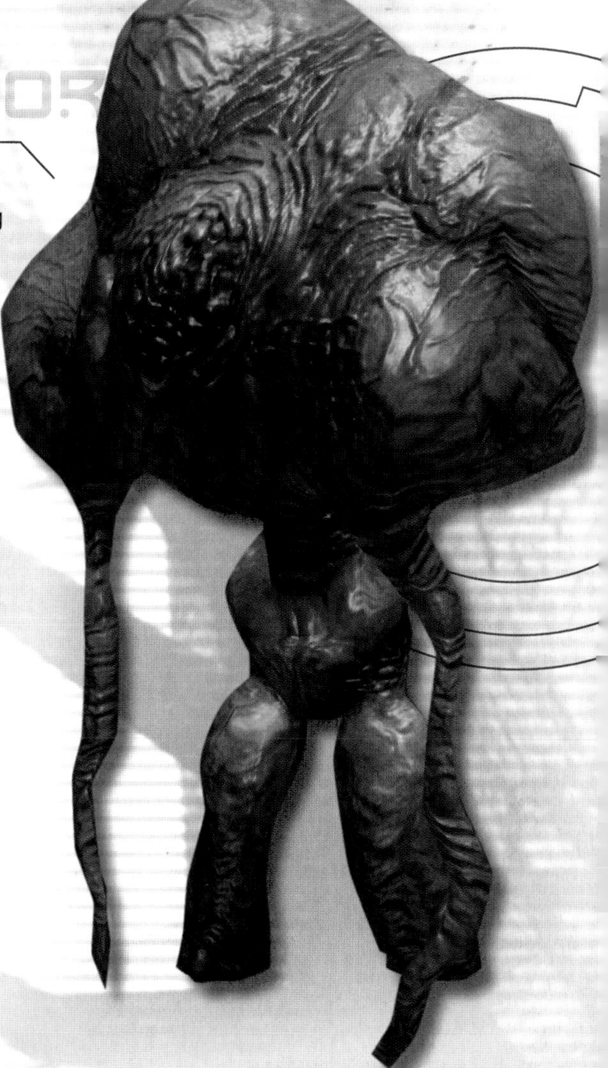

TIPS

- Don't get caught in their explosions: shoot the Carrier Forms before they reach you.
- The presence of Carrier Forms amidst a mass of Flood offers a tactical opportunity. As they explode when shot, you can aim your fire at them and maximize your firepower in a spectacular way. Learn to judge the best time to do this: against the overpowering Flood, you need every break you can get.
- There's a trick for exterminating both Carrier Form and Infection Form in one fluid movement. Throw a grenade at its feet or stick a Plasma Grenade to its body, then instantly open fire with a weapon. The Carrier Form will explode, but so too will your grenade, killing the Infection Forms immediately.

04

05

3 Laboratory No 2

Don't forget to destroy all Combat Form bodies on your way. In the second lab, a small group of Heretics is fighting against the ever-advancing Flood. Don't even think about siding with the Heretics – they are, of course, still your enemy – but you could at least intervene from above (Fig. 4). Attack the Flood and avoid being seen by any of the Heretics. Keep in mind that the Combat Forms are eminently capable of jumping up to your raised vantage point. Others, meanwhile, will fall from above. Watch your back! Sooner or later you'll have to drop down there and finish the battle off, because the exit from the laboratory will only open after every Flood and Heretic combatant is dead. Don't forget about the Arbiter's Active Camo!

There will be further attack waves at regular intervals. Don't underestimate the Carrier Forms! They may look fairly harmless, but if one of these mutants self-destructs in close proximity to you, the consequences will be more than uncomfortable. If you like, you can use the Plasma Cannons at the end of the hall, but only if the Flood advances from the other side (Fig. 5). Don't forget to destroy prone Combat Form bodies to reduce the reincarnation rate, so to speak. You'll know that this battle is almost over when the exit on the lower level opens and Heretics rush out of the gate and into the hall. Dispatch them with cold precision, then leave this area through the entrance they came through.

4 The Hunt Continues

Mission Objective: Find the Heretic Leader

On the bridge, Flood will fight against Heretics. A Phantom will deploy SpecOps soldiers to support you. At the end of the bridge, turn to the right (Fig. 6) to finally find the Heretic Leader in his shelter in the center of the station. Unfortunately, your prey is hiding behind an energy screen. Defeat all enemy forces in the hall. The Arbiter will now reveal his plan in a cutscene.

06

5 The Perfect Plan in the Perfect Storm

Mission Objective: Cut the three cables holding up the station

The mining facility seems to be suspended by cables fastened to a space station in orbit around the planet. This is strange – it's redolent of a Heath-Robinson contraption – and quite bizarre to behold, but who are we to judge the Forerunners? The plan of the Arbiter involves cutting these cables to make the station fall down… which, in turn, will cause the Heretic Leader to leave his hideout. Follow the Commander (Fig. 7). You can swap his Energy Sword with any weapon you have at the moment, but only if it contains ammo, of course. Alternatively, you can wait until you reach the hall – you can find two lying on the floor. Run up the slope and activate the elevator at the top.

07

6 "Hey, Watch This!"

In the hall on the top of the station, go from one cable to the other and cut them with the Energy Sword (Fig. 8). You can also achieve this with melee attacks using any other weapon, but that will take more time. As soon as you've cut all three cables, return to the elevator in the middle of the hall and head back down.

Mission Objective: Pursue the Heretic Leader back to the hangar

As soon as you arrive, search for the passage with the energy screen that the Heretic Leader hid behind (Fig. 9) on the ground floor. The energy screen that was once in front of it has disappeared – and so has the Heretic Leader. He's truly a shy guy, isn't he? Don't let yourself be detained by the Heretics and Sentinels – just jump down into the elevator shaft inside the hideout. Once down there you'll have to reach the other end of the hall to see another cutscene. In hot pursuit, the Arbiter leaps into a Banshee. This flight will only be a short one. Just fly over to the left, to the launch pad on the opposite side (Fig. 10).

08

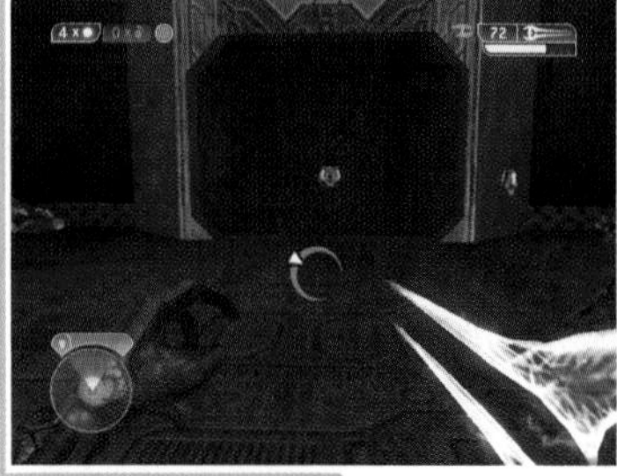

09

10

7 "Dead or Alive... Actually, Just Dead"

After the short flight, you'll be on the Banshee launch pad that you left at the end of the previous level (The Arbiter). You are now expected to get back up to the hangar with the Seraph. The Flood is abundant throughout the station. From time to time, pockets of Heretics and Sentinels will still fight against it.

The exit of the first hall is on the lower level on the right. Continue further to the right. In the next great hall (Hall B, Fig. 11), run to the left. The exit is on the right side, shortly before the hall ends. Behind it, you'll find a corridor leading upwards. Keep to the right. In the next hall (Hall A, Fig. 12), the exit is far away on the left. Now you're in another corridor going upwards. Again, keep to the right. Finally, you'll catch up with the Heretic Leader. He is accompanied by the holy Oracle – an old acquaintance from Halo: Combat Evolved...

11

12

8 Showdown

Mission Objective: Kill the Heretic Leader

The hunt is finally over: it's time for a final showdown with the Heretic Leader. He'll create two holograms of himself who will begin firing at the Arbiter as soon as the cutscene is over (Fig. 13). Sidestep as soon as you regain control. You only need to kill the actual Heretic Leader to finish the mission.

The Heretic Leader and his doubles are armed with two Plasma Rifles each. They are also equipped with jetpacks that allow them to hover through the hall. The Oracle will show up as an ally on your Motion Tracker, but this is not of any consequence during this fight. You should grab the Sentinel Beam or both Needlers lying on the floor behind the ship (Fig. 14). If you chose the Needlers, you'll only have to fire in the vague direction of the Heretic Leader – the needles will home in on their target while you sidestep incoming attacks (Fig. 15). There is another Needler that you can grab for extra ammunition when required: it's on the right of the upper level in front of a door. You'll see it if you look from the gate of the hangar in the direction of the ship. If you strike quickly, you can take out one or both holograms with a quick assault at the very start of the fight: kill one with the Energy Sword and stick a Plasma Grenade to the other. In general, you should run from cover to cover. Don't stand in the open, and use your Active Camo if you need to recharge your shields.

Ostensibly there's no difference between the Heretic Leader and his two doppelgangers. Only by subjecting a target to a sufficient amount of sustained fire can you reveal its true nature: hologram or actual Heretic Leader. If it's a hologram, continue your assault to make it disappear once and for all. Occasionally the Heretic Leader will land on the floor, which is a huge tactical mistake. If you've got an Energy Sword, you should attack him with critical hits right now. Don't forget that he's an Elite as well: you'll have to overload his full-body energy shield until he yells angrily. When this happens, attack with renewed vigor – should he manage to evade your attacks, his shield will recharge. This battle is rather more difficult on Heroic and Legendary skills settings. On these levels, the Heretic Leader will retreat when his shields are depleted, then return with them at full power twice and four times respectively. Furthermore, his dual Plasma Rifles are far more potent – so stealth is far more important. When you've finally defeated him, the story will return to the Master Chief. He's on board the In Amber Clad, and is just about to make a historical discovery...

13

14

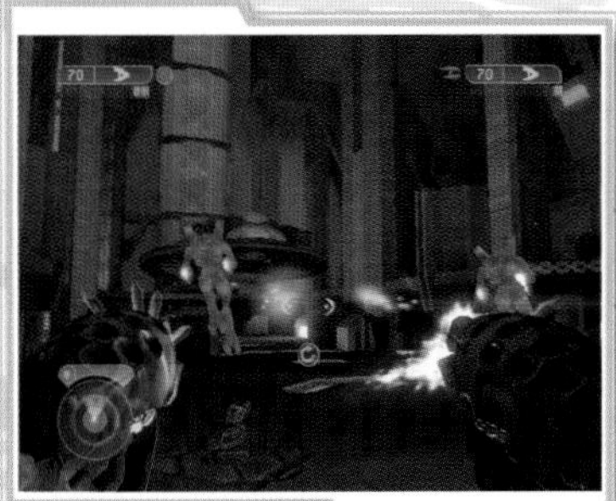

15

Delta Halo

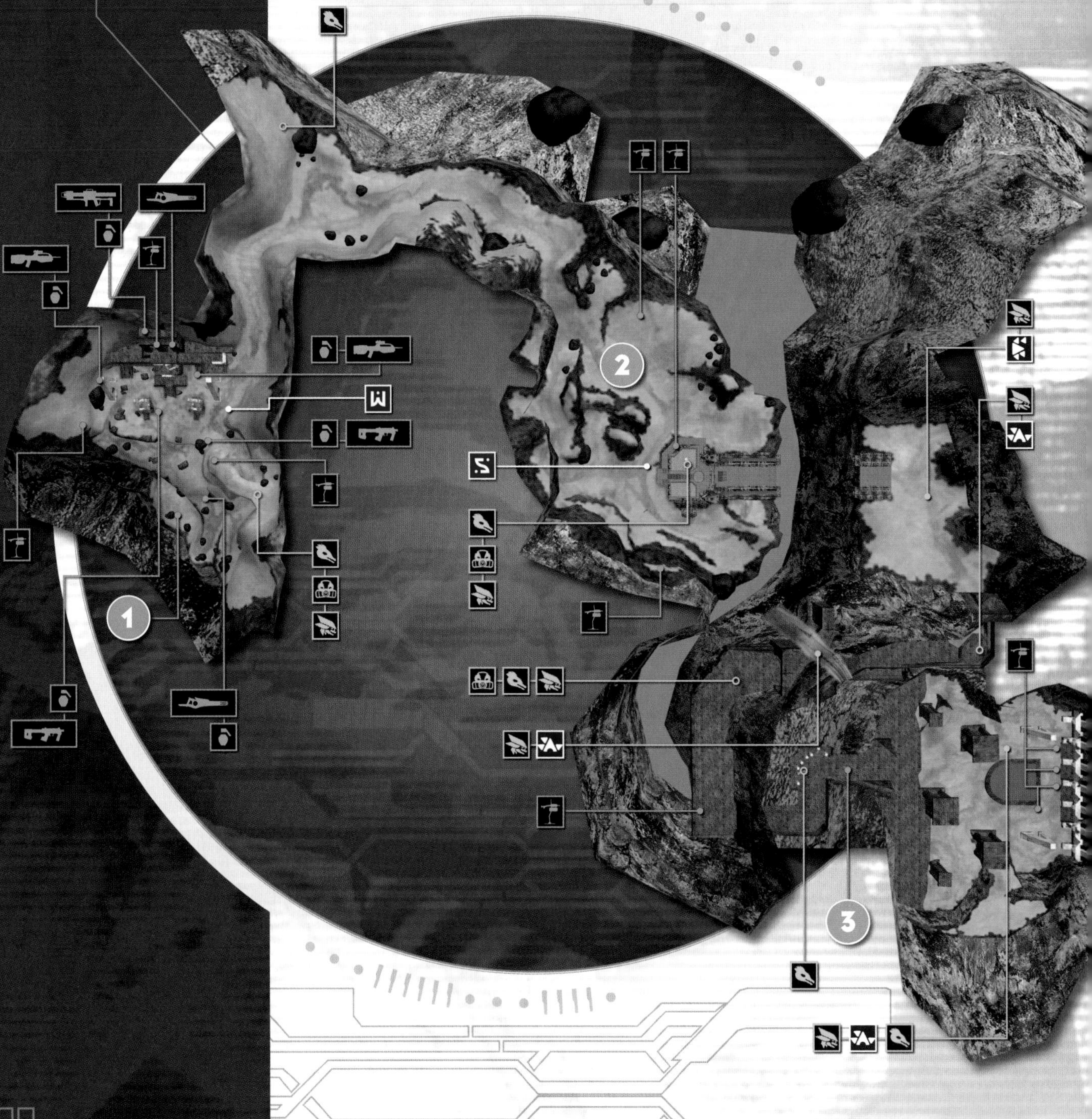

1

2

3

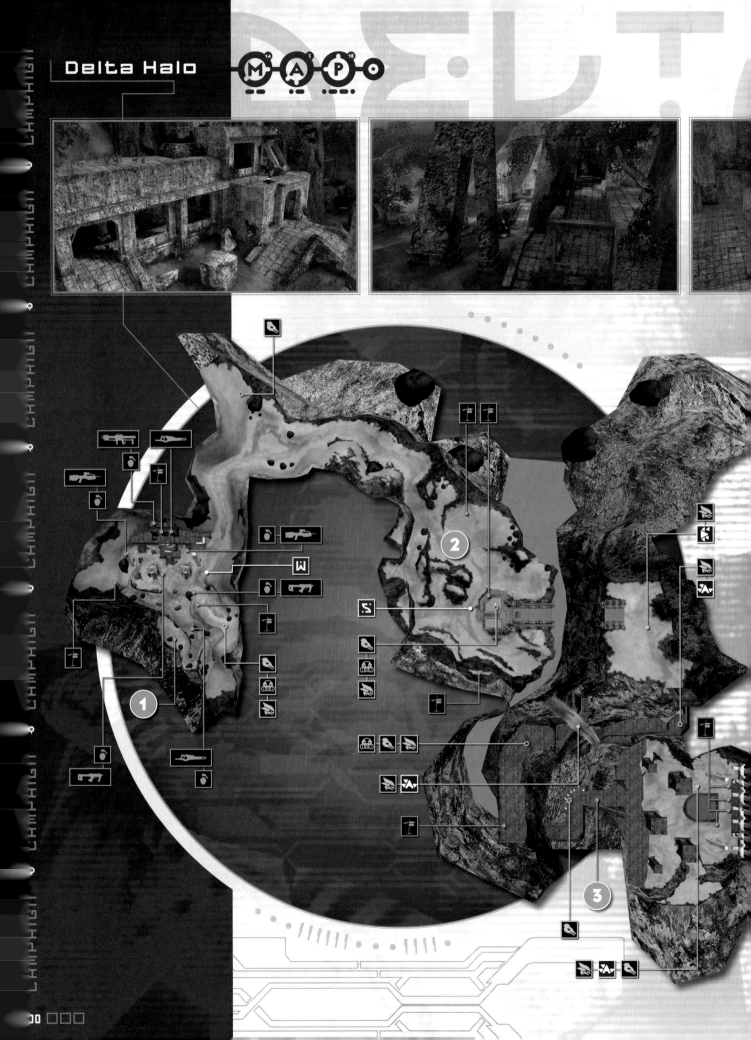

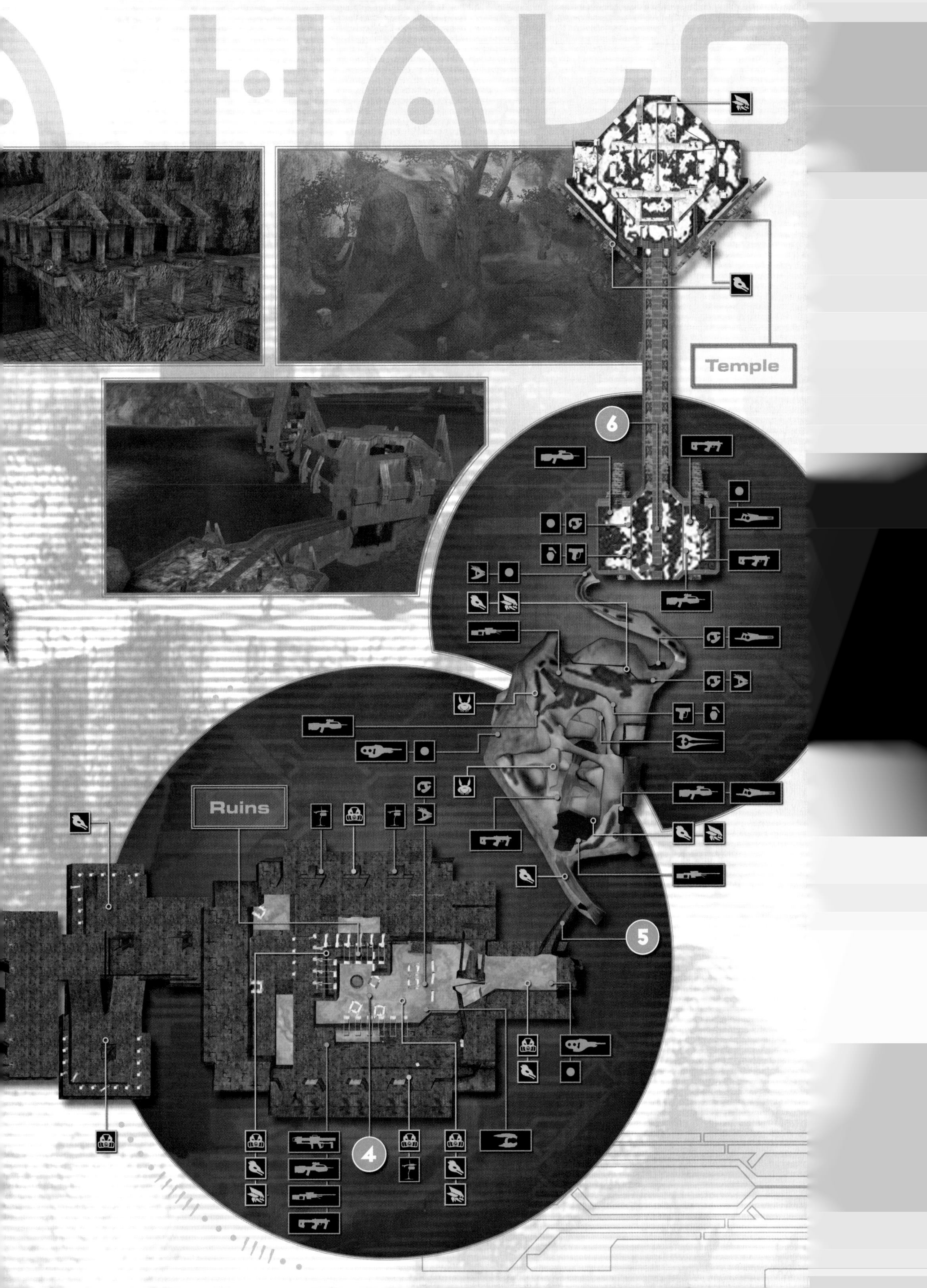

Temple
6
Ruins
5
4

MISSION 7

Delta Halo

A Covenant army stands between you and your target: the Prophet of Regret

MISSION BRIEFING:

Master Chief, neutralize the enemy artillery. Hold your position and wait for reinforcements. Gain control over the bridge and advance through the ruins occupied by the Covenant to the temple in the middle of the lake.

01

02

1 "Helljumpers"

Mission Objective: Clear the landing zone for the Pelicans

The Master Chief begins his mission on the Halo ring equipped with an SMG and a Rocket Launcher. Your objective is to destroy or capture the two Covenant ordnances (expect more on higher difficulty levels). Several ODSTs (Orbital Drop Shock Troopers) will accompany you. The turrets are protected by energy shields, but can be neutralized with a direct hit by a rocket or a well-placed grenade (Fig. 1) – the turrets will, of course, be destroyed in the process. If you want to capture and use these swiveling, multi-directional "plasma hoses", you should instead shoot their operators from behind, or make a precise headshot, aiming just above the shield.

As soon as you've killed all the Grunts, Jackals and Elites in front of the building, Phantoms will deploy enemy reinforcements. You'll find more ammunition for your Rocket Launcher on the rooftop of the building (Fig. 2). You can get up there if you start from the balcony to the right and then jump up. Destroy the cannons on the dropship as soon as possible so you can concentrate on fighting the troops as soon as they land. The turrets are perfect for this job, and will help you conserve ammunition. The first troops will be deployed on the left as seen from the building (Fig. 3), the second on the right side. After you have suppressed this resistance, wait for a Pelican to drop a Warthog as a reward for your labors. Drive past the building on your right side and proceed to the bridge. You can skip this objective if you like and continue to the bridge on foot.

TIP

The passenger in the Warthog is quite useful but, equipped with a weapon like an SMG or an Battle Rifle, they won't be able to do much damage. You can easily change that. Get out of the vehicle, go to the passenger side and force your comrade out by pressing Ⓧ. Now swap weapons with him. The best thing you can give your ally is a Rocket Launcher. Even if it is loaded with a single rocket, in the hands of an AI-controlled soldier it will have unlimited ammunition. Now go back and take the driver's seat again. When riding a Scorpion you can only act as the driver and you can't evict your passengers from their seats. If you want to change the weapon of a soldier riding on the side of a Scorpion, you'll have to lure him away from the tank – you could, for example, jump behind the wheel of a nearby Warthog.

03

2 The Bridge

Mission Objective: Extend the bridge and cross the chasm

Drive your Warthog up and down in front of the building to finish off the Ghosts, turrets and infantry. Don't forget however that the Wraith on the other side of the chasm can shoot at you. You'll have to activate the switch inside the building to lower the drawbridge. There are a number of different entrances to the building: one on ground level at the front, one the left side, and one at the back. Additionally, a big opening on the roof allows you to attack the Covenant in the room where the switch is located (Fig. 4).

After activating the switch (Fig. 5), a Pelican will deploy a Scorpion in front of the building. Get into it and set off as soon as your passengers have taken their places on its sides. Destroy the Wraith immediately with long-range shots. You'll have sufficient space for dodging in this area and on the broad bridge. Now follow the path to the ruins by going through the cave on the right. You'll meet many Ghosts and infantry on your way. You should take Elites very seriously: these clever warriors are capable of boarding your tank, and should be dispatched as soon as possible.

04

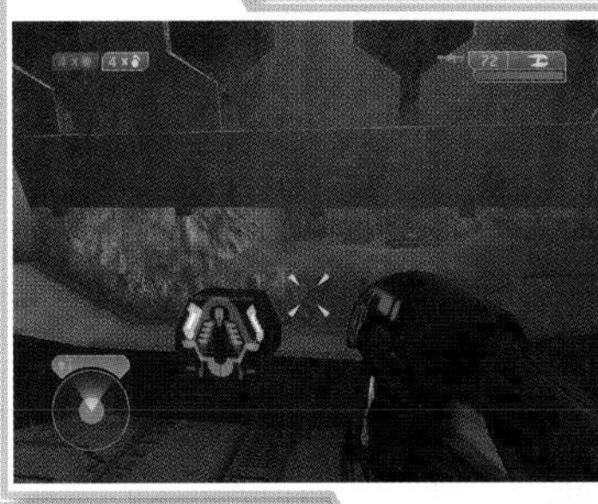

05

TIP

You'll see several holograms of a Prophet on Delta Halo (Fig. 6). When you've killed all the enemies in its vicinity you can stop and listen to the liturgy. At some point the Prophet will interrupt the choral ceremony to tell you some background information about the Covenant and the Great Journey.

06

3 "You Break It, You Buy It"

Mission Objective: Push through the Covenant-controlled ruins

On your way to the ruins you'll have to cross a valley that is defended by turrets and a whole fleet of Ghosts (Fig. 7). The Scorpion will just, praise be to an unknown Forerunner architect, fit snugly through the columns.

At the end of the next tunnel you'll find the ruins you've been searching for. Approach them with caution because the defenders are categorically not pleased to see you. The narrow entrance is on the left end of the walkway you'll see directly in front of you (Fig. 8). You won't be able to get through there with your tank, so you should use its cannon to pummel enemy forces before jumping out.

A secondary goal on your way to the center can be found on the right side of this structure. Drive up on the ramp to get as close to the arcades as possible. A Pelican will drop Weapon Capsules (Resupply Canisters) there. These torpedo-like containers are filled with weapons like Sniper Rifles and Rocket Launchers (Fig. 9). Help yourself! As soon as the area is safe, Marines will be deployed – they'll support you on your way into the center (Fig. 10). The entrance is designed for pedestrians only, but it's entirely possible to squeeze through with a Ghost.

07

08

09

10

4 Through the Ruins

After you've advanced to the center of the ruins, you'll have to fight your way through the Covenant. Use every bit of cover the ruins can offer you. Grenades are quite effective in the close confines of this area. In case you lose your way, here are some directions: in one corner of the inner courtyard a slope will lead upward (Fig. 11). Follow the slope up and then just follow the path. Don't be lulled into a false sense of security by the deceitful silence: there are Jackals and other enemies hiding between the rocks (Fig. 12). Finally, leave the area through the narrow crevice on the left side.

11

12

5 "Off the Rock, Through the Bush, Nothing But Jackal"

Shortly after the mission name has been displayed on your screen, you'll meet a Jackal sniper who is careless enough to show his back to you. His Beam Rifle will prove very useful. Have a good look at the basin in front of you. On the opposite side you'll see a small cave (Fig. 13). On the level above it, there are several Covenant crates and containers. Up there you'll also see a large cave tunnel – the exit! You can reach it via the left side of this valley. The natural bridge in the middle of the valley will help you to orientate yourself here. Between its lower end and the small cave, a path will lead steeply upwards. At the upper end of this path, keep to the right and you'll reach your goal (Fig. 14).

Use the Beam Rifle to kill all the Jackals you can see. Keep an eye on the area below your original position. There are several Covenant down there – and not only Jackals, but Elites as well. Use your scope to shoot enemies from the largest possible distance. If you are being fired at by snipers, move to a new position and examine the clearly visible traces of each shot – they will betray the position of the hidden marksmen. Occasionally Drones will attack you, too. You'll hear their characteristic noise before you see them, giving you time to switch to another weapon – and, ideally, one with a suitably high rate of fire.

13

14

6 Honor Guards!

Mission Objective: Reach the towers in the lake

Help yourself at the Weapon Capsules before entering the complex (Fig. 15). There are Jackal Snipers on the rooftop. As soon as you've killed them – and, should you attract their attention, swatted a swarm of Drones as well – get ready to meet the Honor Guards. These Elites are trained to protect of the Prophets, and are truly fearsome. Several of them carry Plasma Rifles, but that isn't really a big problem. Others, however, are carrying Energy Swords – like the two waiting for you in the building (Fig. 16).

You shouldn't get into a fight in these narrow rooms: those swords are absolutely deadly, and the Honor Guards will charge towards the Master Chief without pause. The best thing you can do is to quickly stick a Plasma Grenade to one of the guards and run backwards until it explodes. You could also simply run outside again once they've spotted you. When the Honor Guards follow you, backpedal up the ramp while constantly firing at them. Once they are dead, take an Energy Sword and kill the Honor Guards armed with Plasma Rifles. When you've dispatched them all, you'll get to see a cinematic interlude.

15

16

Temple No. 2
B
4
A
3
Gondola
2
Temple
1

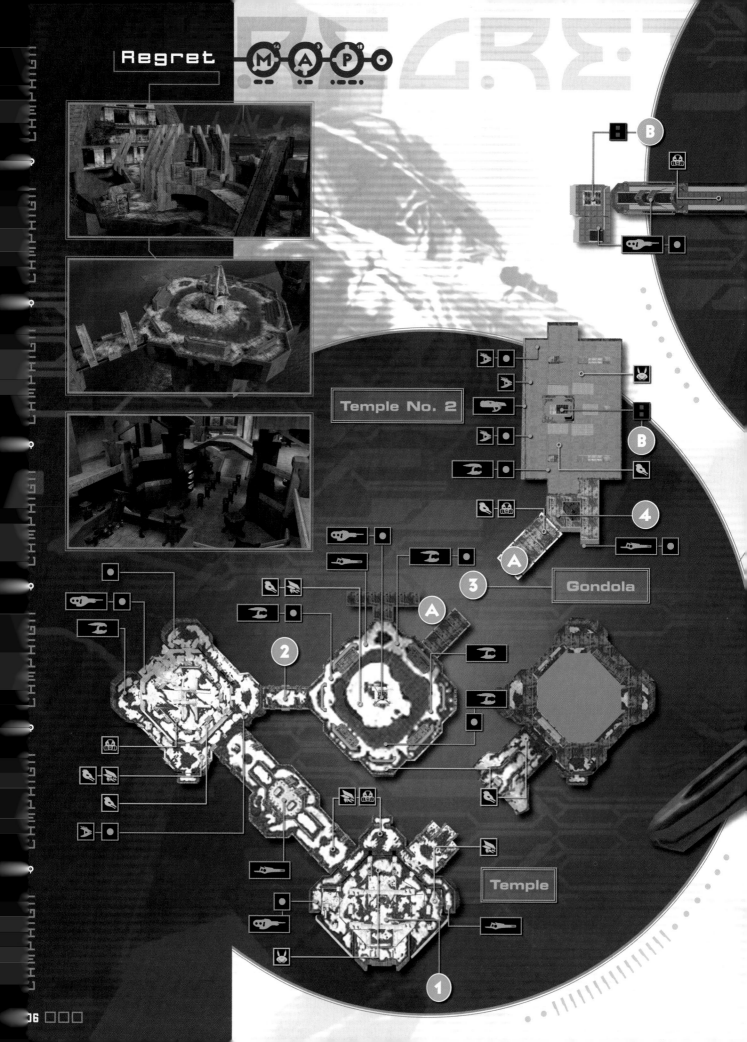

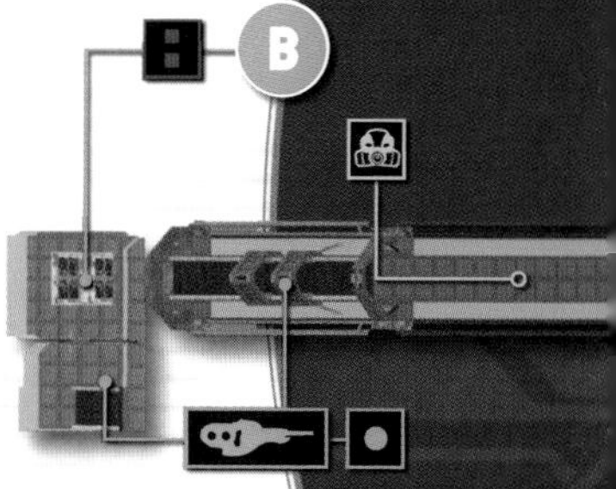

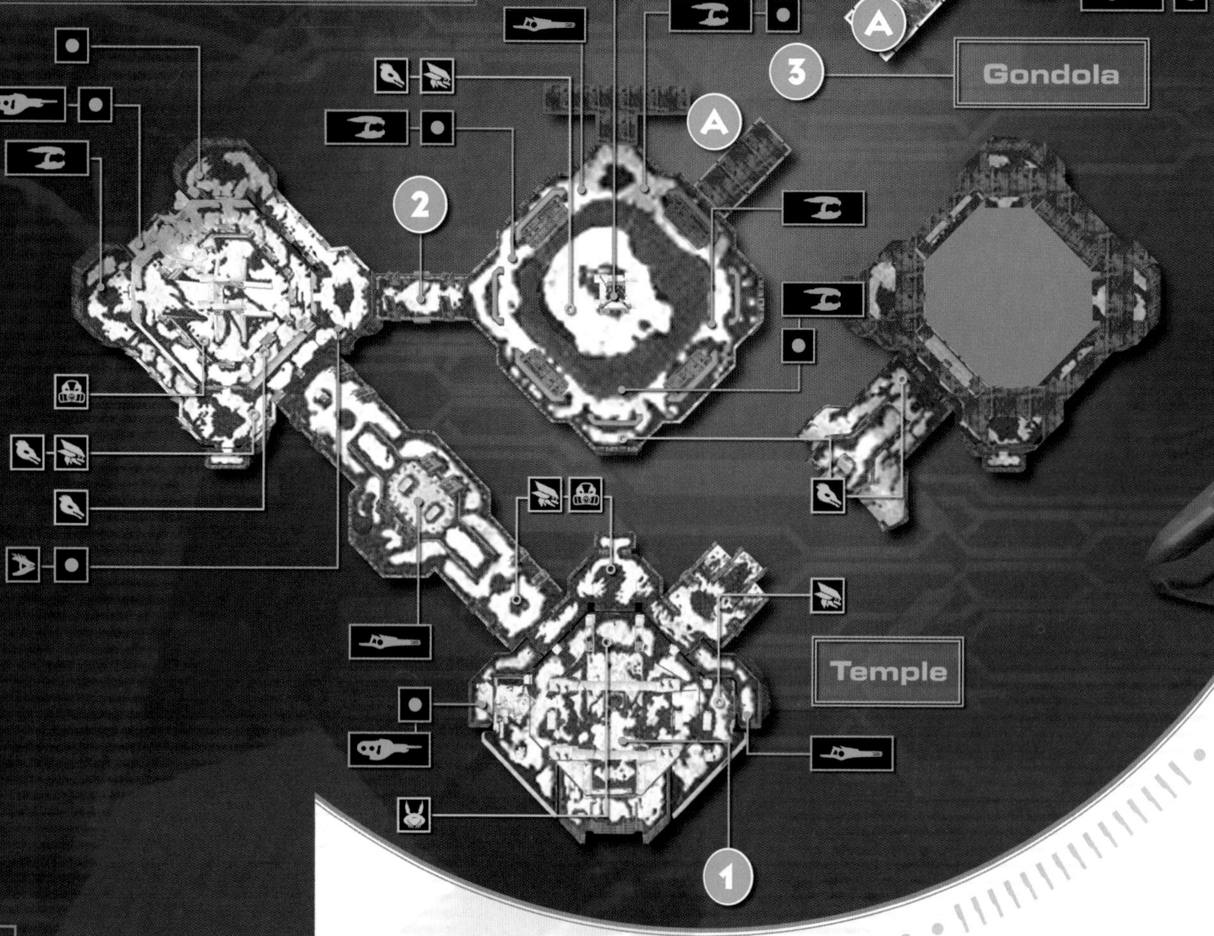

5
Submerged Section
Hologram
C
Main Temple
Gondola
D
7
D
6
C

MISSION 8

Regret

You heard the lady: locate the Prophet, take him down

MISSION BRIEFING:

Master Chief, fight your way through this building. Take the gondola and drive to the next tower and cross through the submerged structures. Get into the Main Temple and put an end to the sermons of the Prophet of Regret. Forever.

1 "Testament"

Mission Objective:
Make your way through the first set of towers

At the end of the cut-scene you'll immediately be attacked by Drones and Elites. They will enter through the door that opened on the upper-right side. Behind the door, you'll find a Beam Rifle. This weapon definitely comes in handy here, because there are several snipers on the other buildings (Fig. 1). Take a good look around. If you're hit by a shot from afar, run behind cover and take care of the marksman afterwards. The rays of the Beam Rifles will give away the position of each sniper.

There is an equally pressing but altogether more immediate problem that requires your attention as you evade and return fire on the snipers: Grunts and Elites will approach from behind the corner on the left side. When crossing the bridge leading to the next building, you should stay on the lower level (Fig. 2). You'll find another Beam Rifle here. Show a little foresight and use the weapon to kill enemies from the largest possible distance. Get to the center of the next building. You can climb across the wreckage (Fig. 3) to an almost completely buried ledge. You'll find two Plasma Grenades and two Carbines here.

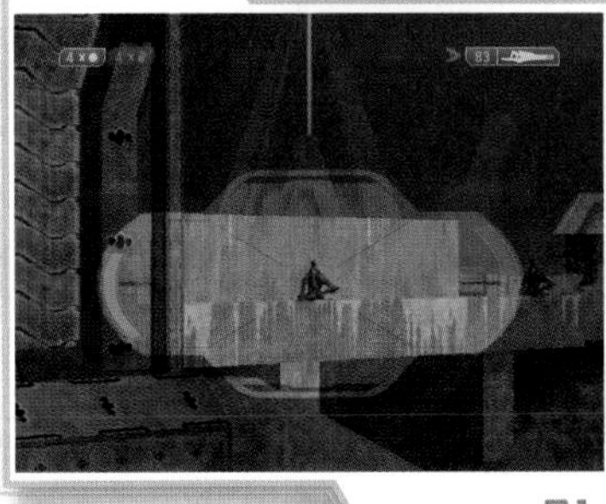

01

02

03

2 The Fellows in the Ring

There are several Elites and Jackals in the area behind the building. As soon as you've terminated each with due prejudice, there will be a small and deceptive hiatus. It won't last long: a Phantom is closing in. Take cover close to the building or under the roof in the middle of the almost completely round battle arena (Fig. 4). The dropship will also deploy a pair of Hunters. If some Marines survived up to this point, they will distract the giants. If this is the case, it's easy to place a deadly shot in their backs with the Beam Rifle or Carbine. A Plasma Sword (which you could get from one of the Honor Guards) can also help you to end this particular gladiatorial bout quickly and cleanly.

After the fight, a Pelican will deploy Weapon Capsules and fresh Marines. Take a Sniper Rifle or a Beam Rifle: you'll need it. Approaching from the direction of the building in the background, a gondola floats closer, and it's packed to the brim with Covenant (Fig. 5). Shoot as many as you can from a safe distance. After the gondola has docked, you can jump aboard and use the switch located in the lower area. The strange vessel will accelerate again.

04

05

3 "One-Way Ticket"

Mission Objective: Ride the gondola to the far towers

From the other "lane", another gondola will approach you. Be warned that there are several Covenant hiding behind the rail. Try to dispatch all Covenant forces on the tower you're driving towards (Fig. 6), as there are turrets and Grunts as well as snipers on its rooftop. When you've shot the operators of the cannons, be aware that others will take their place. There will also be enemies down at the entrance.

4 The Two Towers

Mission Objective: Pass through the submerged structures

There is a huge rock in the entrance area, and you can jump on it. From there, jump up to a ledge lying in the dark which will lead you to the turrets outside. Make sure that no Covenant can sneak up on you here. In the center of the building you'll have to kill all the Drones and Jackals. Shortly afterward, a glass elevator will appear. There are some Jackals inside (Fig. 7), so throw a grenade into it as soon as it opens. Before you get into the elevator and use the switch to get the thing going, there's a very special weapon waiting for you nearby. Climb up the slopes to the very top and go out on the ledge. Your reward is a mighty Fuel Rod Cannon.

06

07

08

09

10

5 The Submerged Structures

The central room of the underwater passage is a huge hall (Fig. 8). In the middle of it there is a large hologram of the Prophet that you are searching for. This projection is of no danger to you, but it's fanatically guarded by Drones, snipers and Honor Guards. You should finish off the snipers and Honor Guards with a Beam Rifle (you'll find one on the right side of the hall). You should take out the Drones (which are a bit further away at the end of the hall) with a weapon that has a higher rate of fire. Behind the door at the other end of the hall, two more Hunters await your arrival. You can shake them off easily: just run through the low corridors at the feet of the hologram (Fig. 9). The monsters will submit to the power of the Fuel Rod Cannon soon enough.

Your main objective here is to leave the hall again through the exit on the opposite side. Just turn your back to the Prophet and then walk left. You don't really have to go through the door with the Hunters – you could use the doors on the upper level instead. The structure of the hallways is a mirror image of the area that led you here. You'll find camouflaged Elites and even Grunts in the water corridor (Fig. 10). Finally, return to the surface in another glass elevator.

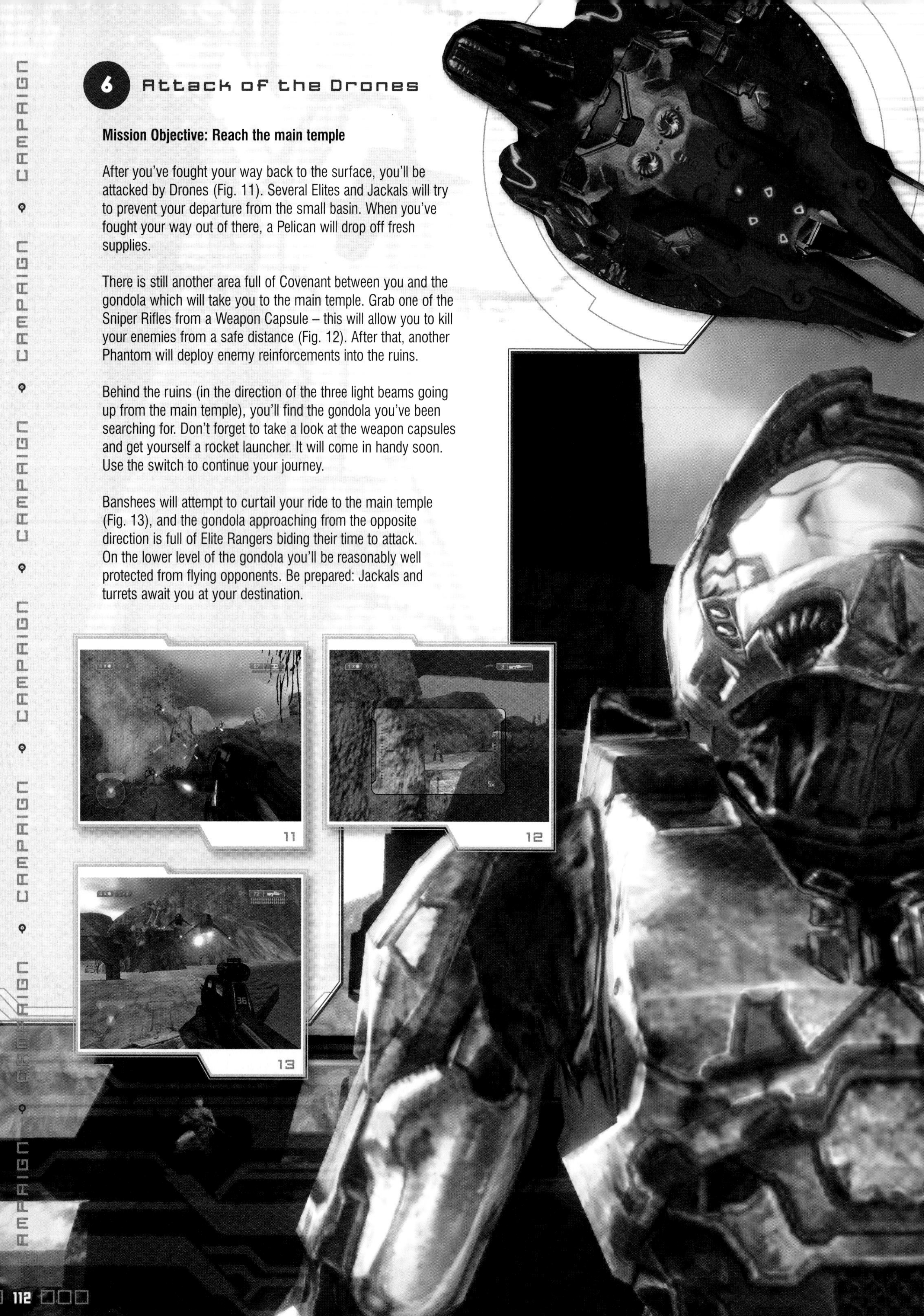

6 Attack of the Drones

Mission Objective: Reach the main temple

After you've fought your way back to the surface, you'll be attacked by Drones (Fig. 11). Several Elites and Jackals will try to prevent your departure from the small basin. When you've fought your way out of there, a Pelican will drop off fresh supplies.

There is still another area full of Covenant between you and the gondola which will take you to the main temple. Grab one of the Sniper Rifles from a Weapon Capsule – this will allow you to kill your enemies from a safe distance (Fig. 12). After that, another Phantom will deploy enemy reinforcements into the ruins.

Behind the ruins (in the direction of the three light beams going up from the main temple), you'll find the gondola you've been searching for. Don't forget to take a look at the weapon capsules and get yourself a rocket launcher. It will come in handy soon. Use the switch to continue your journey.

Banshees will attempt to curtail your ride to the main temple (Fig. 13), and the gondola approaching from the opposite direction is full of Elite Rangers biding their time to attack. On the lower level of the gondola you'll be reasonably well protected from flying opponents. Be prepared: Jackals and turrets await you at your destination.

11

12

13

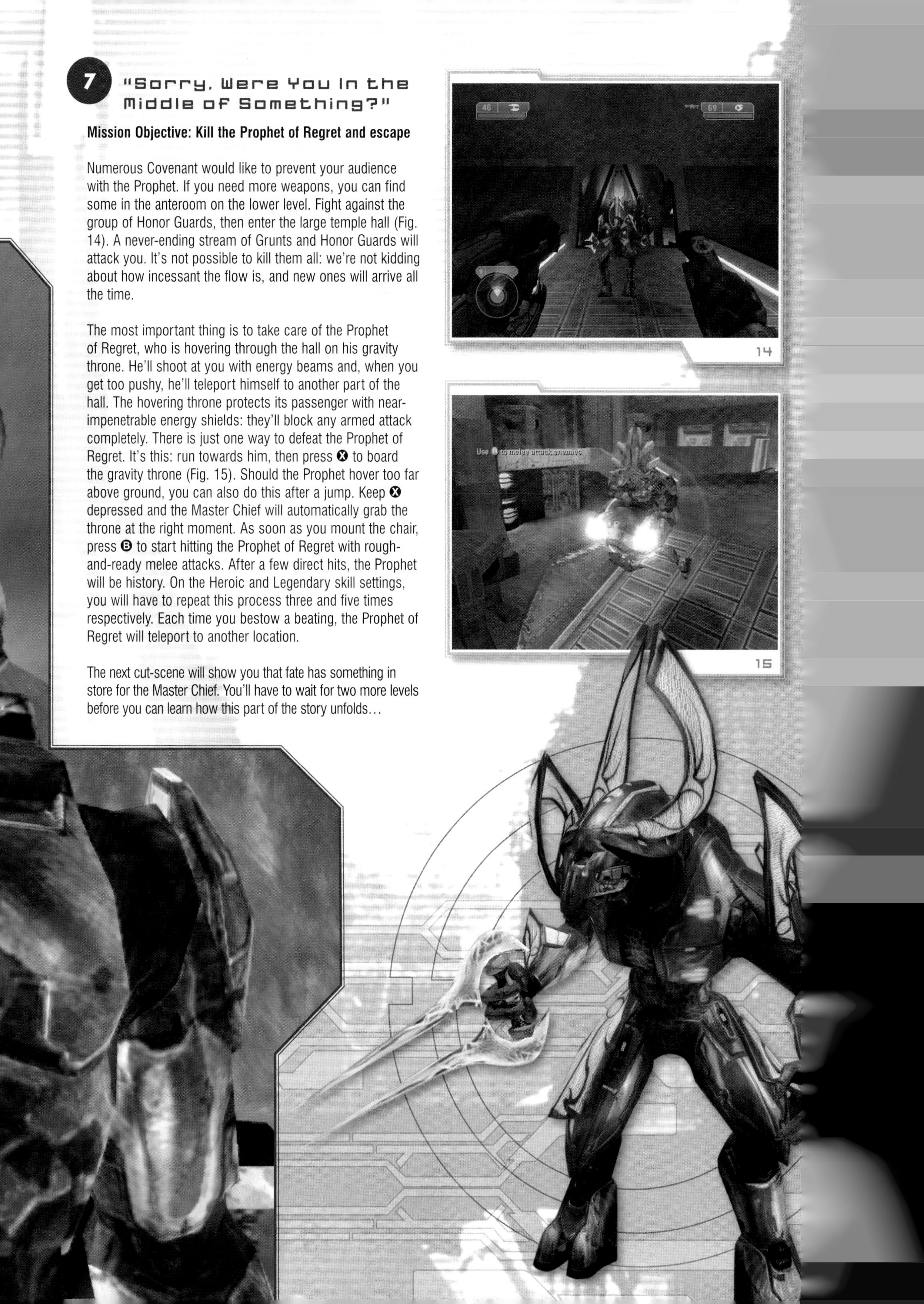

14

15

7 "Sorry, Were You In the Middle of Something?"

Mission Objective: Kill the Prophet of Regret and escape

Numerous Covenant would like to prevent your audience with the Prophet. If you need more weapons, you can find some in the anteroom on the lower level. Fight against the group of Honor Guards, then enter the large temple hall (Fig. 14). A never-ending stream of Grunts and Honor Guards will attack you. It's not possible to kill them all: we're not kidding about how incessant the flow is, and new ones will arrive all the time.

The most important thing is to take care of the Prophet of Regret, who is hovering through the hall on his gravity throne. He'll shoot at you with energy beams and, when you get too pushy, he'll teleport himself to another part of the hall. The hovering throne protects its passenger with near-impenetrable energy shields: they'll block any armed attack completely. There is just one way to defeat the Prophet of Regret. It's this: run towards him, then press ⓧ to board the gravity throne (Fig. 15). Should the Prophet hover too far above ground, you can also do this after a jump. Keep ⓧ depressed and the Master Chief will automatically grab the throne at the right moment. As soon as you mount the chair, press Ⓑ to start hitting the Prophet of Regret with rough-and-ready melee attacks. After a few direct hits, the Prophet will be history. On the Heroic and Legendary skill settings, you will have to repeat this process three and five times respectively. Each time you bestow a beating, the Prophet of Regret will teleport to another location.

The next cut-scene will show you that fate has something in store for the Master Chief. You'll have to wait for two more levels before you can learn how this part of the story unfolds…

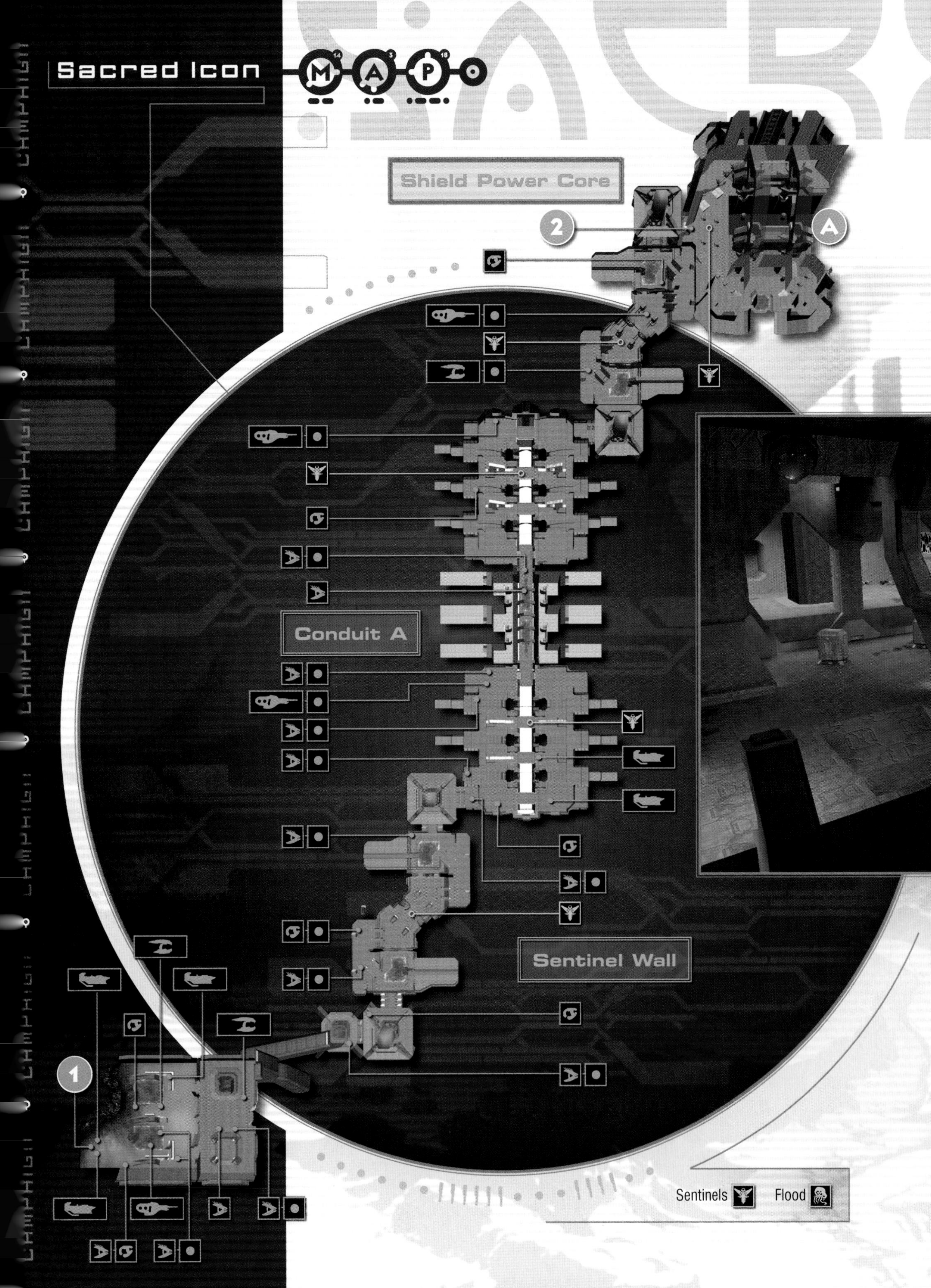
MAP
Shield Power Core
2
A
Conduit A
Sentinel Wall
1
Sentinels
Flood

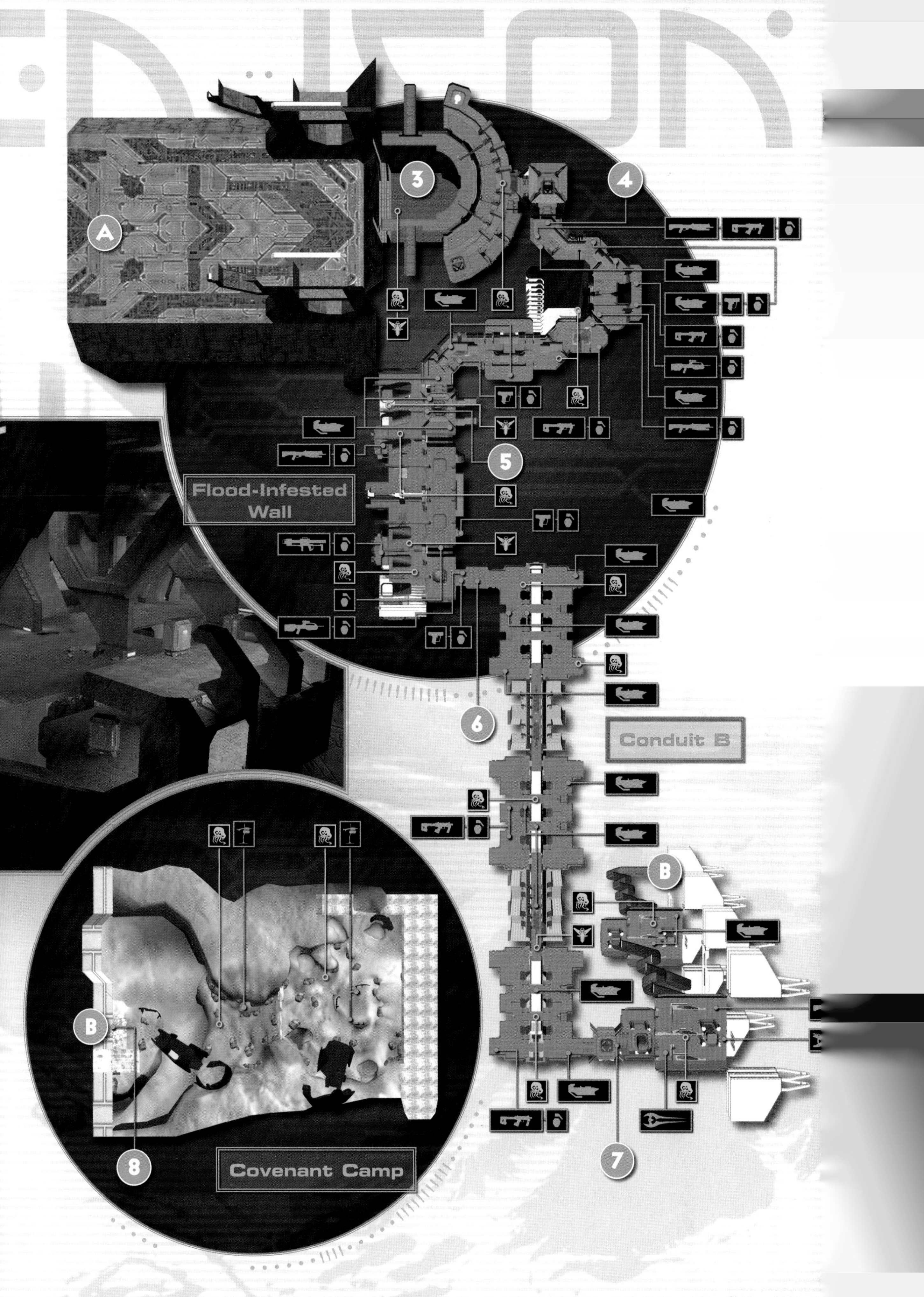

3
4
A
5
Flood-Infested Wall
6
Conduit B
B
7
8
Covenant Camp

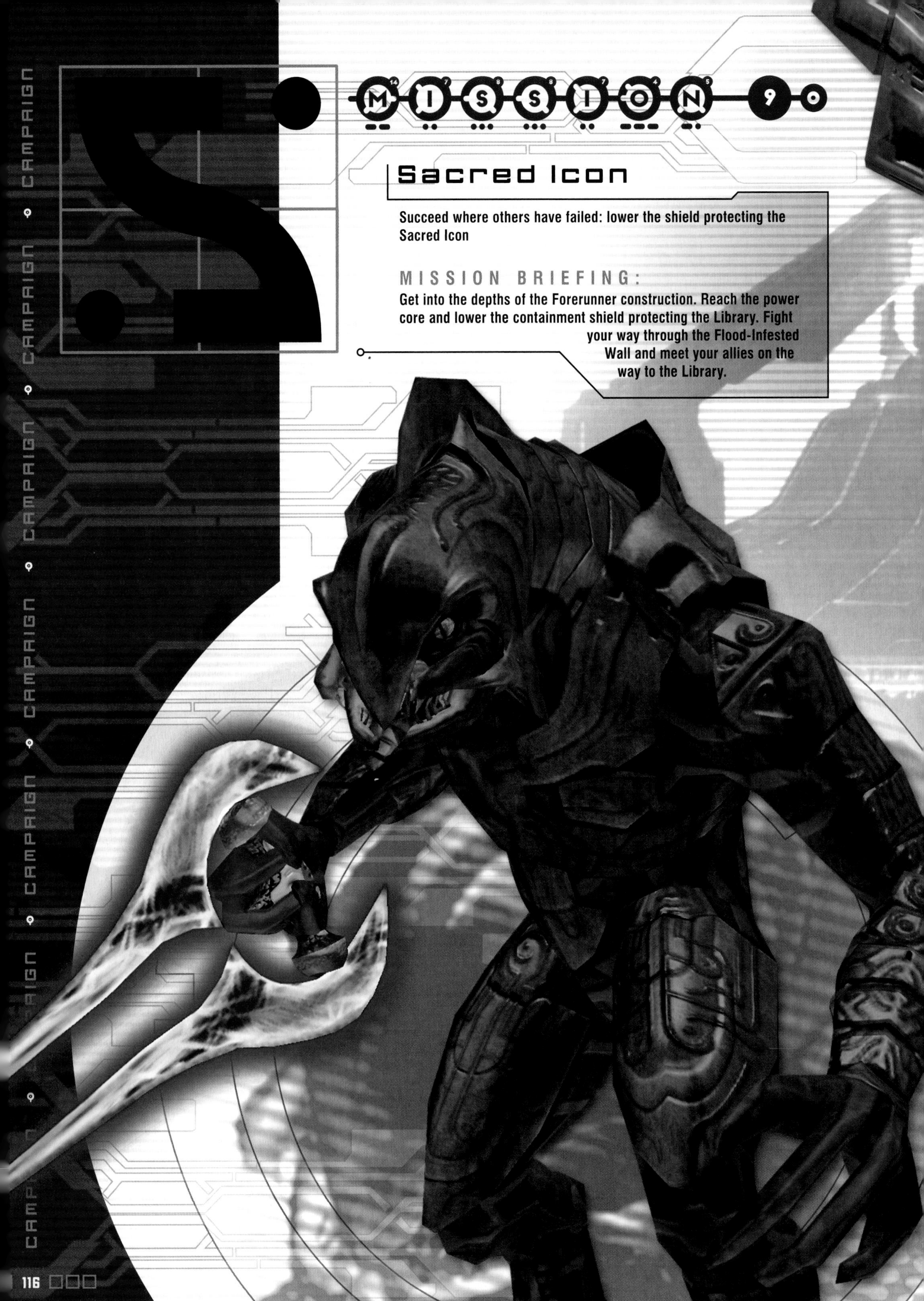

MISSION 9

Sacred Icon

Succeed where others have failed: lower the shield protecting the Sacred Icon

MISSION BRIEFING:

Get into the depths of the Forerunner construction. Reach the power core and lower the containment shield protecting the Library. Fight your way through the Flood-Infested Wall and meet your allies on the way to the Library.

1 "Uncomfortable Silence"

Mission Objective: Lower the Containment Shield

You'll start the level with a Carbine and a Plasma Pistol. As you're the Arbiter again, remember that you are now allied with the Covenant. Don't forget that you can activate your Active Camo by pressing ◯. Turn around and take a look at the wreckage. There is a Sentinel Beam lying at your feet. In the background, small Constructors fly around. If you attack these harmless Forerunner devices, Sentinels will be deployed (read the tip at the bottom of this page).

The exit is under the large, rectangular column on the far left side of the room. Stand right in front of the column and, as the onscreen prompt says, hold ⊗ to Activate Piston. Alternatively – and this is mandatory on higher difficulty levels – you can also shoot at the glowing spot (Fig. 1) until the mechanism snaps in and the column drives up. Sometimes it's also opened by Constructors. Jump into the shaft. Down there is another piston, and it won't be the last you'll have to open during this level. Many Sentinels will try to stop the Arbiter (Fig. 2). You could try to destroy every Sentinel and every Sentinel Launcher, but this isn't necessary. The Launchers often hang high up on the ceiling and are easily overlooked. Occasionally, you'll meet allies like Jackals or Grunts – they will offer their support.

TIP

A Sentinel Launcher is a device that can dispense an unlimited number of Sentinels. When a hatch opens (Fig. 3), you'll hear a characteristic sound. Every time you hear it, new Sentinels will be deployed somewhere close to your position. You can shoot the Sentinel Launcher off the wall when the hatch is open, or just use a Plasma Grenade. It will stick to the device and explode.

01

02

03

2 Lethal Enforcer

Mission Objective: Power up the four Absorbers to lower the Containment Shield

The shield power core is guarded by an enormous machine: a Sentinel Major, also called an Enforcer by the Covenant. Tartarus will inform you via a radio transmission that it's pointless to attack an Enforcer from the front, because its shields are so strong. His recommendation is that you should "Stay in the shadows, wait until it loses interest. Then strike the beast when its back is turned." Actually, you won't necessarily have to be that cautious.

You can crash the Sentinel Major's energy shield, as usual, with a charged shot from a Plasma Pistol or with continued fire from other weapons. The latter, obviously, will take longer to achieve the desired effect. Without its shield, the Sentinel Major is particularly vulnerable at the glowing fields on the lower end of its arms, and the arms themselves (Fig. 4). You can shoot them off one by one. Hits on its metal body will also count. Since the Enforcer is rather large, it's relatively simple to hit it with Plasma Grenades (Fig. 5). When things become too dangerous, draw back into the corridors at the side of the hall where you can find fresh weapons.

Your primary objective should be to loosen the four mountings of the power core. This is similar to the pistons faced earlier. Stand right in front of the columns and do as the prompt tells you: hold ⓧ to deactivate Plug Lock. If you prefer a more aggressive approach, you can also shoot the glowing areas on the column (Fig. 6) until they turn green and the columns are pulled up. After the fourth column, a switch will appear which will allow you to lower the Containment Shield of the Library (Fig. 7). Before you do that, you should grab some fresh weapons if you need them, because a gate in the wall opens and the platform you're standing on will move to another part of the Sentinel Wall.

04

05

06

07

SENTINEL MAJOR

A Sentinel Major is much more than a simple Sentinel upgrade: its capabilities far exceed those of its more common counterpart. It is an impressive device. It can fly, and its mighty claw arms can even grab vehicles – with deadly consequences. It has two built-in weapon systems. The first is a light energy beam, which is relatively weak. The second is a mortar device that should be avoided at all costs.

3 "Buyer's Remorse"

Mission Objective:
Make your way through the Flood-Infested Wall

The way to the Library is open, but when Tartarus attempts to pick you up with a Phantom, a Sentinel Major forces him to retreat. Additionally, Sentinels protected with light energy shields will attack – and the extra protection does make a difference (Fig. 8). Continue fighting until the large gate opens.

08

As soon as you reach the corridor behind it, the wall behind you will close and from another opening Combat Forms will stream into the hall (Fig. 9). You will face mainly human victims of the Flood, so the majority of weapons that you find will be of the UNSC variety. Battle Rifles and Magnums are not particularly useful for fighting the Flood because their rate of fire is fairly low. Other enemies you will encounter include Sentinels and occasional Infection Forms. Turn to the right: there's a piston at the end of the hall. You'll continue your quest one level deeper.

09

4 Biohazard

The number of Combat Forms will rise constantly. Combat Forms carrying Shotguns are especially dangerous, and should be killed as quickly as possible. While you can easily identify a Rocket Launcher carried by an enemy, it's a lot harder to notice a Shotgun. Because of this, it's common for a Combat Form to rush towards you and knock you out cold with a Shotgun blast over a short distance. You should, therefore, be very careful while using an Energy Sword for close quarters combat. The Carrier Forms will always approach you slowly (Fig. 10). Shoot these cauliflower-like monsters so they explode while close to other Flood creatures. Additionally, as there are Infection Forms here, take the time to insure that defeated Combat Forms are completely immobilized.

10

5 On the Edge

The rooms at the edge of the Infested Wall are open on one side, which allows an Enforcer to fire on the Flood. Slopes lead down to a lower level (Fig. 11). There are numerous Sentinel Launchers under the ceiling, but some of them are already destroyed. Although these surroundings are equipped to contain outbreaks, the Flood is still present in large numbers. You can try to keep out of the whole battle by engaging your Active Camo. Run to the left, following the wall, and jump into the next opening on the left and into the corridor (Fig. 12). At the end, the passage will lead you outside, to a room just like the one you've left behind. The exit from here is on the far left side.

11

In the passage between the two great rooms you'll see four openings in the back wall (Fig. 13). The openings in the middle are connected with each other, but the ones on the outer sides end in a shaft leading downward into the lower levels of both great rooms. These passages can be useful if you have to shake off pursuing foes.

12

13

6 Conduit B

Don't simply concentrate on the Combat Forms on the floor in the first hall of Conduit B (Fig. 14). Thanks to their enormous jumping ability, the Combat Forms up on the gallery are always more than ready to leap down. You can sneak through this hall by activating your Camo. There is a snag: if you activate a Checkpoint and are discovered at that very second, you might be in serious trouble. The enemies behind you won't see the funny side when they notice that you've fooled them with your invisibility trick.

At the end of the second hall, you'll encounter Combat Forms and Sentinels – as well as dead humans (Fig. 15). The exit piston is on the far left side, so follow the light beam to the very end.

14

15

7 Down to Earth

At the end of the Infested Wall is a hall that looks like the starting room of this level (Fig. 16). You can see the impressive Library in the background here. Grab some useful weapons, like the Energy Sword or the Shotgun, before going down to the next deep opening below a column. Down there, you'll have to kill numerous Flood before you can leave the structure through a final shaft.

16

8 "100,000 Years War"

Mission Objective: Rendezvous with your allies in the Covenant camp

You're now a lot closer to the Library. In the snowy landscape, allies will fight against the Flood. Watch out for Combat Forms armed with Rocket Launchers. To reach the camp you'll have to get across the gorge and walk through the small tunnel, behind the turret, leading through the wall (Fig. 17). In the camp on the other side you'll have to kill all Flood before you can meet the SpecOps Commander near the turrets. He'll be wearing his usual white ceremonial armor.

Together, you'll have to defend the camp until the reinforcements arrive. More Combat Forms will jump down from the walls. Several of them will have Energy Swords. The turrets can be quite useful when defending your position (Fig. 18). Finally, the long-awaited Phantom will show up in the sky as another level draws to a close...

17

18

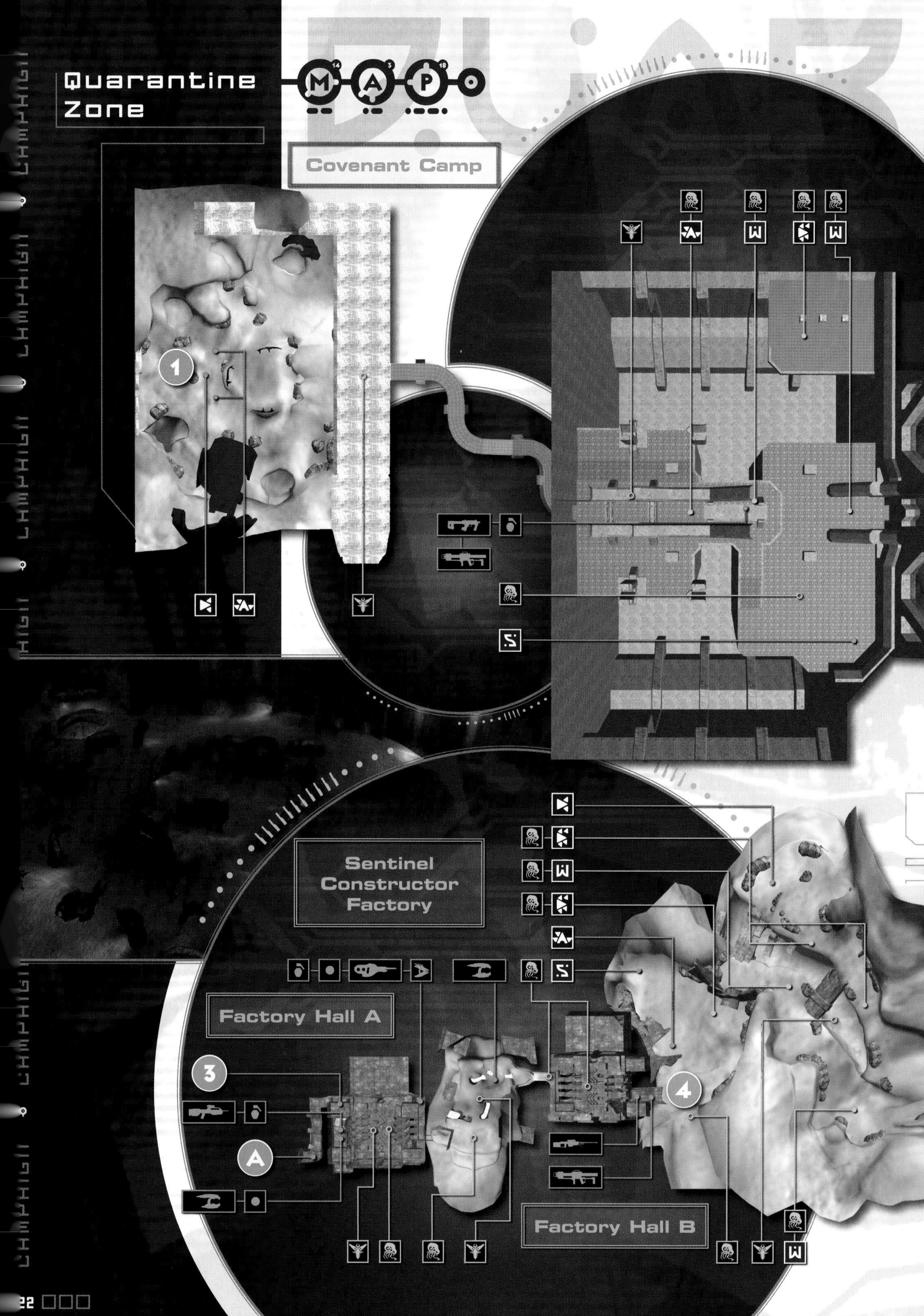

Quarantine Zone
MAP
Covenant Camp
1
Sentinel Constructor Factory
Factory Hall A
3
A
4
Factory Hall B

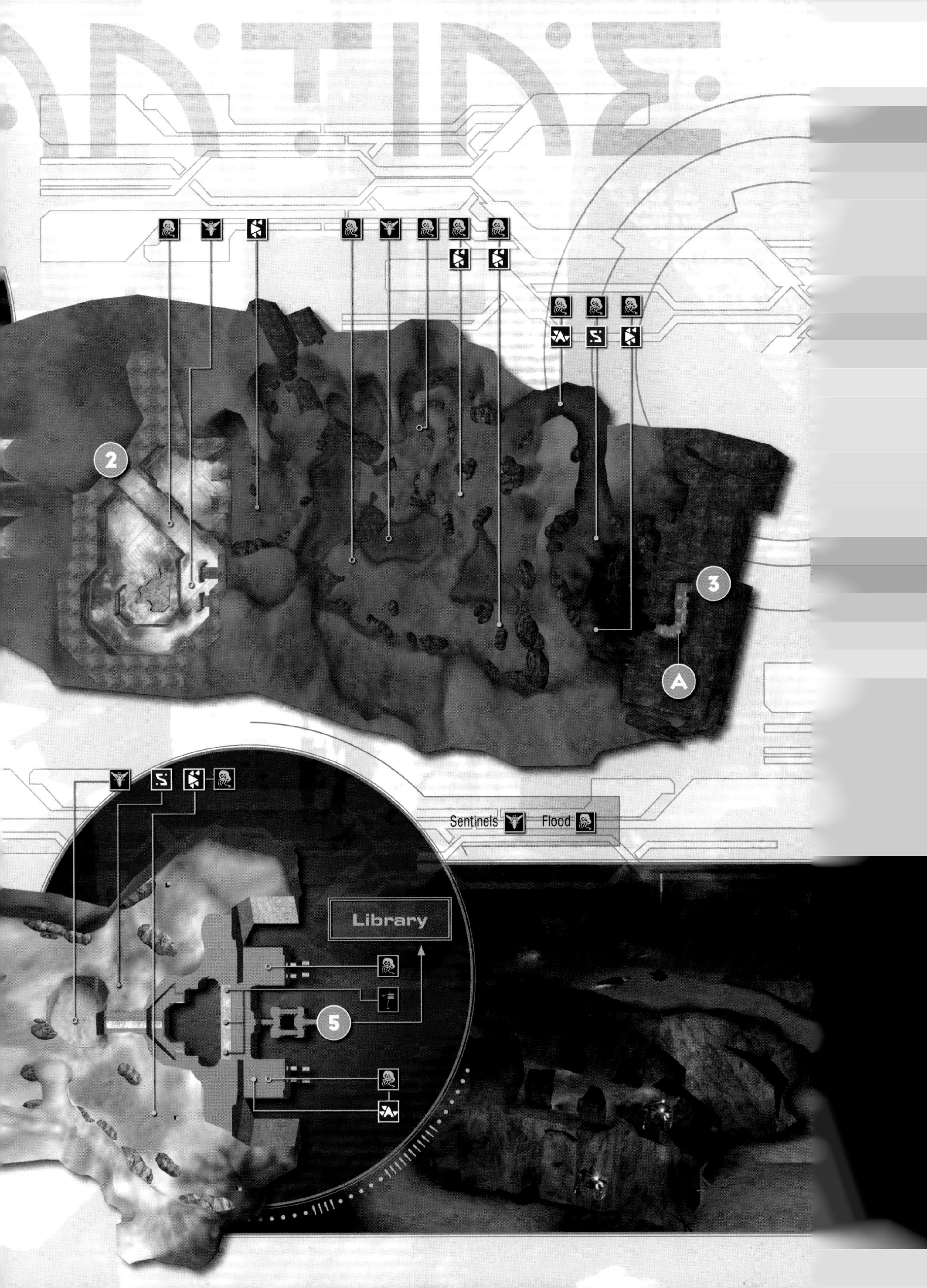

2
3
A
Sentinels
Flood
Library
5

Quarantine Zone

Parasites, humans – no matter. The Icon must be found

MISSION BRIEFING:

Fight your way through the Flood-infested area. You must advance into the Library and hold the Sacred Icon in your hands.

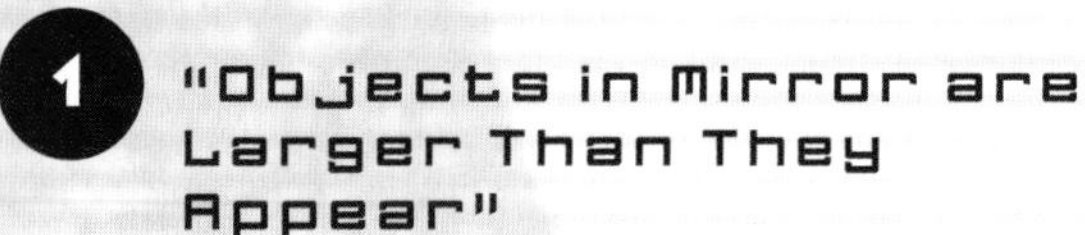

1 "Objects in Mirror are Larger Than They Appear"

Mission Objective: Push through the Quarantine Zone towards the Library

This is your chance to drive a Spectre. Get behind the wheel, sit in one of the passenger seats or take control of its cannon – the choice is yours. If you'd prefer to take a good old Ghost, you can do that, too. The gate in the wall opens and two Sentinels hover out of it (Fig. 1). Don't drive directly under the Sentinel Major – unless you want to have first-hand experience of its anti-vehicular capabilities, that is.

You'll encounter a new danger in the hall: the Flood at the wheels of vehicles (Fig. 2). These include Warthogs and even a Scorpion piloted by human Combat Forms. There are more Sentinel Majors, too. You can try to board the tank – just jump on the vehicle and attack the driver. As the Sentinels and the Flood are fighting against each other, it's entirely plausible that the driver of the Scorpion could be killed by the robot guards. If that is the case – and, naturally, if the tank remains in working order – then feel free to appropriate it for your own use.

01

02

2 "Healthy Competition"

Outside the great hall, the Flood versus Sentinels versus Arbiter battle continues. Don't forget that the Combat Forms can board vehicles – especially when you're driving a slow tank. The large metal gates up in the wall are actually hangar doors. Occasionally, brand-new Sentinel Majors will float from them (Fig. 3). Follow the path down and enter one of the two sluice gates (Fig. 4). As soon as the gate on the other side opens, you'll see the impressive Library again (Fig. 5), and the burning wreckage of a spaceship in front. It's actually a Sentinel Constructor Factory. (On leaving the Infested Wall, you can see the flying factory crash out of the sky.)

This is where you need to go. Enter it through a cave at the opposite end of the valley. Cross the first bridge. Now you can either walk on foot via the route on the left to get to the cave (Fig. 6), or grab a vehicle and take the slightly longer path on the right across the second bridge. Behind the cave you'll find a small valley with the entrance to the burning wreck (Fig. 7). Here, the Flood is fighting against Sentinels – and don't be surprised to encounter a Scorpion and a Wraith. The entrance is too small for larger vehicles, but you can try to squeeze yourself through in a Ghost.

03

04

05

06

07

3 Sentinel Constructor Factory

You'll have to take care not to lose your sense of direction here. In front of you are two factory halls which look very similar. They are separated by a rather symmetrical basin. In Hall A, Sentinels are fighting against Combat Forms. The exit is diagonally on the opposite side – it's a large hole in the wall on the lower level (Fig. 8). The tunnel behind it ends in a valley. The exit of this area (which is the entrance to Hall B) is diagonally on the opposite side as well (Fig. 9).

The Sentinel Beam, Energy Sword and Shotgun are very useful for fighting the ever-present Combat Forms. The Sentinel Beams will empty with alarming speed on constant fire, so you shouldn't leave your finger on the trigger any longer than is necessary. Fortunately, there are many Sentinels in this area, so you'll find a ready supply of these weapons. The exit of Hall B is in the middle of the back wall on the upper level (Fig. 10). There are a number of human transport containers standing in the passage leading outside. Help yourself to the weapons you'll find here. A Sniper Rifle is useless against the Flood, but a Rocket Launcher can be very handy at times – especially as there are enemy-controlled heavy vehicles to face in the not-too-distant future...

08

09

10

11

4 Into the Library

Mission Objective: Link up with the SpecOps Leader and break through the Flood barricade

Now that you've left the second hall, you're a lot closer to the Library. In the area directly in front of you are several vehicles which are, mostly, still occupied by the Flood. Don't concentrate too hard on the action on the left side, because some Combat Forms will jump down from the right any moment now. Take care of them, then grab yourself a vehicle – a Ghost, for example. Take it and drive through the tunnel behind the Wraith (Fig. 11).

The Library is now on your right side. If you want to contact the SpecOps Commander first – it's not mandatory that you do, though – drive straight across the bridge after arriving through the tunnel. A Phantom will deploy the Commander, a Spectre and some reinforcements. Now head in the direction of the Library. You'll access it via a large building. Its entrance area is heavily defended by the Flood with, among other things, turrets. You can break through their lines with relative ease if you surprise the enemy with speed and determination. If you harbor ambitions of destroying the Flood presence here, however, things will be far more difficult. As well as their sheer weight of numbers, the Flood also have heavy vehicles. One way or another, once you reach the entrance (Fig. 12), a large gondola will transport the Arbiter to the Library.

12

TIP

Until you reach the cut-scene at the Library gondola, you could actually race through the Quarantine Zone level on a Ghost – and without firing a single shot. At the exit of the factory, you might find that you can't squeeze through the military containers. Fortuitously, the next Ghost is only a few feet away – on the left side behind the exit.

5 "Shooting Gallery"

Mission Objective: Retrieve the Sacred Icon before the Humans

The gondola will take you slowly through the huge, awe-inspiring Library. After you pass through the first gate, the Flood will be upon you again. Combat Forms will jump down to your level from the left side (Fig. 13). Get into position and throw a grenade at the appropriate time. You should, as a rule, avoid hurling Plasma Grenades at the Flood because the Combat Forms always charge so relentlessly, which could lead to you being caught up in the resultant explosion. You should be extra-careful whenever enemies have an Energy Sword or a Shotgun, because they'll be lethal at close range. Occasionally, Tartarus's Phantom will open fire on the Flood. Be sure that you don't get in the line of fire.

The second wave of Flood appears in the middle of the gondola, on the lower level (Fig. 14). Combat Forms are entering through the hole in the back wall. You can get up into the tube here as well, and then you'll be largely safe from attacks (Fig. 15). After the gondola passes through a second gate, the journey will continue upward. Once you arrive, you'll move horizontally for a short time before you pass through the last gate. The gondola will now dock at its destination.

"That Old, Familiar Feeling"

The gondola finally reaches its destination: the heart of the Library, where the Sacred Icon is kept. You'll have to get through a smaller hall, where countless dead bodies are lying on the floor. Apart from a few Infection Forms, nothing moves. As soon as you enter the central room through a rather inconspicuous passage (Fig. 16), a long cut-scene will begin. This cinematic interlude shows the extraordinary meeting of the Master Chief, the Arbiter and the Gravemind – which appears to be the central "consciousness" of the Flood...

13

14

15

16

Gravemind

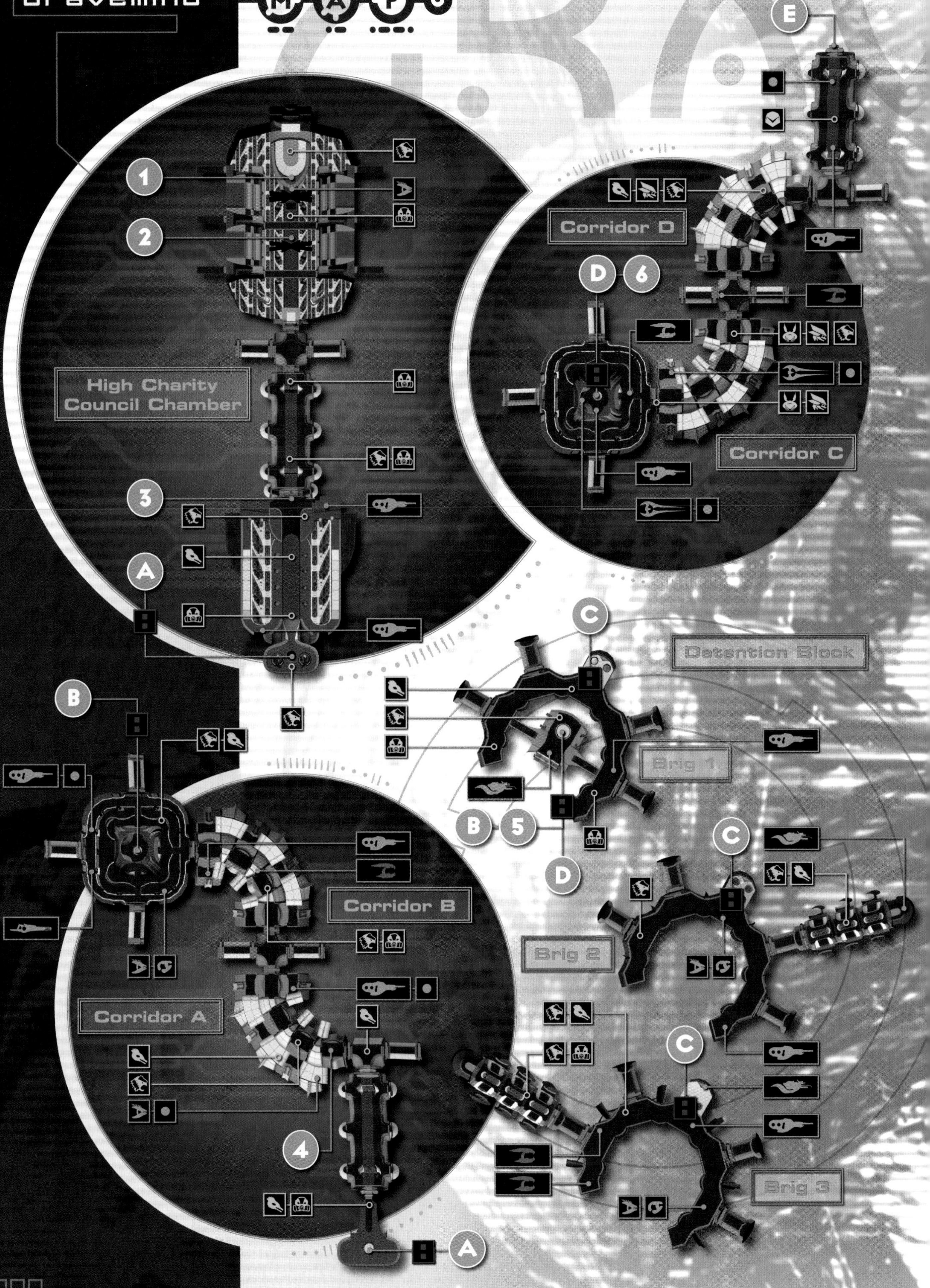

MAP

High Charity Council Chamber

Corridor D

Corridor C

Detention Block

Brig 1

Corridor B

Brig 2

Corridor A

Brig 3

1
2
3
4
5
6
A
B
C
D
E

F
Mausoleum
Mid-Tower
9
11
G
Hanging
Gardens A
Far Tower
10
8
Hanging
Gardens B
7
E
F

MISSION 11

Gravemind

The Prophets have the Index and plan to use it? Over your dead body

MISSION BRIEFING:

Master Chief, find the Prophet of Truth and take the Index from him. Free captured Marines from detention cells on your way. Follow the signal of the Prophet of Truth through the hanging gardens up to the Mausoleum of the Arbiter.

1 "Inside Job"

Mission Objective: Locate the Prophet of Truth and the Index

After meeting the Flood creature Gravemind, the Master Chief is suddenly transported into the lion's den: the center of the Council Chamber of the Covenant! The only weapon he is equipped with is a single lousy Needler – but there is another one just a few steps behind the Chief's starting position. Open fire immediately on the Honor Guard Brutes (Fig. 1). You must be sure that enough needles hit them in rapid succession for an explosion to take place, as not even a Brute can weather that storm easily. As soon as the first Brute dies, get some distance between yourself and the second one. When it charges towards you in a berserk manner, retreat as effectively as you can while maintaining constant fire. You can't escape a berserk Brute with simple sidesteps, as it will react immediately and attack again. The best method for slaying these animalistic aliens when so enraged is to shoot them as fast as you can.

The Brutes will leave their Brute Plasma Rifles behind. These red weapons have a much higher rate of fire than their blue Elite equivalents – but as a direct consequence, they overheat very quickly. However, if you dual-wield two Brute Plasma Rifles and pull alternate triggers in a measured fashion, you'll find that they form a potent weapon combination. Once you take out the Grunts, a second wave of attacks will begin (Fig. 2).

01

02

2 The Demon Is Here

Show the Covenant what a SPARTAN-II is made of. Shortly after defeating the first row of opponents, another group will storm into the room. After that, a third wave will arrive. At this point, a Brute will appear on the spectator stand. If you find it difficult to shoot him from below, jump on a pedestal (Fig. 3) and from there up to the stand. After you've killed all enemies, Cortana can get to work. Move to the exit at the end of the hall. Cortana will now enter the network of High Charity and open all the important doors for the Master Chief. Fight your way through to the next room until you reach a balcony.

03

3 Et Tu, Brute!

Only a few feet away a Brute Honor Guard (Fig. 4) awaits you. His helmet protects him from headshots but, after a few hits, his helmet will eventually fall off. The best thing you can do is to stick a Plasma Grenade to his fur – but be aware that Brutes can reciprocate in kind. You'll have to clear this balcony very thoroughly. In the left corner you'll find a container with two Carbines. You could also employ agility and superior firepower up close with two Brute Plasma Rifles or Needlers in a dual-wield configuration. You should take out the Grunts as early as possible – they'll come floating down from the grav-lift in the background. Several of them will tow Plasma Cannons.

04

After you've dispatched a certain number of enemies, a Brute Captain will arrive from below via the lift. He's equipped with a Brute Shot (Fig. 5). Usually you could kill him with a few headshots using a Carbine, but his weapon can fire grenades quickly over great distances – and this affords you precious little time to take aim. The simplest way to deal with this situation is a frontal assault. Charge at the Brute Captain, evade his grenades, then stick a Plasma Grenade to his body and take cover. After defeating him, you have the opportunity to use a Brute Shot. When you use it, take care to bounce the grenades on the floor in front of your opponents to improve your accuracy.

After you've taken out all the enemies on the balcony, Cortana will access the elevator to change its direction – it will now take you down. Collect the Brute Shot and simply jump into the hole. While you're slowly floating down, Jackals will enter through the door on the lower level (Fig. 6). If you still have grenades, hurl some on your enemies. The next room is empty, but you'll hear the transmission of a Brute, and Cortana will comment on it. Shortly afterwards, several Jackals will run through the corridor behind the exit. If you stay out of sight and wait a short while, you can avoid this particular fight.

05

06

TIP

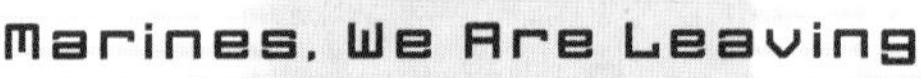

If you keep waiting in front of the grav-lift, Cortana will find warm words of encouragement for you.

4 Marines, We Are Leaving!

You'll enter another corridor (Corridor A) which bends to the right. There are some Jackals and a Brute here. Use the pedestals in the corridor as cover (Fig. 7) to get close enough to the Brute to kill him from behind. If the patrols notice you, they'll raise the alarm – and if they do, numerous reinforcements will arrive in the corridor.

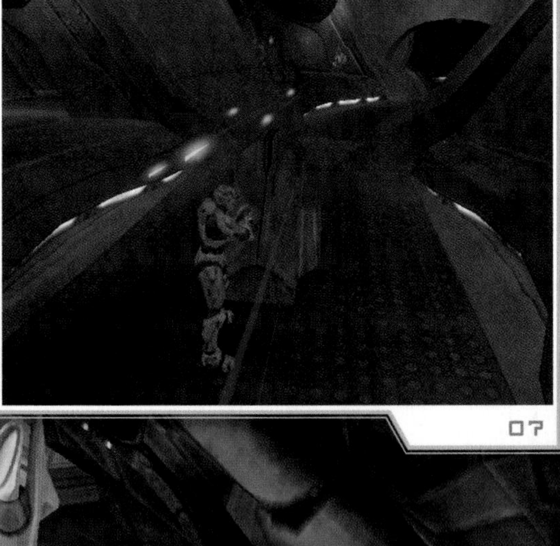

07

Mission Objective: Rescue the Marines being held in the Detention Block

At the crossing in front of the next corridor (Corridor B), Cortana will notice the signals of captured Marines. Get through the next hallway (it's full of Grunts and Brutes) to reach the small elevator – it's in the middle of the room on the lower level (Fig. 8). Step on it and you are transported up a few meters, to the platform above your head (the upper level in the same room). Wait for a second, and Cortana will change the direction of the elevator. It will then transport you down.

08

5 Detention Block

There are two groups of Marines in the cells on three different levels. Kill the Brute standing with his back facing you by hitting him from behind. On the other side of the elevator there is a weapons container holding Brute Shots. Slaughter as many sleeping Grunts as you can before more alert enemies notice you. Once you have dispatched these hostiles, Cortana will locate the first group and tell you to go to the middle or lower level. Use the small grav-lifts to change levels (Fig. 9). The one in front on the middle level leads down, and the one behind leads up.

09

On the level in question, the door to the room with the cells is already open (Fig. 10). Once you've killed all the guards, Cortana will open the cells. Now you'll have to search for the second cell block. That done, you can leave the Detention Block via the main lift – but only after killing off the reinforcements that arrive that way. Reload the Brute Shot before you float up there yourself.

10

6 Covenant Civil War

Mission Objective: Follow the Prophet of Truth to the far tower

The area you'll arrive at after the Detention Block looks just like the passage you already passed through. But it only looks similar: you really are on a different level now. As soon as you get close to the door, Elites and Drones will storm through it. Greet them with grenades (Fig. 11).

11

From this juncture, the situation changes. You'll soon notice in Corridor C that Elite Honor Guards are fighting against Brutes and Drones (Fig. 12). In Corridor D, Jackals will also join the fight. The regular radio transmissions made by the Prophet of Truth will explain the reason behind this: civil war has broken out among the Covenant! Elites and Grunts will fight against Brutes and their allies, Jackals and Drones. While divided, be aware that they remain united in their hatred for the Master Chief. You can, however, hold back and allow battles to unfold – there is no need for you to leap headfirst into each and every confrontation between the warring factions. The most effective technique is to wait until the majority of combatants are dead, then attack the weakened remnants from afar with grenades or long-range weapons.

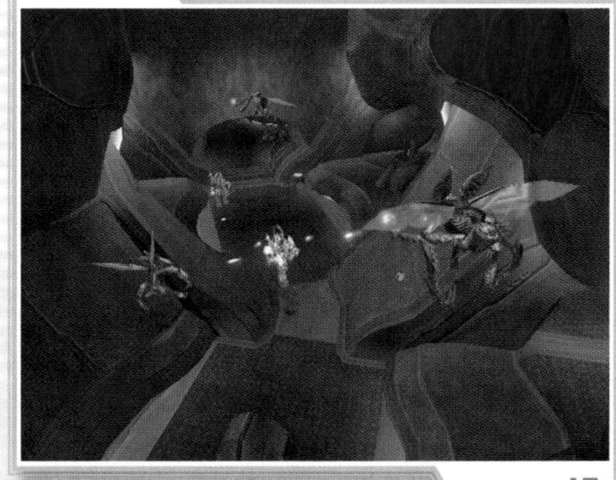

12

In the last room before you leave the building, you'll meet two Hunters (Fig. 13). You can actually just run through the room and bypass them entirely. If the very idea of such prudence (or cowardice) offends you, go find some weapons which are good for shooting these monsters accurately in the back. Now walk past the wall standing opposite the entrance, keeping it on your left side. The Hunter should turn its back to you and you can score some free hits – a great start to this particular fight. In truth, it's actually advisable to kill them here and now: if they discover you, the Hunters will follow you doggedly wherever you go.

13

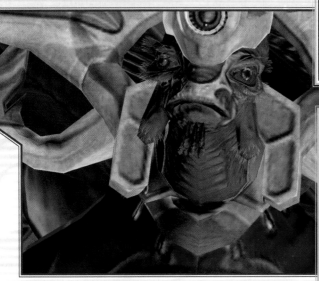

7 Valley of Tears

On the other side of the Hunters you'll see a basin, filled with numerous Brutes and snipers fighting against Elites, Rangers, Honor Guards and Hunters. The exit is on the other side – just behind the wall you see on the opposite side (Fig. 14). Right in front of you, a Brute and a Honor Guard will fight against each other. The Honor Guard usually wins. Kill him while he remains weakened from the fight. A Plasma Grenade will work wonders here.

14

You could experience a very interesting fight in this valley, competing against all the varied enemies and their differing abilities. Alternatively, you could simply run straight forward, jump down, run to the right, pass through under the arch, up the slope to the left and sprint to the exit (Fig. 15). If you start running right away, you'll meet a Brute with a Brute Shot who will enter through this opening.

15

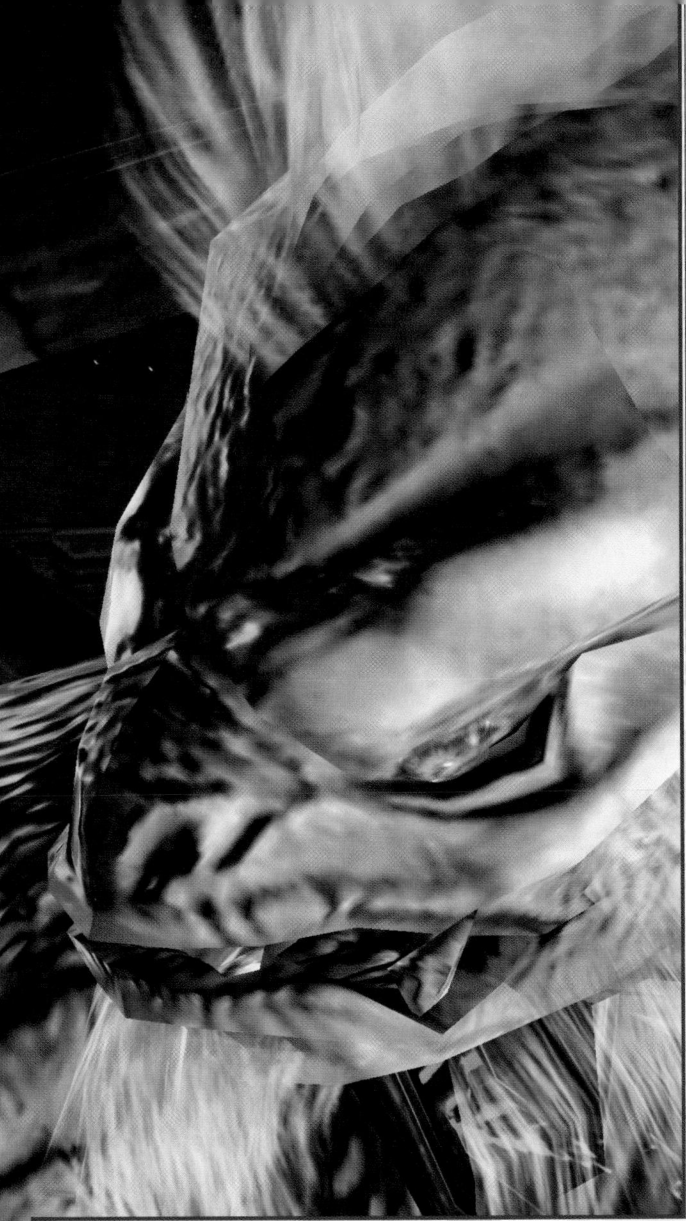

8 The Hanging Gardens

Go across the long light bridge (Fig. 16) and you'll reach Hanging Gardens A. The battle between Elites and Grunts against the rest of the Covenant is also raging here. After you've taken out the "welcoming committee", help yourself at the weapon containers. A Beam Rifle would be useful: you could, for example, shoot the combatants in the middle of this construct (Fig. 17) from afar. Depending on how quickly you progress, you'll meet two Elite Rangers at the end of the middle part, or some time later. Plasma Pistols and Needlers (or a combination of both) are a good choice when fighting them. Homing ammunition and the shield-depleting ability of charged plasma shot are a lethal combination. Try to fight under the arches to give yourself some cover (Fig. 18).

The gardens are built symmetrically, but you're not in danger of running in the wrong direction. You can maintain your sense of direction with ease by keeping an eye on the well-lit structure (Fig. 19). As long as it's on your left, you're on the right track.

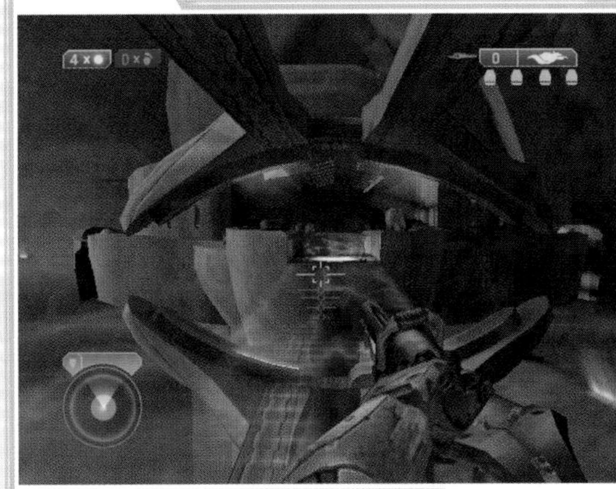

16

17

18

19

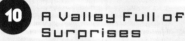

9 Mid Tower & Gardens B

In the center of the Mid Tower, several different Elites (Rangers among them) fight against Drones. Brutes and Jackals will come to the aid of their allies – they'll storm through the corridor on the opposite side. As you have to go through there, you should wait in the entrance area and watch how events unfold (Fig. 20).

In the Hanging Gardens B, Brute Berserkers hunt down Grunts. You'll have to cross the last light bridge to reach the Far Tower, where the Prophet is rumored to be located.

10 A Valley Full of Surprises

Mission Objective: Stop the Prophet of Truth from boarding his Phantom

Enter the first room. There's a steep slope going upward, and Brutes will arrive through the exit up there. They are armed with Brute Shots (Fig. 21). Stay in the entrance, but quickly grab a Carbine from the container on the left if you don't have a sniper weapon. Kill the Brutes with headshots from a safe distance.

Now walk through the gate. You'll be standing in front of a wall, and there's probably a Jackal behind it. There is another valley on the other side of the gate, just like on the other end of the garden. This time, the exit will be on the opposite side (Fig. 22). Before you go there, you should watch the action in the valley. Take your Beam Rifle or Carbine and fire into the masses, but watch out for the little Grunt carrying an enormous Fuel Rod Cannon. You can make good use of this weapon later on. On your way up the incline leading to the exit (Fig. 23), you'll meet Stealth Elites – you'll also encounter them in the anterooms of the Mausoleum. Take note of the Fuel Rod Cannon on the floor in the second room. Save it for bad times.

20

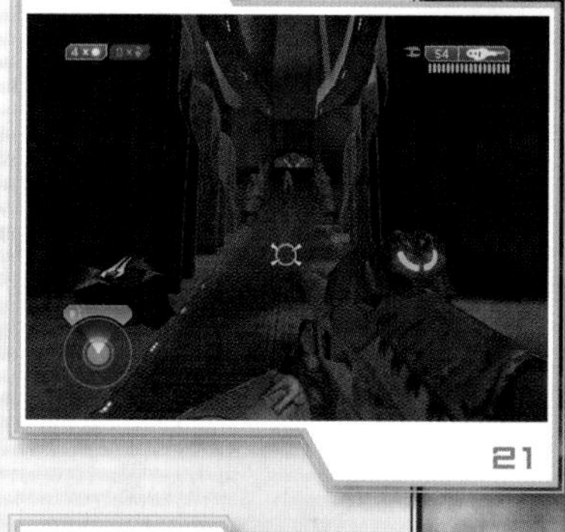
21

22

23

24

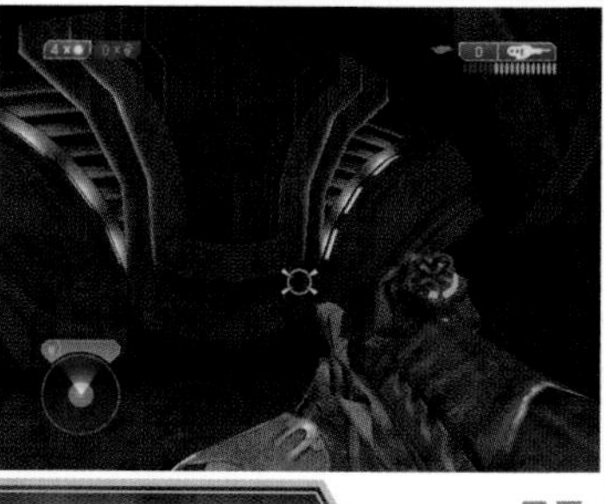
25

11 The Last Battle

There's another battle between Brutes and Elites taking place on the bridge in front of the Mausoleum (Fig. 24). A short time later, Drones will arrive. Kill Brutes standing with their backs facing you with a simple hit to their heads. After that, the best thing to do here is to sit this battle out, then finish the survivors off with some grenades.

Many Elites and Grunts will rush from the gate at the end of the bridge (Fig. 25), and some of them carry Fuel Rod Cannons. At this point, the Fuel Rod Cannon we discussed earlier will be very handy. Destroy the turret on the left side immediately, and fire into the masses. Watch out for enemy Plasma Grenades, and be sure to throw some yourself. After a short time, reinforcements will pass through the gate, and their numbers include two Hunters. Kill them with the Fuel Rod Cannon.

12 Mausoleum

In the holy halls of the Arbiter, Brutes and high-ranking Elites fight against each other. Many Fuel Rod Cannons and Energy Swords can be found here. The Elites dressed in white can withstand and inflict a lot of damage: two precise Fuel Rod hits from a short distance are barely enough to take one down. You'll even need to make two lunge attacks with the Energy Sword to kill them, too. The Brutes don't stand much of a chance in this exchange, especially when two Hunters enter the fray to support the Elites (Fig. 26). The Brutes will also receive some reinforcements.

Again, you can sit this battle out and watch how it develops. Usually, though, it works quite well if you run to the right immediately and attack the back of the Elites while they concentrate on the Brutes (Fig. 27). You can even, if you're quick and subtle, hit one on the head with a melee attack before you are noticed. Now use the Fuel Rod Cannon from a short distance – but not so close that you are caught in the blast (Fig. 28). Your attacks should be swift and silent. When you're noticed, retreat immediately. Should one of the Elites pull out his Energy Sword, backpedal rapidly and neutralize him as quickly as possible.

If the Elites notice you immediately, you'll have to try a more cautious approach. You'll find a Plasma Pistol on the lower level at the right end, which is useful for disabling shields. Finally, the entrance will remain open, so you can return to the bridge whenever you need to equip other weapons. If you're lucky, the Brutes will kill the Hunters; if not, you've still got the Fuel Rod Cannon at your disposal...

As soon as the Master Chief is the last combatant standing, Cortana will open the exit. Watch out! Stealth Elites will enter through it, followed by a Elite Councilor (Fig. 29). You could use the old run-like-the-wind tactic here, if you wish. You only have to dash a few feet across the bridge behind the Mausoleum to initiate the concluding cut-scene.

26

27

28

29

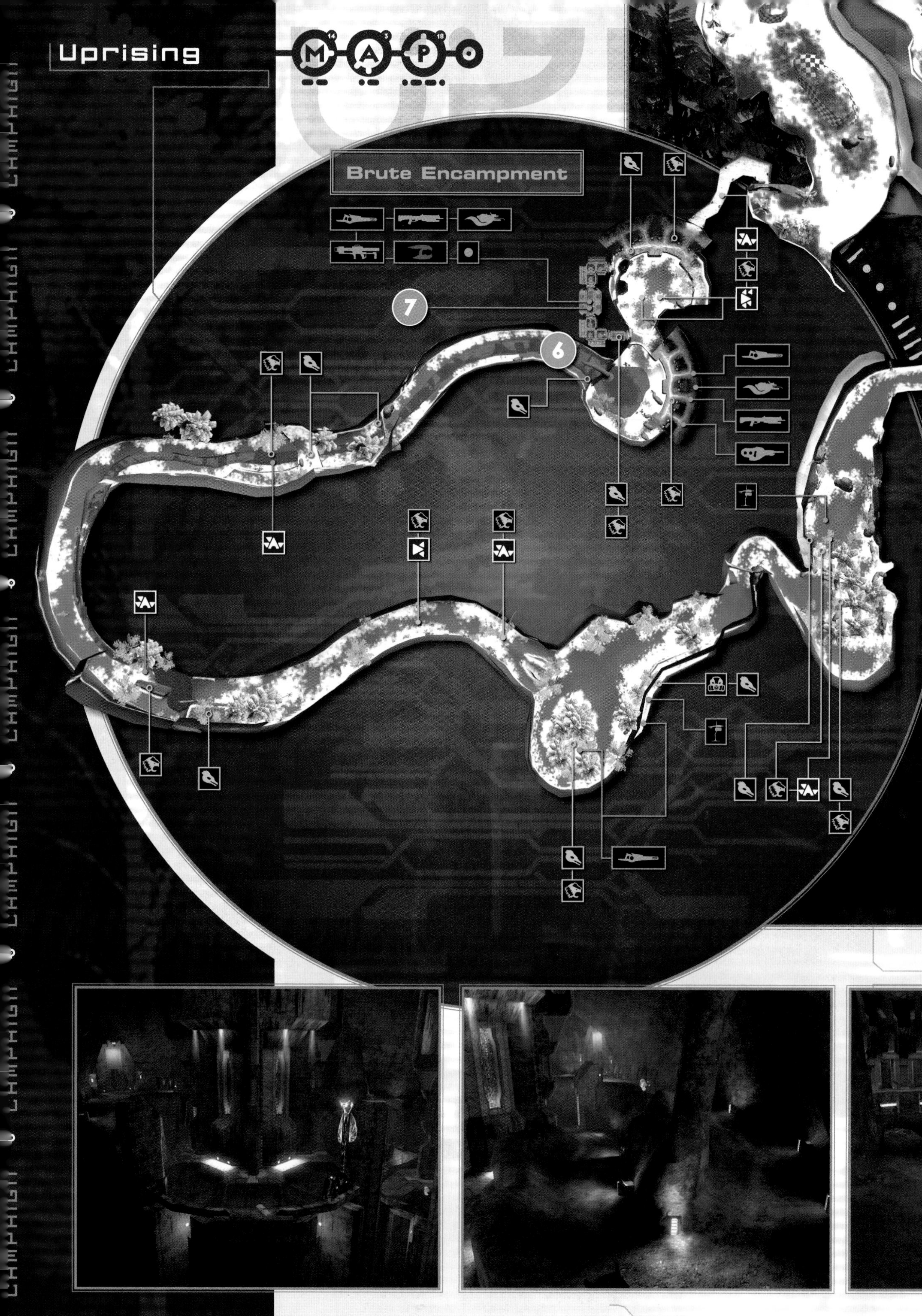
Brute Encampment
7
6

5
4
3
2
1

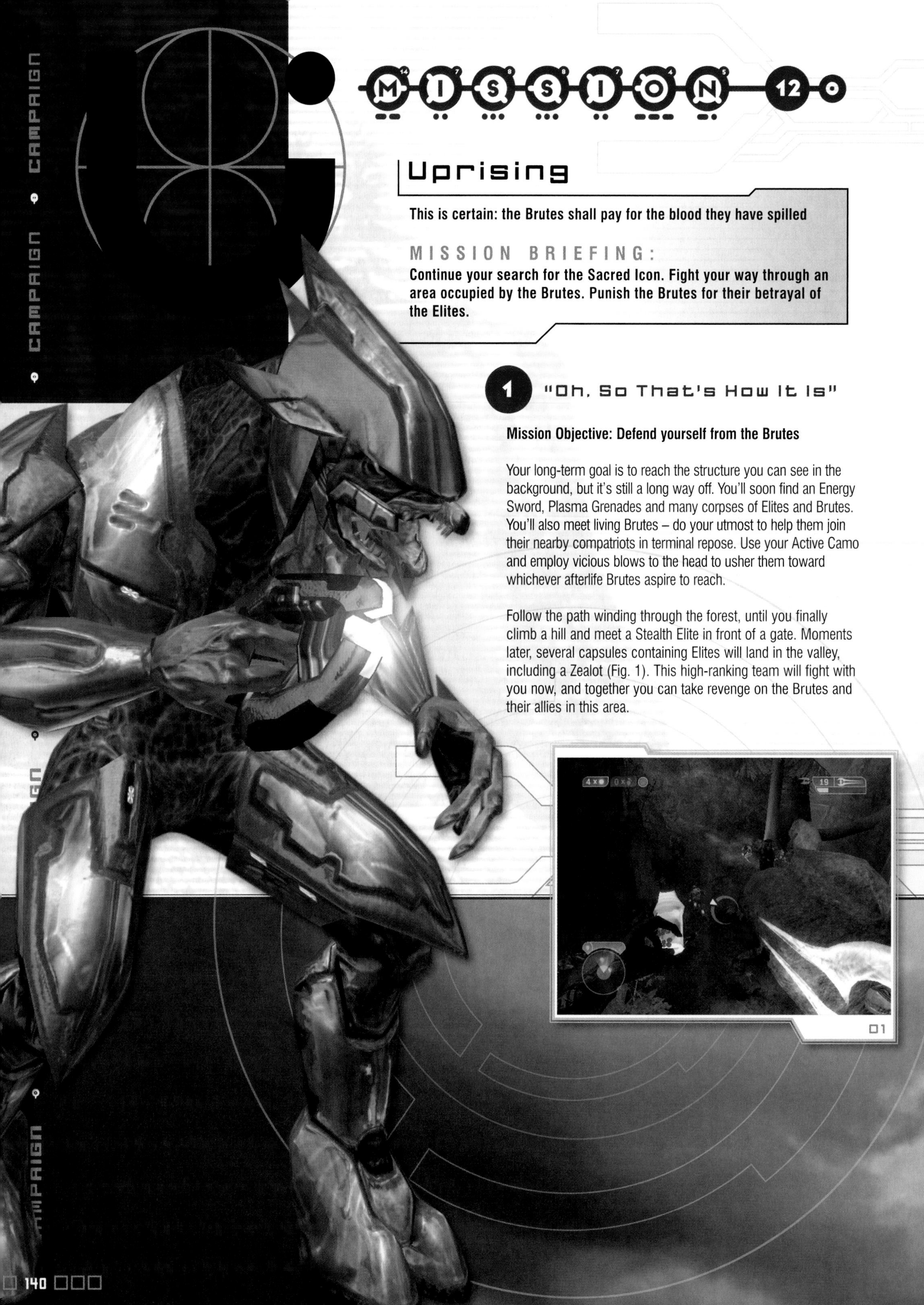

Uprising

This is certain: the Brutes shall pay for the blood they have spilled

MISSION BRIEFING:

Continue your search for the Sacred Icon. Fight your way through an area occupied by the Brutes. Punish the Brutes for their betrayal of the Elites.

1 "Oh, So That's How It Is"

Mission Objective: Defend yourself from the Brutes

Your long-term goal is to reach the structure you can see in the background, but it's still a long way off. You'll soon find an Energy Sword, Plasma Grenades and many corpses of Elites and Brutes. You'll also meet living Brutes – do your utmost to help them join their nearby compatriots in terminal repose. Use your Active Camo and employ vicious blows to the head to usher them toward whichever afterlife Brutes aspire to reach.

Follow the path winding through the forest, until you finally climb a hill and meet a Stealth Elite in front of a gate. Moments later, several capsules containing Elites will land in the valley, including a Zealot (Fig. 1). This high-ranking team will fight with you now, and together you can take revenge on the Brutes and their allies in this area.

01

2 The Elite Fighting Force

Mission Objective: Exact vengeance on the Brute traitors

Your powerful collective will encounter enemy contact in the large cave (Fig. 2). Caution isn't a virtue that your new colleagues possess – expect them to employ their mighty Energy Swords immediately. As strong as they are, they'll need the aid of the Arbiter, especially when you meet Brutes. If you are dealing with a group, always greet them with an initial rain of Plasma Grenades. Don't be frugal: they are plentiful in this area. Note that the Grunts will be panicked and unwilling to fight. Your proximity will convince them to side with you – that, or the deaths of all of the enemies in the area and the cessation of fighting. You can find the exit on the other side of the two gigantic columns on the upper level.

3 Step by Step

In the room behind the cave, you'll find several Brutes and Jackals down at the exit (Fig. 3). You'll be standing on a level several feet above them, and on one side a steep slope leads downwards. The best thing you can do is to throw grenades from above. Don't forget that the Grunts are no longer your enemies. Keep an eye on the boxes and containers: you'll find quite a lot of them here. Some will explode when you fire or hurl grenades at them.

The next (and larger) room has four huge stairs. Push the explosive containers over the edge (Fig. 4) – they will detonate on impact. Keep in mind that there is an overhang on all the stairs, so an enemy could be standing directly below you. Always use Active Camo when you jump down. Ignore the doors on the sides of these rooms – you can't use them. The exit is at the lower end of the room. The third room looks like the first one you encountered (Fig. 5). This time, though, there is a turret downstairs. Destroy it with a grenade. Watch out for the Brute reinforcements – when they arrive, they will rush your position on the upper level.

TIP

Always take care where you activate Checkpoints. If your comrades are too brave and rush to their subsequent doom, you can simply select Revert to Last Checkpoint and try to prevent their demise on your next attempt. Don't forget that senior Elites are a lot more useful than, for example, Marines. The Zealot is a hugely experienced warrior. His golden armor does not signify rank alone: it indicates that he has killed countless enemies in battle. The Arbiter himself was a Zealot before he received his "calling".

02

03

04

05

4 "Step Aside, Let the Man Go Through"

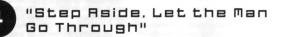

Mission Objective: Fight your way to the canyon floor

On your way to the exit you'll find two Fuel Rod Cannons – be sure to pick one up. As soon as the exit of this structure opens, Brutes and Jackals (Fig. 6) are waiting to ambush you only a few feet away. This is another good opportunity to test the mettle of your foes with a few grenades. Behind the enemy lies a deep abyss. You'll see the building you encountered during the cut-scene at the beginning of this level on the right. To reach this destination, you have to head in the opposite direction: go to the left and downhill.

At the first corner you'll meet a large group of Brutes and Jackals (Fig. 7). They are armed with Brute Shots, Plasma Grenades and even Shotguns! They may keep you busy for quite some time. A Fuel Rod Cannon is very useful here. Remember the oft-repeated phrase common to all levels featuring the Arbiter: "Don't forget your Active Camo!"

TIP

It's often the case that enemies are particularly vulnerable to the effects of weapons they use themselves. This doesn't apply to Brutes armed with Shotguns – quite the opposite, in fact. Shotguns are extremely ineffective against Brutes. You'll be better served by a weapon like the Carbine, using it to make headshots with pinpoint accuracy.

5 Caution, Ghost Driver!

After the battle with the Brutes, collect some weapons and grab yourself a Ghost. You'll find one standing close to the path. In front of you is a long canyon leading down the mountain. You'll encounter resistance after the first left turn: numerous Brutes and snipers will try to end your joyride (Fig. 8). Behind the rock in the middle there is even a turret. If you have a Beam Rifle, you might want to consider getting out of the vehicle to kill the annoying snipers – you've already got enough to contend with in the form of Ghost-driving Brutes.

Further down the canyon you'll have to pass yet another turret – it's standing on the left side on a slope. You can destroy turrets with a speedy frontal attack. This isn't always necessary, though. Kill the Jackal here, and the Grunt close to him will use the turret to support you (Fig. 9). Take a Beam Rifle from the weapon container and start fighting the enemies further down. As soon as you've cleared the way, a Spectre will come towards you in the area after the next bend to the right. Evade it to the best of your abilities.

After some steep climbing, you'll espy another ambush – but this one is a little more subtle. The Brutes have arranged explosive containers and hope to blow them up as you drive past. Destroy these containers immediately (Fig. 10). Race your Ghost up the slope on the right and simply drive over the edge. Keep Ⓐ depressed to stabilize the vehicle during the long flight.

06

07

08

09

10

6 "Fight Club"

Mission Objective: Raze the Brute encampment

Your Ghost ride will soon end. At the end of the canyon, snipers guard a valley. Take out the Jackals and observe the scene before you. In the valley, a slope starting on the right will lead you around a bend to the left and into the Brute encampment (Fig. 11). This is where you have to go. You could conceivably drive your Ghost there, but you should kill the Brutes first. This is best achieved with several headshots with a Beam Rifle. As soon as Brutes no longer trouble your crosshair with their ugly faces, or you run out of ammunition, climb back into the Ghost.

11

There are several Wraiths in the valley on the left, and they'll soon notice your arrival. You'll find a suitable remedy for this headache up on a slope in one of the niches – a Fuel Rod Cannon. It's possible that you may encounter Brutes up here that you didn't slay earlier with the Beam Rifle. If a Brute tries to board your Ghost, jump out and allow your opponent to take the controls. Now immediately board the vehicle again, drive a few feet back and kill your attacker. You should also watch out for the snipers firing on you from the neighboring valley.

7 Weapons Depot

You'll find a weapons depot guarded by Brutes and Jackals in this structure (Fig. 12). Along with weapons like Beam Rifles, Brute Shots and Plasma Grenades, you'll also find human munitions like Shotguns and Rocket Launchers. These are trophies gathered by the Brutes. Take everything you need for your fight against more Brutes and Jackals. If you haven't destroyed them yet, you should also equip yourself to deal with the two Wraiths. Now continue on your path.

12

The exit will lead you outside to a slope which leads around the rim of the second valley (Fig. 13). The exit to this valley is further behind on the left side. Go through the tunnel to reach your destination. Doing so will end this level. Should you run out of ammunition before you reach this point, you can return to the weapons depot at any time.

13

High Charity

MAP

Inner Sanctum
4
A
5
Conduit
Flood

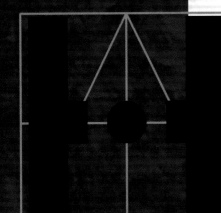

MISSION 13

High Charity

Cortana can handle the Index – stopping Truth is up to you

MISSION BRIEFING:

Master Chief, you have to reach the Forerunner spaceship and stop the Prophet of Truth. Every living creature on Earth depends on you! Get back to the Mausoleum Tower and fight your way through the Flood-infested halls of High Charity.

1 "Cross Purposes"

Mission Objective: Fight your way back inside the Mausoleum Tower

You begin on the Phantom landing platform. You have to get into the building on the right side, but countless Infection Forms and Combat Forms want to prevent you from doing just that (Fig. 1). Several Combat Forms might actually still have the energy shields of the Elites they once were. The Plasma Pistol is one of the weapons you start this level with and, although it's normally ineffective against the Flood, it's going to come in handy here. From a large distance, fire at the Flood with a Carbine. This allows you to both identify those wearing shields and kill the standard Flood as quickly as possible. As soon as you can, grab a better weapon from one of these monsters – for example, an Energy Sword. You'll find Frag Grenades, a Shotgun and a Rocket Launcher in front of the structure at the site of the crashed spaceship. Fight your way through the first room and get into the grav-lift.

01

TIP

The blade of the Brute Shot is a powerful melee weapon when employed against Combat Forms, just like the Energy Sword. Unlike the Energy Sword, though, a Brute Shot remains an efficient close combat tool even when its supply of ammunition is exhausted.

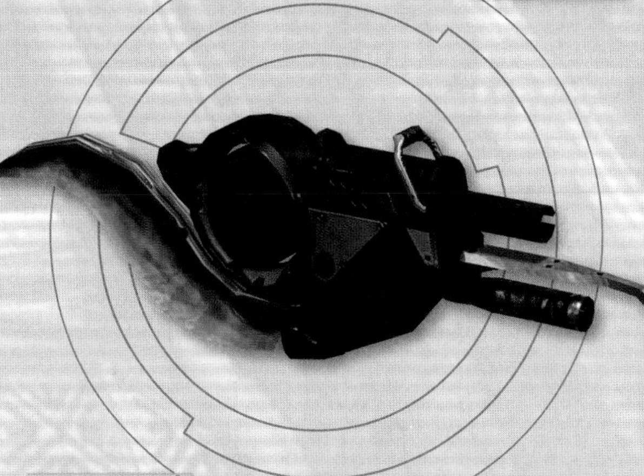

2 The Great Hall

You'll find a Covenant container with two Beam Rifles – in the space between the elevator and the great hall above – in the Mausoleum Tower (Fig. 2). This is convenient, because you can make good use of this weapon in the hall. At the platform on the left side, Drones fight against Flood. You can shoot the survivors of this battle from a safe distance. Cross the plasma bridge and enter the platform with the shining circle. This will activate the next plasma bridge which will automatically take you to the platform on the left side (Fig. 3). Now step into another shining circle to be transported to the next platform. From there you can leave this hall. Be cautious, though: behind the exit, several Combat Forms are waiting to surprise you!

02

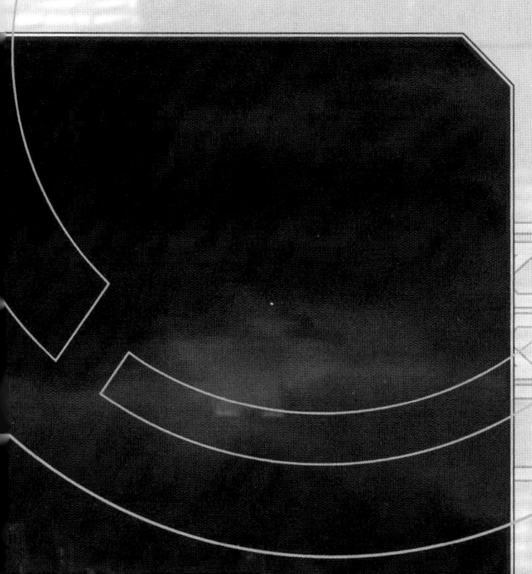

03

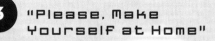

3 "Please, Make Yourself at Home"

Mission Objective: Stay ahead of the wave of Flood sweeping through High Charity

From now on, you'll have to get through areas of High Charity where the Flood has become fully entrenched. Spores in the air will obscure your view, so you'll have to use your flashlight (Fig. 4). Watch the Motion Sensor with extreme vigilance and listen very carefully to everything you hear, because the Flood will attempt to make sudden attacks. You will also still encounter Brutes and Jackals in these dark chambers. In the corridor bending slightly to the right, you should take the slightly higher side walkways (Fig. 5) – Brutes usually prefer the middle of the main hallway. As a rule, you should never simply stand and wait until Flood and Covenant combatants have killed each other off, because more Flood will arrive regularly from behind.

Your next task is to get through a cave-like hall. As long as you stay on the path, you won't get lost. If you become disorientated, note that the windows should always be on your right side. Behind the hall, a tunnel winds further downward. It ends in a hall almost identical to the one you've just passed. There is a significant difference, however: you see gigantic, root-like growths when you look out of the window here (Fig. 6). You will again encounter Human Combat Forms, and they'll be armed with Shotguns and Rocket Launchers. On the other side of the second hall, you'll arrive at an intersection. The branch to the left leads upstairs. Behind the door you'll find an elevator. Activate the shining switch to travel to the Inner Sanctum.

04

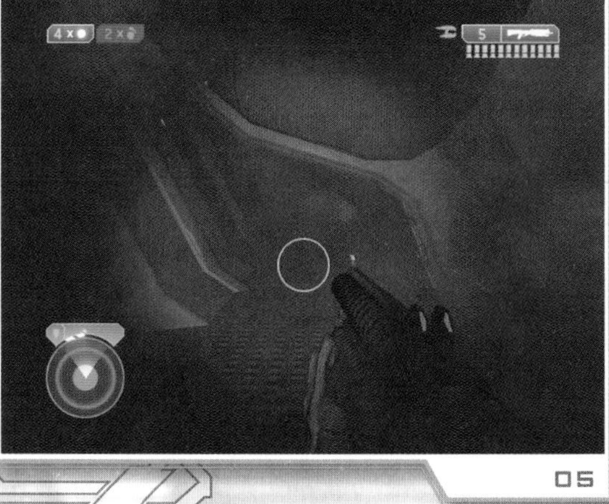

05

06

4 "Sanctified"

Brutes and Jackals have built up a last defensive line inside the Inner Sanctum (Fig. 7). In principle, you have to wait in the hall long enough for Cortana to open the exit. Don't hang around: this will happen exactly at the point when the Master Chief becomes the sole living creature in this area. You can jump from the pedestals to one of the balconies to observe the situation from above (Fig. 8). You won't be protected from enemy attacks here, but at least you're not standing in the middle, with Flood on one side and Brutes on the other. After you've killed the last enemies in the hall, get over to the opening gate.

Mission Objective: Find a way onto the Forerunner Ship

You'll find a lot of weapons in the room behind the great hall. Don't forget the Energy Sword lying on the shining pedestal in the middle of the room – it's easily overlooked (Fig. 9). Take what you need and enter the grav-lift leading to the Conduit.

07

08

09

5 "Once More, With Feeling"

Cortana will have already revealed the secret of the tower in the middle of High Charity: it's a Forerunner spaceship, and the Prophet of Truth plans to use it to fly to Earth. The Master Chief has to board it if the Earth is to be saved. Your mission is to reach the opposite end of the hall. Brutes and Flood are fighting against each other there (Fig. 10). If you've selected the Normal difficulty level, you can simply charge through to your destination. The Master Chief will be transported onto the ship at the very last second. Cortana, meanwhile, stays behind…

10

The Great Journey
MAP
Scarab
2
A
B
4
1
5
C
CAMPAIGN

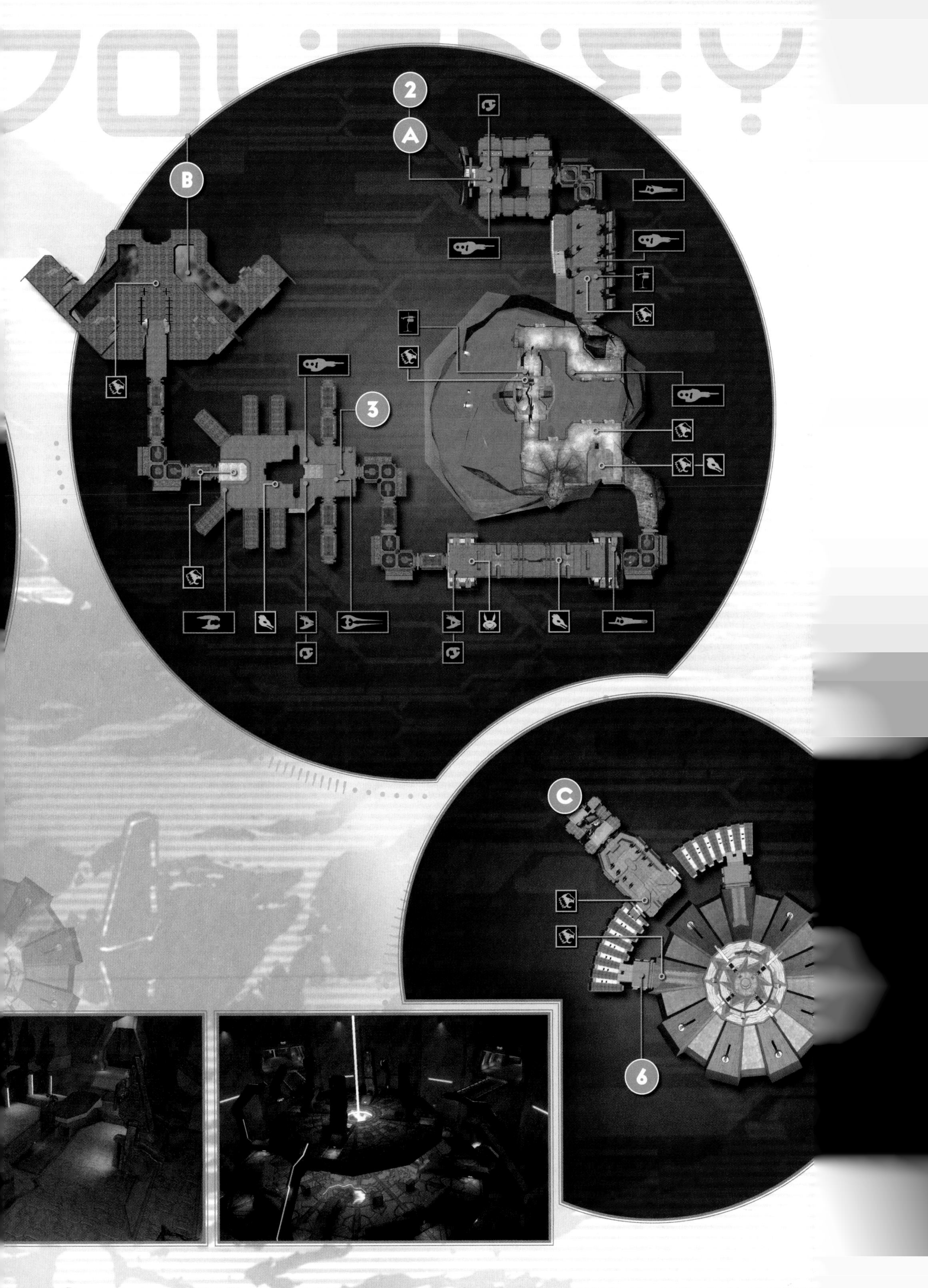

2
A
B
3
C
6

M I S S I O N 14

The Great Journey

Form an unexpected alliance; prevent Tartarus from activating the ring

MISSION BRIEFING:

With the aid of the Scarab, gain access to the Control Room. Stop the Brute Chieftain Tartarus and prevent Delta Halo from being activated!

1 "Your Ass, My Size-24 Hoof"

Mission Objective: Crush any Brutes in your path

You will see the building where the Halo can be activated with the Index in the background. To get there, you first have to go in the opposite direction. You can choose to drive a Wraith if you like, or would you prefer a Spectre? You can be the driver, a passenger or the gunner of the Spectre. You are, however, not that well protected if you opt for the latter, so the best option is to get into the Wraith. On your way to the Scarab, you'll have to take out numerous Ghosts and Wraiths that are controlled by Brutes (Fig. 1). Keep an eye on all the Brutes that survive the destruction of their vehicles. The SpecOps Commander (who will accompany you in the Spectre) will usually take care of pedestrians, but you shouldn't rely too heavily on his assistance.

You can't do much against the Scarab from ground level, because it's simply too huge. You'll have to find a way to the platform close to where the Scarab is parked. Continue driving to the left. At the end of the cliff you'll find a gate in the rock wall (Fig. 2). It is guarded by Brutes and Wraiths and – complicating matters to the nth degree – you'll also be attacked by a Phantom. Use the cover of the rocks to avoid fire from the enemy vessels. Destroy your enemies and collect their weapons. Now prepare to storm into the last bastion of the Brutes.

01

02

2 Bastion of the Brutes

Mission Objective: Commandeer the Scarab

Your campaign against the Brutes is now supported by Hunters. Their aid is truly welcome, as you will soon discover. In the first room you enter with your allies, there is a ramp on the right side. At the upper end of this area numerous Brutes await you (Fig. 3). Watch out for containers that can explode. This first encounter is a mere warm-up, a gentle aperitif, because the real army is waiting in the next hall. Don't forget to engage the Active Camo of the Arbiter at regular intervals.

The exit on the opposite side is defended by a large collection of Brutes (Fig. 4). Hurl several grenades over to thin their

03

numbers. Your opponents are no fools, though, and will try to do the same. They will also bombard you with their Brute Shots. The path to the exit bends to the right and, halfway there, a turret has been installed (Fig. 5). You should definitely save at least one grenade so you can throw it right behind its protective energy screen.

Behind the hall you'll reach a bridge. Jackals are holding it. Take a Beam Rifle out of the container close to the entrance. You can aim at the heads of the Jackals (Fig. 6) over the walls. Cross the bridge quickly – there is a Phantom closing in on the left side.

04

3 Bulwark of the Brutes

There is only one room left between you and the Scarab, but don't jump for joy just yet: you face stiff opposition here. Behind a partition, Jackals are patrolling. In front of the exit, several Brutes have made themselves more or less comfortable (Fig. 7). As soon as you killed them – no small task in itself – reinforcements will arrive through the gate. This fight could get rather difficult but, luckily, you can count on some support here. Observe the energy shields in front of the passages to the left and to the right of the Brutes. Behind them, Hunters and Elite Councilors are imprisoned. To free them, fire on the plasma shield generator locks you find on the floor in the middle of the shields (Fig. 8). Destroy them all quickly, because a few allies won't be of much against the Brutes.

05

In front of the Scarab, kill the last Brutes. You don't have to pay much (if any) attention to the Marines. As soon as the situation is cleared, an unlikely alliance will be forged between the Arbiter and Sergeant Major A.J. Johnson…

06

4 Backseat Driver

Mission Objective: Escort Johnson's Scarab to the Control Room

Two Banshees will land close to you on the platform. Get into one and start flying. The Scarab will need your support as an escort. Destroy the three Wraiths blocking the path of the gigantic war machine first (Fig. 9). Approach and fire at these tanks from the side – this way, you won't be shot at by several cannons simultaneously. This makes staying alive that bit easier, and you can destroy your targets with both Banshee weapons – especially the Fuel Rod Cannon.

07

08

Using this method, you can inch step-by-step closer to the Control Room as you fight against Spectres, Banshees and turrets. Use Ⓐ to perform aeronautical maneuvers to help you dodge enemy fire. If your Banshee sustains too much damage, you'll find others parked close to the enemy turrets on the ground (Fig. 10) and in other places along the floor of the canyon.

10

TIP

If your fragile Banshee is repeatedly shot down, you can instead take one of the Wraiths. The tank will take you close to the Control Room in relative safety. As soon as the gate is opened, an allied Banshee will land nearby. You can take it to make the flight up to the entrance.

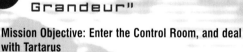

5 "Delusions and Grandeur"

Mission Objective: Enter the Control Room, and deal with Tartarus

As soon as you've escorted the Scarab safely to its destination and Johnson has opened the gate, fly over to the landing platform and get out of the Banshee. Climb through the wreckage and enter the small hall, where you will meet with a last-ditch attempt to prevent you from entering the structure. When you get close to the door on the right at the end of the hall, a small group of Brutes will enter the fray (Fig. 11). Engage your Active Camo immediately and throw grenades into the group, then kill the Brutes from behind.

11

Use the architecture of this hall to your advantage. There is another level under the glass floor. You can jump down through several different openings at the upper and lower ends. Use these corridors and your Active Camo to both flee from your persecutors and to ambush them (Fig. 12). This tactic is especially important when the second group of Brutes arrives. Don't forget that your opponents can employ Plasma Grenades with accuracy. Once you've killed all the Brutes, the door will open. Finally, you now have the chance to prevent Tartarus from activating Delta Halo.

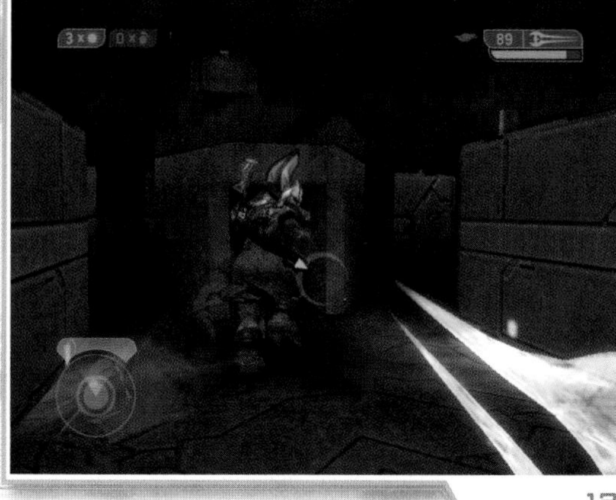

12

13

6 Tartarus, Chieftain of the Brutes

14

15

Many Elites will aid the Arbiter in his fight against Tartarus. This mighty Brute is protected by a very powerful energy shield (Fig. 13). Targets hit by his Gravity Hammer don't stand much of a chance. Even a single hit is enough to send the Arbiter on the Great Journey prematurely. It's not enough to merely evade a single shot, because Tartarus can use the Gravity Hammer regularly.

The arena has three tiers, the top level smaller than those below. If you were to liken it to a classic wedding cake design, you wouldn't be far wrong. A grav-lift in the middle will take you upward. If you want to leave the uppermost tier, drop down to the level below at the edge. Don't jump too enthusiastically – falling into the bottomless pit is not advisable. On the second level you can jump through the holes in the floor.

Initially, it might seem that you can't do anything to harm Tartarus. This isn't the case. Simply hold back while the Elites are killed one by one, because a steady attack will do the trick. Johnson will fire his Sniper Rifle on the Brute at regular intervals from a safe distance. After a while, the energy shield will finally fail (Fig. 14), but only for a short duration. You need to be there at that precise moment to hit the Brute with everything you have.

If you are close enough, deal him a mighty blow to the head from behind. This is something you should only do while the Brute is distracted. After making your hit, find cover immediately – it certainly won't be enough to defeat Tartarus, and he'll be keen to return the sentiment in kind. It's safer to use a weapon from a larger distance (Fig. 15). Brute Plasma Rifles, used alternately, work rather well. Aim for the head. Listen to the shouts and advice of Johnson – he'll tell you when Tartarus will be vulnerable. Repeat your attacks until you kill this monstrously tough and aggressive Brute. On higher difficulty levels, don't concentrate on Tartarus alone – on Heroic and Legendary modes, more Brutes will jump to the platform and come to the aid of their chieftain.

After your victory you'll see the credits, which end with a cliffhanger. It's a very open ending, leaving a number of questions unresolved. Will Spartan 117 save the Earth? Will Cortana prevent the activation of Halo, or will all sentient life in the entire galaxy be erased? Will humanity share the destiny (and ultimate fate) of the Forerunners? Is there a future for Johnson and the Arbiter? To learn the answers… drum roll… we'll just have to wait. To help endure the suspense, why not try playing through Halo 2 on higher difficulty levels? In the Heroic mode, many situations in the game are altered – you'll encounter more enemies, and they're stronger, not to mention more intelligent. Should you choose to attempt the Legendary setting, you'll find Halo 2 an almost entirely different game – it's truly that challenging. Good luck!

3: MULTIPLAYER MODE

Multiplayer matches in Halo 2 can be enjoyed by up to 16 players simultaneously via three distinct options: Split Screen, System Link and Xbox Live. Although its multiplayer component shares weaponry and many gameplay principles with the single-player Campaign mode, Halo 2 is a very different challenge when enjoyed with human participants. From casual, free-for-all melees to epic, highly strategic squad-based clan battles, this play mode offers virtually boundless depth and diversity of experience. There are seven different Game Types, and you can modify the rules of each to an astonishing degree if you wish. The true beauty of Halo 2's multiplayer mode is that it has a magnificent wealth of options… and yet, should you so desire, you can ignore them all and just *play*.

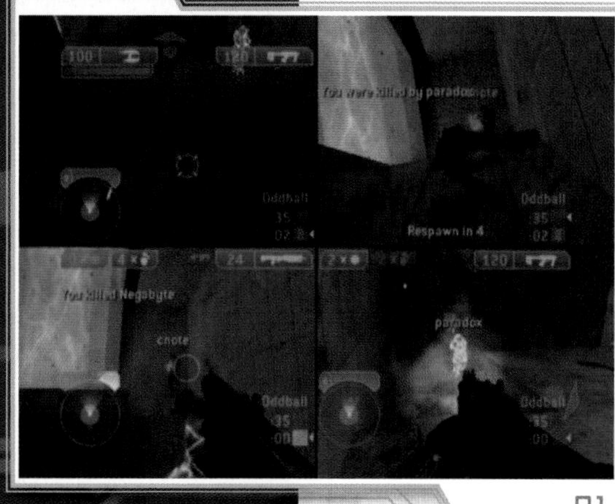

01

02

Split Screen

You can play with a maximum of four players via Halo 2's Split Screen option (Fig. 1). All you need is one Xbox, a single game disc and up to four controllers. Before combat begins, all participants will need to select – or first create – a Profile to continue, as explained on page 180. This done, you'll find yourself in the Pregame Lobby – see page 160 for further details – where you can choose a game variant, alter rule settings and begin a match.

System Link

You can connect two Xbox consoles with a System Link Cable to facilitate matches featuring up to eight players. With the addition of an Ethernet hub and relevant cables, you can even connect up to 16 Xbox consoles (a feat explained in your Xbox manual) but the maximum number of players is limited to 16. After each player has selected a profile, you'll arrive in the menu Available Games. From here you can browse and join games played on your local Xbox network, or select Create New Game to visit the Pregame Lobby and create a new match. If you don't have Xbox Live access, you can skip the following paragraphs and continue reading on page 162.

Xbox Live

If you want to fight online multiplayer battles against players from all over the world, you'll need access to Xbox Live (Fig. 2). A high-speed internet connection is a requisite if you want to experience Halo 2 multiplayer at its best, though – you can find more information on this at http://www.xbox.com. To begin, select the option Xbox Live and choose your Gamertag (or register a new one if you have yet to do so). Three additional gamers can, if you like, play as guests on your account. Alternatively, people can use their Gamertags (if they have them) to sign into Xbox Live – they don't have to be guests. Once the number of players is finalized, you can proceed to the Xbox Live menu.

SECTION 10

Xbox Live Main Menu

When you play Halo 2 via Xbox Live, the game's code will insure that neither you nor other players are unduly disadvantaged. This is achieved by matching you up with potential opponents or team members of the same approximate level and internet connection speed. If you want to leap fearlessly into the first available conflict, you should select the Quickmatch option. If you crave a more specific encounter, OptiMatch will allow you to select your preferred kind of game from a list of those available. If you would like to design your own battle, choose Create Party. This will take you to the Pregame Lobby.

Quickmatch

When choosing Quickmatch, you'll be sent into any game available at the moment based on a random selection. If you've played a Playlist with OptiMatch before, a game from this Playlist will be preferred.

OptiMatch

You'll find several different Playlists in the OptiMatch menu (Fig. 3). The available Playlists will be modified and extended by Bungie as time goes by. Choose the Playlist you like best. (A "Playlist" is a matchmaking utility, a single file that contains (among other things): whether players are ranked or unranked, whether the games are team-based or every man for himself, the minimum and maximum allowed team sizes and maps and games that are available for random selection.) There are variants like Head to Head (one-on-one Slayer duels), Rumble Pit (free for all matches, everyone against everyone else), Team Skirmish/Minor Clanmatch (two small teams fight for victory) or Big Team Battle/Major Clanmatch (two large teams of eight fight against each other). As soon as you've selected a Playlist, "Matchmaking" will automatically search for appropriate opponents with similar levels and connection speeds. As soon as the players are ready, the current Quick Options will be displayed on the screen and the game can start.

CHOOSE MATCHMAKING PLAYLIST
Rumble Pit
Team Skirmish
Head to Head
Big Team Battle
Minor Clanmatch
Major Clanmatch
Training Ground
Pick your preferred matchmaking playlist and get matched with others that chose the same one.
Training Ground
Practice your skills in unranked games. Guests allowed. Plays the same games as the Team Skirmish playlist.
FRIENDS
SELECT BACK
03

A Playlist contains a large amount of possible games. Usually, you can't determine exactly which kind of game you are going to play on which map, but you can get into a game with friends or a Clan (see Friends and Create Party on page 160).

Level: Your Halo 2 Xbox Live ranking will be determined by your results in Quickmatch and OptiMatch battles. Your level will reflect your ability in the currently active Playlist, and will make it possible for you to join matches with players of a similar standing. Even if you are a highly experienced gamer, it will take a great deal of time and no small amount of skill to climb the rankings. If you are interested to learn how your level is determined, find all there is to know about this topic from page 220 of the Extras Chapter.

You can find very detailed information about your success in online matches. You can also see extensive statistics at www.bungie.net.

Create Party

Using this menu, you can send Party Invites to friends: it allows you to all get into one group and play together or against each other online. Choose Custom Game, then select your game variant, the exact rules, and the map where you want to play it. The options available to you here are described in the Pregame Lobby: Game Setup section that begins on the next page. It's also possible to arrange for your party to fight against other teams via the Matchmaking option.

Content Download

Download new stuff to your hard drive. Halo 2 developer Bungie plans to release additional maps. As soon as they are available, you'll be told about it on the Xbox Live Main Menu or at the www.bungie.net homepage.

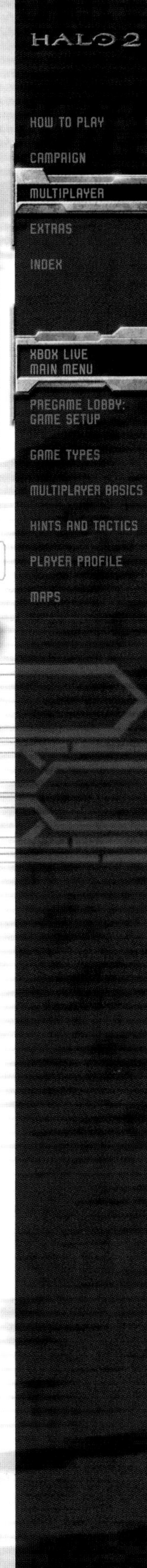

Friends

Use Ⓨ to call up the Friends Menu at any time (Fig. 4). It consists of three lists: Friends, Clans and Players. Players will list all the people you've played with recently. The symbols in the lists will tell you immediately if other players are online or not, if they use the communicator, or if you have any messages.

How to recruit friends: If you want to send a Friend Request to a teammate or opponent, you can select their Gamertag in the Player and Clan lists. It is also possible to send a direct invite to someone: just enter their Gamertag manually. The other player will then receive a Message with your offer of friendship.

04

If they accept, they will be added to your Friends list, and you'll be added to theirs. You can send messages to everybody on your Friends list, or invite them into a Party. Of course, you can also refuse a request. You can block all further messages from certain players if you need or want to, or even choose to mute the voices of particularly annoying individuals. The Friends list can contain up to 100 entries, and you can remove Friends from it whenever you like.

How to organize a Party: You can send Party Invites to the people in your Friends List. The members of a Party can take part in Custom Games together or play team matches. When you've sent the invites you will be the Party Leader, and you get to choose the game for the group. When selecting Custom Game, every player can decide which team they want to be in. Press Ⓧ in the Lobby and choose a team color. You can even change teams during the game – just select the option in the Pause menu. Leaders can disband the Party if they want to, or hand the leadership to someone else.

How to found a clan: A clan is a special group of players and, unlike the Party, a clan is designed to be a long-term affiliation. A clan can have up to a hundred members, and every player can join one. Read more about clans in the menu Clan Details on Xbox Live. You can't be a member of several Halo 2 clans at the same time. You can find statistics and information on clans at www.bungie.net.

Pregame Lobby: Game Setup

The Pregame Lobby is the multiplayer control center in Split Screen or System Link modes (Fig. 1). You'll find this menu under the heading Create Party on Xbox Live.

You'll see on the lower left-hand corner of the screen which game variant is currently selected, while the column on the right will show you all gamers currently in the Party. You can begin play by selecting Start Game. If you want to play another game variant or Map, select Game Setup and create a Custom Game. The following options will be available.

01

Change Map

Before choosing a map, be sure to consider how many players will be involved, and what type of combat will suit you best. If you have a relatively small number of players, one of the more expansive maps could lead to large periods of inactivity. Similarly, a smaller map crammed with a full 16 players might feel somewhat overcrowded, yet could also be incredibly intense. You'll find an overview of Halo 2's maps at the end of this chapter.

MAPS

MAP	PAGE
Lockout	206
Ascension	182
Midship	210
Ivory Tower	202
Beaver Creek	186
Burial Mounds	188
Colossus	194
Zanzibar	216
Coagulation	190
Headlong	198
Waterworks	212

Change Rules

Choose one of the seven game types and, if required, fine-tune further individual settings. Every game variant offers a different gaming experience.

TYPE

GAME TYPE	PAGE
Slayer	162
King of the Hill	163
Oddball	165
Juggernaut	166
Capture the Flag	167
Assault	168
Territories	169

You can choose from built-in variations for every basic game type – for example, you'll find variants like Team Slayer in your Slayer menu. Furthermore, you could also play Rockets, which lets you enjoy Slayer with the Rocket Launcher as the default weapon. It's also possible to modify rules and create your own very individual match. Select the option Settings in the Main Menu, then choose Game Variants.

Quick Options

You can modify eleven game rules in the match you've selected by choosing Quick Options – for example, how many points are needed to win or which weapons will be available. The rules will stay modified until the Party Leader changes them again or the Party disbands.

Switch To: Co-Op Game

Using this option in the menu, you can leave the normal multiplayer mode and get into the Campaign with a second player (see page 8). This mode is only available if you're playing on an Xbox via a Split Screen view.

Switch To: Matchmaking

When you've created a Party with Friends on Xbox Live, you can also switch with this option to Matchmaking and, together, fight against other teams.

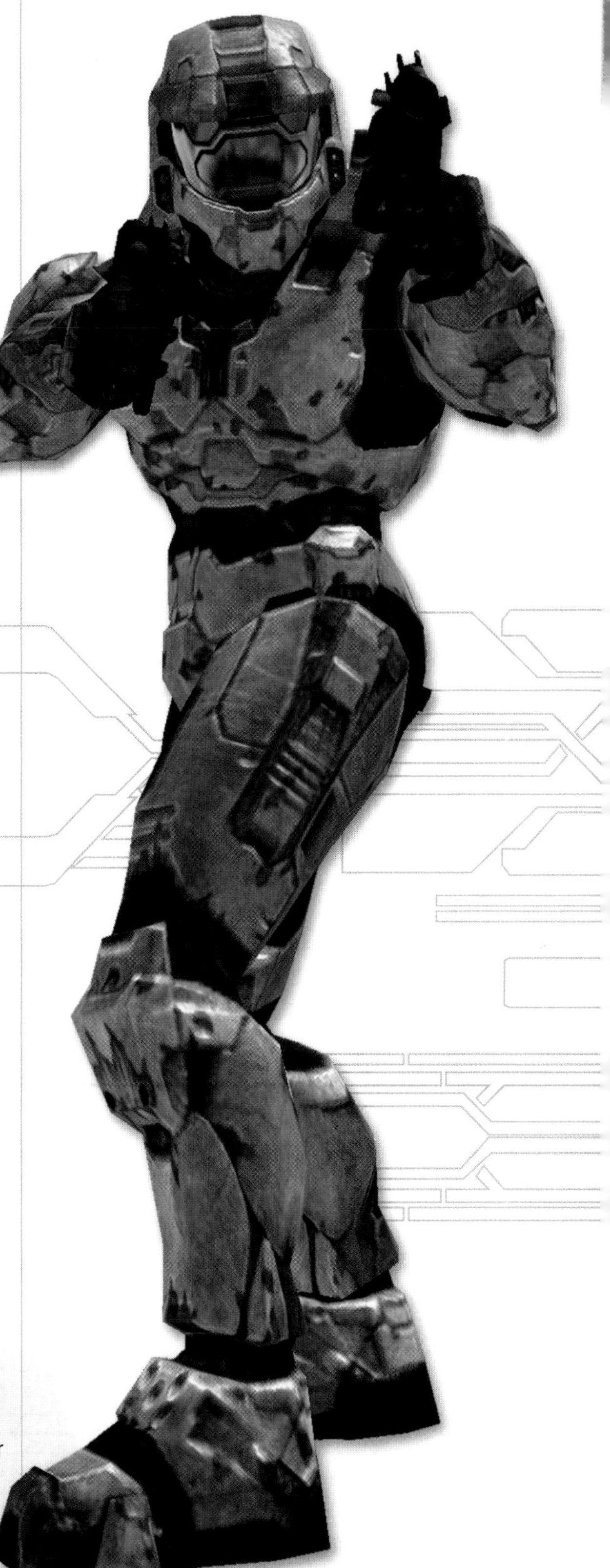

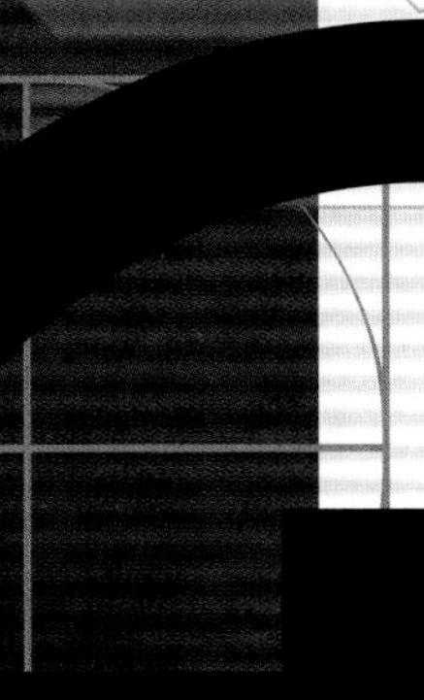

Game Types

There are seven different game types in Halo 2's multiplayer mode. The array of options may seem initially bewildering, but worry not: you'll soon come to appreciate the flexibility on offer. Be aware that if you are joining a game of Quickmatch or OptiMatch via Xbox Live the rules are predetermined and cannot be modified by you.

The following text details the various basic multiplayer game modes.

01

Slayer

This is a classic deathmatch – a true battle of life and death, with the simple objective being to kill as many of your opponents as possible (Fig. 1). Successful kills will be rewarded with points. A maximum of 16 individuals can play this game at once. If you're opting for a Team Slayer match, you can have teams of two versus two, four versus four or even eight teams of two competing against each other.

SLAYER

BUILT-IN VARIANT	RULES
Slayer	A classic Slayer duel to the death. Everybody tries to kill everybody else. 25 points to win.
Team Slayer	Small teams fight against other enemy teams. 50 points to win.
Rockets	Rocket Launchers are the only weapons. There are no motion sensors. 25 points to win.
Swords	Energy Swords are the only weapons. Everyone has Overshields. 25 points to win.
Snipers	Sniper Rifles and Beam Rifles are the only weapons. There are no motion sensors. 15 points to win.
Phantoms	All players are wearing Active Camouflage. 15 points to win.
Team Phantoms	The team version of Phantoms. First team to 25 points wins.
Elimination	The solitary survivor wins the battle.
Phantom Elimination	The team version of Elimination. You have just one life and everyone is invisible. Last player standing wins a round. First to win three rounds is the victor.

QUICK OPTIONS

Score to Win Round	Determines how many points are needed to win a round.
Round Time Limit	A round can be set to end after a specified amount of time has elapsed.
Starting Weapon	Determines which primary weapon players start the game and respawn with.
Weapons on Map	Determines the set of weapons that is available on the map. Can also be turned off entirely.
Motion Sensor	When the Motion Sensor is turned off it no longer detects or indicates movement.
Bonus Points	Players can earn additional points for notable achievements like double kills and killing sprees.
Starting Grenades	When this setting is on, players will start the game and respawn with grenades.
Secondary Weapon	Determines if the players start the game and respawn with a backup weapon.
Max Active Players	Controls how many players are active in the game at once.
Primary Light Vehicle	Choose the primary light land vehicle (Warthog, Gauss Warthog, Ghost, Spectre, random, none).
Primary Heavy Vehicle	Choose the primary heavy land vehicle (Wraith, Scorpion Tank, random, none).

Generally, the most important thing to do in Slayer is to kill as many opponents as possible. Unless you're playing Elimination, where stealth and measured attacking play is a virtue, there's little to gain from hiding yourself in the quietest corner that you can find.

You should also be aware if the game variant you're playing punishes your death by deducting points from you. Generally, it's much more important to act than to merely react.

Also keep in mind that suicide will be punished by a deduction of points (although not with Rockets). Usually you'll get a penalty of five seconds. This is added to the standard respawn time of five seconds.

02

By selecting the Quick Option "Bonus Points", you can determine that special achievements will be acknowledged and rewarded with additional points. This may include the honor of being awarded one or more of several Medals – have a look at these on page 173. In the default settings this option isn't activated. You can only enable the appearance of vehicles on a map if it was designed to support them. In Lockout, for example, the option to include them is not available.

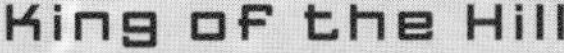

King of the Hill

In this play mode the objective is to conquer and maintain control of a designated area of the map. The action will be fast and furious as your rivals attempt to wrestle it from your oft-tenuous grasp. If you can remain at your post for a designated time, you'll win. The "Hill" is always a specific place on the map marked with a border (Fig. 2). In a team game, if someone is standing on the Hill, the color of the borderline will change into that player's team color. Announcements in the form of text messages will inform you of events on the Hill – for example, when control shifts from one group or individual to another, and how much time remains before a player or team wins a round.

KING OF THE HILL

BUILT-IN VARIANT	RULES
King	Conquer the Hill and occupy it for specific amount of time.
Team King	Several groups fight to control the Hill. The team must control it uncontested for one minute.
Phantom King	Players wear Active Camo. The Hill must be held for one minute.
Crazy King	The Hill changes its position from time to time.
Team Crazy King	The team version of Crazy King.

QUICK OPTIONS

Score to Win Round	Determines the amount of time you must stand on the Hill in order to win a round.
Team Play	Determines whether this is a team game or a free-for-all.
Uncontested Hill	When this option is on you can only earn time on the Hill when there are no enemies contesting it.
Moving Hill	Determines if the Hill will change to a new random location after a set interval.
Weapons on Map	Determines the set of weapons that is available on the map.
Team Time Multiplier	Determines if you will earn time faster when you have more teammates on the Hill.
Damage Resistance	When Damage Resistance is on, a player on the Hill will be tougher than normal.
Starting Weapon	Determines the primary weapon players start and respawn with.
Secondary Weapon	Determines the backup weapon players start and respawn with.
Force Even Teams	Each team will only have as many active players as the team with the fewest players. All other team members must wait their turn to respawn.
Starting Grenades	When this setting is on players will start the game and respawn with grenades.

When you've activated the Uncontested Hill option, a player can only collect time if there are no opponents within the boundaries of the Hill. If Moving Hill is selected, the position of the Hill will change after a certain period of time.

The position of the Hill will be marked with a Waypoint Indicator. Its color will show you which team is occupying the Hill at that time. You don't usually have to spend all your time on the Hill all at once. It can be quite a good idea to leave your position for a short time to grab more ammunition or to fight an attacker.

If you're on the Hill and a number of opponents are closing in on you, consider backing off and letting them fight it out, then returning to clean up the stragglers and reclaim your place. Many of the Hills contain obstacles that can serve as cover. You don't always have to fight on the Hill. The winner can often be the player that crouches down and hides better than anyone else...

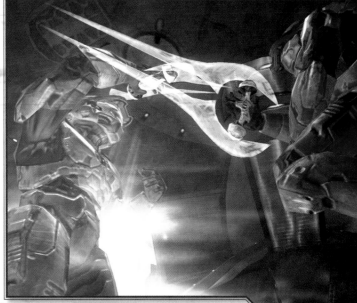

In the game Crazy Hill the option Moving Hill is activated. This means that the Hill will change its position after a specified interval and will reappear in a random location. There are, however, only a limited number of places where it could conceivably be positioned. Remember where these spots are so you can react quickly.

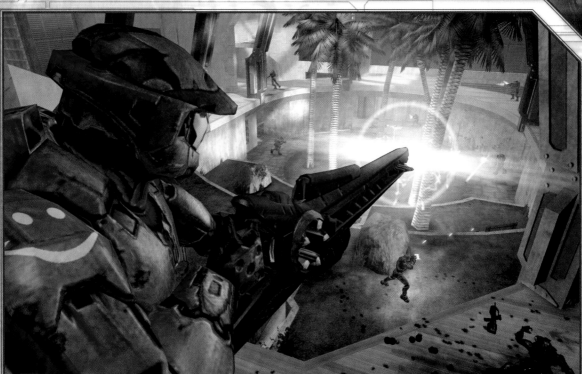

Oddball

Find the Oddball and hold it for a specific amount of time (Fig. 3). The "ball" is actually a skull, and its position is marked with a Waypoint Marker. Hold ⊗ to pick it up. There's a catch, though: the person holding this widely-coveted object is unable to use weapons while it is in their grasp, and will soon find every other combatant bearing down on their location. You can use the skull to beat your opponents up if you're quick and clever, though…

ODDBALL

BUILT-IN VARIANT	RULES
Oddball	Find the ball and hold it for two minutes in total to win.
Rocketball	Rocket Launchers are the only weapons. Hold the ball for one minute to win.
Swordball	Variant with Energy Swords and without a Motion Sensor. 30 seconds of holding the ball wins the round. Three rounds to win.
Team Ball	Up to eight teams compete against each other. The team holding the ball for two minutes in total wins.
Low Ball	Everyone in the team has to hold the ball for at least thirty seconds to win.
Fiesta	You respawn with random weapons. Earn two minutes of ball control time to win.

QUICK OPTIONS

Score to Win Round	Determines the amount of time you must hold the ball in order to win a round.
Team Play	Determine whether this is a team game or a free-for-all.
Ball Count	Controls the number of balls in the game.
Starting Weapon	Determines the primary weapon players start and respawn with.
Secondary Weapon	Determine the backup weapon players start and respawn with.
Weapons on Map	Determines the set of weapons available on the map.
Motion Sensor	When the Motion Sensor is turned off it no longer detects or indicates movement.
Ball Indicator	Controls if an indicator reveals the location of the ball (always on, dropped ball, team control, off).
Speed with Ball	Determines the speed that a ball carrier moves in relation to other players (slow, normal, fast).
Toughness with Ball	When Toughness with Ball is turned on, a player carrying a ball will be tougher than normal.
Damage Resistance	When Damage Resistance is on, everyone will be tougher than normal.

This skull is a quite formidable blunt weapon, but it can be a trial to get close enough to an opponent to use it. Remember: you don't have to keep it in your hand constantly, as it's not necessary to collect all the time at once. Don't hesitate to drop the Oddball in order to defend yourself. To do so, press a fire trigger to switch to the last weapon you used. You should also bear in mind that the skull can be moved around with projectiles and explosions.

The Oddball will always reappear on the same spot. If the ball leaves the map – if, for example, it falls into the abyss on Lockout – it will appear again at its point of origin. If you are about to be killed, you could throw the ball into a suitable "out of bounds" area. This means that your attackers won't be able to grab it immediately – and you get the pleasure of knowing that your executioners haven't profited from your demise!

Likewise, if you're nowhere near the ball, sometimes you can wait for it to go out of bounds and then be first to snatch it when it reappears.

Like King of the Hill, sometimes the best strategy is to not be the center of attention. If a number of opponents are closing in on your position when you have the skull, just drop it and take cover. Let your enemies fight it out. Then, when they're weak, make your move and reclaim your prize.

Juggernaut

One player takes the role of the so-called Juggernaut. All other players have only one task: to hunt down and kill the Juggernaut. The person who kills the Juggernaut will become the next Juggernaut (Fig. 4).

If the Juggernaut kills one of his adversaries, he'll get a point. Only the Juggernaut can accumulate points and win the game.

04

JUGGERNAUT

BUILT-IN VARIANT	RULES
2 on 1	One player is the Juggernaut, the other two are teammates. Only the Juggernaut can score. Ten points win the game.
3 on 1	One player is the Juggernaut while three others are teammates. Earn ten points as the Juggernaut to win the game.
Ninjanaut	The Juggernaut has constant Active Camo and a Motion Sensor. You don't, so work together to corner him and take him out. Ten points to win.
Phantom Fodder	You're invisible, but you have no motion sensor. You're being hunted, so watch out! Three rounds wins, five points wins a round.
Dreadnaut	The Dreadnaut is faster, has damage resistance, extra damage and an Overshield. 20 points to win.

QUICK OPTIONS

Score to Win Round	Determines how many points the Juggernaut needs to win a round.
Juggernaut Overshield	When Overshield is on, the Juggernaut has abnormally powerful shields that recharge over time.
Juggernaut Active Camo	When this option is on the Juggernaut has Active Camo.
Juggernaut Movement	Determines the Juggernaut's speed relative to that of other players (slow/normal/fast).
Juggernaut Infinite Ammo	When Infinite Ammo is on the Juggernaut will never run out of ammunition.
Juggernaut Damage Resistance	When this option is activated, the Juggernaut is extra tough.
Juggernaut Extra Damage	When Extra Damage is on the Juggernaut's weapons do more damage than normal.
Juggernaut Motion Sensor	This setting controls whether or not the Juggernaut has a Motion Sensor.
Starting Weapon	Determines the primary weapon players start and respawn with.
Secondary Weapon	Determines the backup weapon players start and respawn with.
Weapons on Map	Determines the set of weapons available on the map.

A message will inform you when you become the Juggernaut. Every other player on the map is now united by a common ideal: to blast you into your constituent atoms with all due haste. Your objective is to take out as many of your opponents as possible. Famous warriors in history and fiction alike have achieved an immortality of a kind by virtue of acts of great heroism, fantastic feats and remarkable skills. In Juggernaut, the trick is to achieve immortality by simply not dying. The Quick Options screen allows you to choose how powerful or vulnerable this lone warrior will be. These settings will overwrite the normal player defaults.

If a Juggernaut commits suicide, another player will be awarded the role. The position of the Juggernaut will not be marked with a Waypoint Indicator, so hunters have to coordinate their search well – and that means lots of communication. The Juggernaut is usually stronger than normal players, so a combined attack will be necessary. Keep an eye on the Team Waypoints. If you can discern from the color of the indicator that someone is shooting or has been killed, you can be sure that the Juggernaut is around there. This game variant is best enjoyed on smaller maps and with smaller groups of players.

In Juggernaut it often pays to not be at the vanguard of a fight. Hang back a little and try to help your teammates out from a distance. If you manage to kill the Juggernaut you'll become the new Juggernaut and conveniently not be a target in someone's sights. Use this tactic carefully, though: if you kill a teammate, you'll lose a point!

When you're the Juggernaut take advantages of your "natural" abilities. If you move faster than other players, use that to get away from trouble. If you have a motion sensor and your enemies don't then it's time to play sneaky, hiding and taking your enemies by surprise.

Capture the Flag

This popular multiplayer game is all about the flag and who's got it. The objective is to grab the flag of an opponent – or a neutral flag – and return it to your home base to score (Fig. 5).

Meanwhile, you have to insure that your flag isn't captured by your enemies. To succeed at CTF you'll need solid offensive and defensive tactical skills. Teamwork and communication are key: without at least a degree of coordination, a humiliating defeat is practically assured...

05

CAPTURE THE FLAG

BUILT-IN VARIANT	RULES
Multi Flag CTF	Defend your flag while launching a coordinated attack on your enemy's flag. Three captures to win.
CTF Classic	Defend your flag while capturing the flag of your enemies. Three points wins, flag must be home to score, flag may be returned.
1 Flag CTF	Take turns on offense/defense. A capture wins a round. Flag may not be returned. Rounds last three minutes. First to three wins.
1 Flag CTF Fast	Intense two-minute rounds of alternating offense/defense. A capture wins a round. Flag may not be returned. First to three wins.

QUICK OPTIONS

Number of Rounds	A game can end after a single round or after a fixed Number of Rounds.
Round Time Limit	A round can be set to end after a fixed amount of time has elapsed.
Flag Touch Return	When Flag Touch Return is enabled you may return your flag to the base by touching it.
Flag Reset Time	The time that must elapse before a dropped flag returns home.
Flag At Home to Score	When enabled, you cannot score a point unless your flag is safely on its flag stand.
Flag Indicator	Controls if an indicator reveals the location of your flag (when uncontrolled, always on, away from home, off).
Vehicle Operation	Determines if a player carrying a flag can drive vehicles or operate turrets.
Overshield	Controls whether or not the Overshield power-up is available on the map.
Active Camouflage	Controls whether or not the Active Camouflage power-up is available on the map.
Force Even Teams	Each team will only have as many active players as the team with the fewest players. All other team members must wait their turn to respawn.
Primary Heavy Vehicle	Choose the primary heavy land vehicle if available (Wraith, Scorpion Tank, random, none).

When you're playing Single Flag one team will be on the offensive, with the goal being to get into the enemy base, steal their flag and take it to a home base. The other team must try to prevent that from happening. When you've selected Neutral Flag, there's only one flag on the whole map, with both teams struggling to transport it to their home base. If the flag carrier wishes to use a weapon, they must first drop the flag – but if you're feeling suitably brave or foolhardy, it's also possible to use it as a crude cudgel. The default options won't allow the flag carrier to drive or ride in vehicles.

With Flag Touch Return activated, a defending team only needs a member to touch the flag in order to return it to its starting position. To do this, though, you must first cause a soldier to drop it. With Flag Reset Time activated, the flag will return to its home base after a specified period of time. If there are enemies close to the flag, the timer will stop; as soon as an opponent picks the flag up, the timer will be reset.

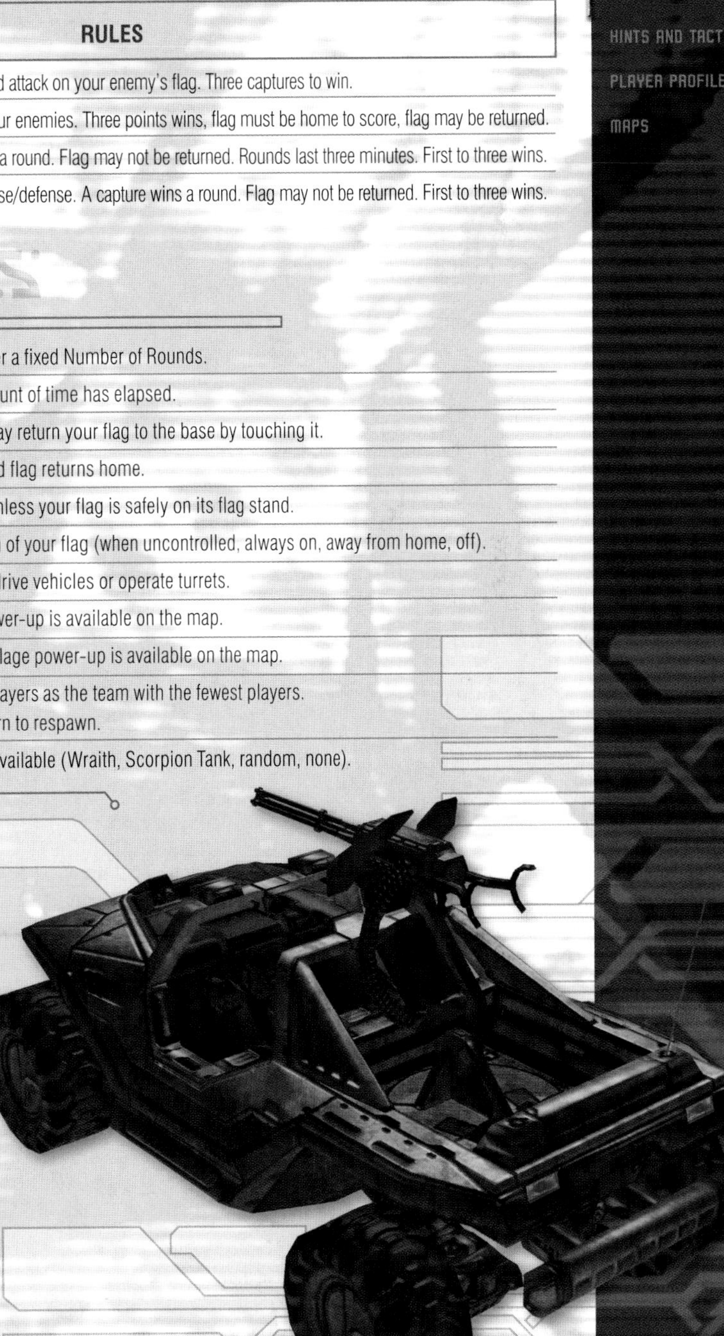

Assault

Assault mode requires you to transport a bomb into the base of your opponent, arm it, then place it in a designated spot (Fig. 6). To arm it, you have to wait for a time in the area around the target… which can prove very tricky indeed.

06

ASSAULT

BUILT-IN VARIANT	RULES
Multi Bomb	Defend your base while trying to deliver your bomb into the enemy base. Three successful bombings wins.
Single Bomb	Take turns on offense and defense. A successful bombing wins a round. First to three wins. No bomb return. Rounds last three minutes.
Single Bomb Fast	Intense two-minute rounds of offense and defense. A successful bombing wins a round. Bomb may not be returned. First to three wins.
Neutral Bomb	There's just one bomb that starts in the middle. Use it to bomb the enemy base three times to win.
Blast Resort	You have just one life and no Motion Sensor in this single bomb game. Ten second arming, three minute rounds, first to three wins.

QUICK OPTIONS

Number of Rounds	Determines how many rounds a game should last.
Round Time Limit	Determines how long one round should last.
Bomb Arm Time	The time it takes to arm a bomb inside the arming zone near the enemy bomb post.
Enemy Bomb Indicator	Determines if defenders have an indicator showing the location of an enemy bomb (always on, when dropped, when armed, off).
Bomb Touch Return	When Bomb Touch Return is on you may return an enemy bomb to its original location by touching it.
Sticky Arming	When Sticky Arming is on you can pick up a partially armed bomb and resume arming it where someone else left off.
Vehicle Operation	Determines if a player carrying a bomb can drive vehicles or operate turrets.
Overshield	Controls whether or not the Overshield power-up is available on the map.
Active Camouflage	Controls whether or not the Active Camouflage power-up is available on the map.
Force Even Teams	Each team will only have as many active players as the team with the fewest players. All other team members must wait their turn to respawn.
Primary Heavy Vehicle	Choose the primary heavy land vehicle, if available (Wraith, Scorpion, random, none).

You could say that Assault is, in a sense, a reverse Capture the Flag game. The same is true for the game types Multi, Single and Neutral. In this game it's necessary to get an explosive into the enemy base. After that, you'll have to arm the bomb. This takes place automatically if the carrier can survive in the vicinity of the enemy "bomb spot" for a specified amount of time.

The carrier of the bomb must stand for a certain amount of time in the designated area around the enemy target. You'll see on your screen how much time must elapse before you can drop it. Naturally, your opponents will try to prevent you from doing so. Remember: the bomb also can be used as an excellent blunt weapon, and you can always drop it by pulling a trigger.

When you're on defense in Assault, don't camp your base, it's in your best interest to range out and try to spot the incoming bomb early, while it's still far from your base. Just remember to leave someone on defense and remember to communicate, or you may suffer a sneak attack. When you're on offense in Assault try creating a distraction far from your bomb, pulling defenders away from the base and allowing a sneaky assault.

Territories

The Territories game type sees participants fighting to gain control of areas on the map (Fig. 7). When you're controlling a Territory, you'll collect time. The first to collect the necessary control time will win the match. Unlike King of the Hill, you won't have to stand in your Territories at all times to accrue time. The more Territories you have under your control, the quicker you'll achieve victory.

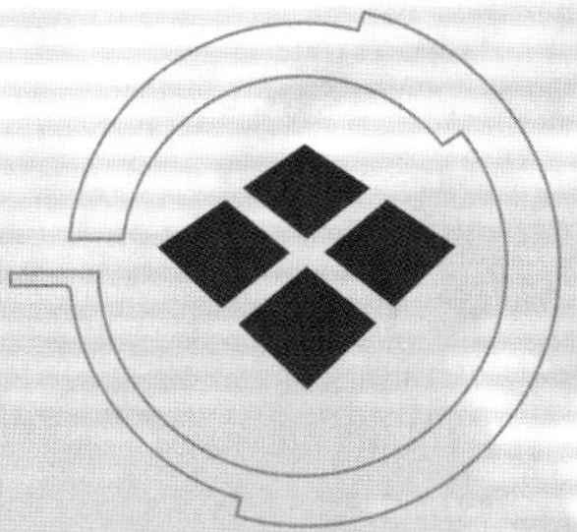

07

TERRITORIES

BUILT-IN VARIANT	RULES
3 Plots	There are just three Territories. Earn three minutes of control time before your opponents do by owning the majority of them.
Land Grab	Own a majority of Territories to earn five minutes of control time before your opponents do.
Gold Rush	Grab your pistol and load your shotgun! Two minutes wins a round. Rounds last three minutes. First to three rounds wins.
Control Issues	Bring out the big guns to fight for control of just two Territories. Everyone has Overshields. Five minutes of control time wins.
Contention	There's just one Territory on the map. Work with your team and control it for two minutes to win.

QUICK OPTIONS

Number of Rounds	Determines how many rounds a game should have.
Score to Win Round	Determines how much control time is needed to win the round.
Territory Count	Determines the number of Territories on the map.
Contest Time	Determines the amount of time it takes to break someone else's control of a Territory.
Control Time	Determines how long it takes to gain control of a neutral Territory.
Force Even Teams	Each team will only have as many active players as the team with the fewest players. All other team members must wait their turn to respawn.
Starting Weapons	Determines the primary weapon players start and respawn with.
Secondary Weapons	Determines the backup weapon players start and respawn with.
Weapons on Map	Determines the set of weapons available on the map.
Active Camo	Determines if all players will be invisible. Firing a weapon or taking damage makes you temporarily visible.
Starting Grenades	Determines whether or not players start and respawn with grenades.

The positions of the Territories are marked with Waypoints. When you enter one of these areas a message will confirm your arrival. As soon as the necessary Control Time is over, the Territory will be yours and your flag will be positioned there. You can even achieve this while inside a vehicle.

The Waypoint leading to this territory will now be adorned with the color of your team. You'll also receive messages when your team members capture Territories. When you arrive in an area controlled by your enemies, you'll have to neutralize the enemy real estate by surviving within its uncontested boundaries for a preset time.

Looking at the bar in the middle of the screen will tell you how many Territories exist on this map. If a field is full, the Territory is controlled by someone. The color will show you which player controls it. If a colored indicator is shrinking, the Territory is currently being seized by someone else.

Game Variants

You can configure an enormous amount of rules and settings for a Custom Game. Choose Settings in the Main Menu and open the sub-menu Game Variants. Now choose one of the seven Game Types. You can now configure a new Game Variant by selecting Create New, or edit a Built-in Variant under a new name. Your own Game Variant will be saved to your hard drive. You can now select it under the heading Custom Games in multiplayer mode and play it with your friends.

In every game there are sub-menus for Match Options, Player Options, Team Options, Vehicle Options and Equipment Options. There are basic options common to all Game Variants, and there are options tuned especially for the individual conditions of each game type – Slayer Options, King of the Hill Options, and so on.

The available options for each setting are described clearly in the Game Variants menu. The only question you might have is what the option **Weapons on Map** might hide. Here's the answer:

Rockets (Rocket Launchers), Shotguns, Swords (Energy Swords), Brute Shots, Halo Classic (Magnum, Battle Rifle, Shotgun, Sniper Rifle, Rocket Launcher, Plasma Pistol, Plasma Rifle and Needler), New Classic (SMG, Energy Sword, Carbine, Beam Rifle, Brute Shot, Sentinel Beam), Heavy Weapons (Rocket Launcher, Brute Shot), All Duals (Magnum, SMG, Needler, Plasma Pistol, Plasma Rifle), No Duals (Battle Rifle, Shotgun, Sniper Rifle, Rocket Launcher, Carbine, Brute Shot, Beam Rifle, Energy Sword, Sentinel Beam), Rifles (Battle Rifle, Sniper Rifle, Carbine, Beam Rifle, Sentinel Beam), Sniping (Sniper Rifle, Beam Rifle), No Sniping (anything but Sniper Rifle and Beam Rifle), Pistols (Magnum, Plasma Pistol), Plasma (Plasma Pistol, Plasma Rifle, Brute Plasma Rifle), Human, Covenant.

SECTION 4

Multiplayer Basics

The basic game mechanics of Halo 2's multiplayer mode are much like those of its Campaign mode. You should absorb the information in the How to Play chapter on page 6 before leaping into the fray – unless, that is, you have a particular penchant for devastating defeats...

Onscreen Display

Your HUD looks just like the one found in the Campaign mode. The color of the display depends on your choice of character (see Player Profile on page 180). The Spartan HUD will be blue, while the Elite equivalent will be violet. The HUD provides you with the following information.

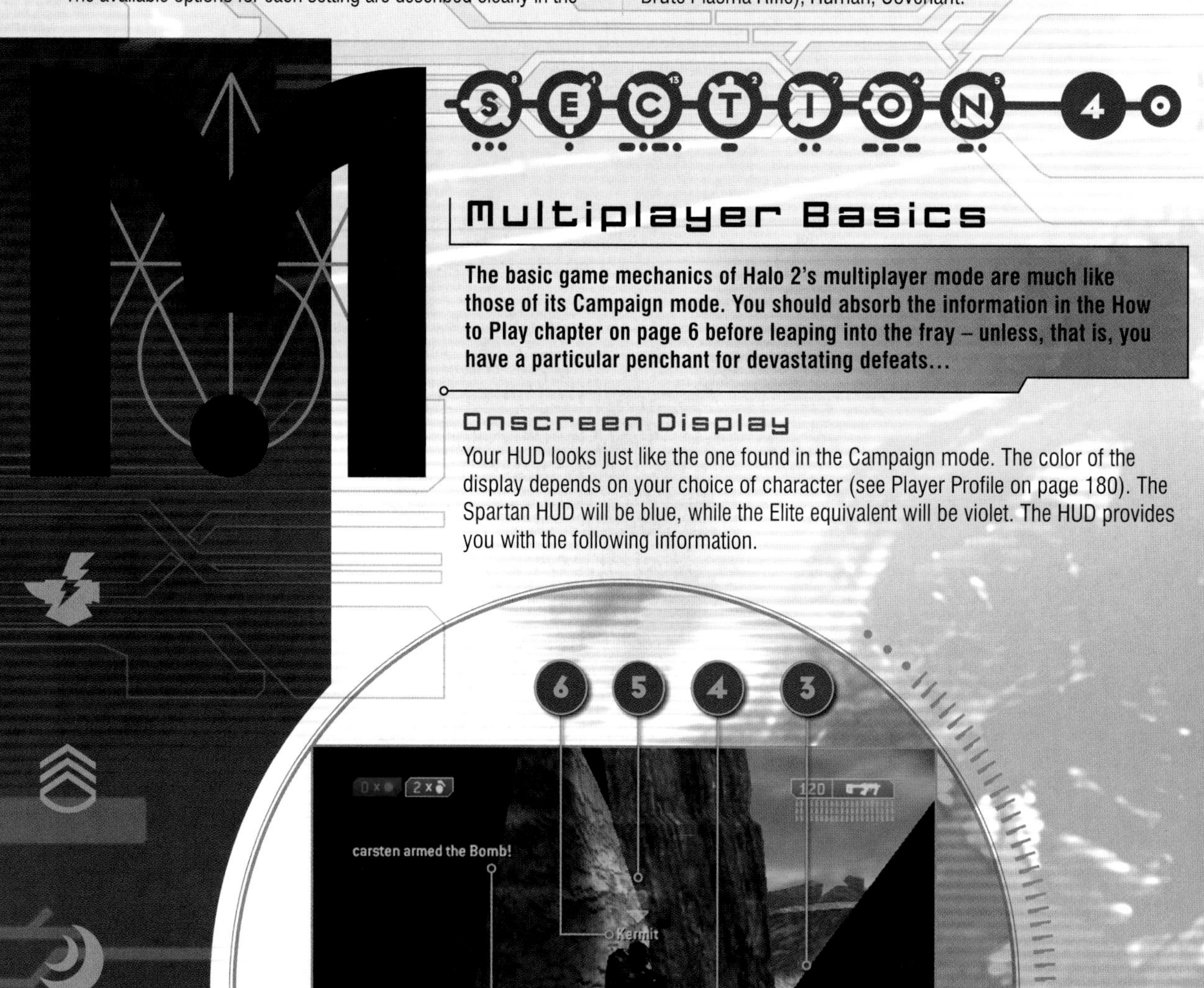

1. The particular **Game Variant** in progress.

2. The **score**: At the bottom-right of the screen you'll find the current high score, and under that you'll find your own score or your team score. While enjoying pole position during a particularly fruitful match, you'll see the total of the team or individual in second place beneath your score.

3. **Warning Indicators**: Keep an eye on the warning indicators for special situations in Assault and Capture the Flag modes:

   - Enemy has Bomb (Assault)
   - Bomb Dropped (Assault)
   - Enemy has Flag (CTF)
   - Flag Dropped (CTF)

4. **Waypoint Indicators**: Depending on the game variant you've chosen, there are a number of symbols which will lead you to the position of the object, place or person you're searching for:

   - Bomb (Assault)
   - Dropped Bomb
   - Flag (Capture the Flag)
   - Dropped Flag
   - Skull (Oddball)
   - Dropped Oddball
   - Hill (King of the Hill)
   - Territory (Territories)
   - Objective

5. **Team Waypoints**: The position of your teammates will be shown with small icons. These will show you the individual Emblem of the player – for example, Seventh Column.

   - Teammate
   - Firing
   - Under fire
   - Killed
   - Communicating
   - Has got the bomb
   - Has got the flag
   - Has got the Oddball

6. **Gamertag**: A Gamertag will be displayed above the head of every player, friend and foe alike.

7. **Information**: Pertinent game events will be reported as onscreen text messages. These will include information on who has killed who, someone taking the lead, the theft of a flag, remarkable acts of derring-do (like a Double Kill or Killing Spree), and much more.

Special Features

When playing multiplayer games, you should be aware that there are certain differences between this mode and the Campaign mode. For example:

- The Banshee is stripped of its secondary weapon to prevent it from being too powerful.
- The Scorpion can't carry passengers. The main cannon has a slower fire rate.
- The Wraith's cannon is noticeably slower and there are no automatic secondary turrets.
- The Energy Sword doesn't run out of plasma energy.
- There are no Fuel Rod Cannons in multiplayer.
- New technology: Teleporters will take you to specific destinations in the blink of an eye (Fig. 1).

01

Active Camo: Active Camo will, when collected, render you or others almost invisible for a short time – but only, and this should not be underestimated, almost. Keen-eyed players will soon learn how to spot the tell-tale (but nonetheless subtle) contortions that indicate the presence of an enemy using Active Camo. It is deactivated when you sustain damage; similarly, firing a weapon will reveal your position. It is best used in conjunction with melee attacks.

Overshield: The Overshield gives your basic shield a single-use boost to three times its usual power. When equipped, your shield gauge will become green. When this green layer is depleted, a red layer will appear; beyond this lies the standard shield. Opponents using an Overshield can be identified by the white glow that surrounds their body. The boost it gives to your shields diminishes over time. You should try to exploit the physical advantage it offers immediately.

Energy weapons are the best counter for Overshields, especially a charged shot from a Plasma Pistol.

Fusion Cores: Keep your eyes peeled for objects in an area which might detonate when hit by shots or melee attacks. The Fusion Cores, for example, don't explode easily, but they can start chain reactions when they do. You can also push these containers to other positions.

Score

You can view the scores of every player in the current match by pressing ◐. If you are playing a Team Match, the colors will tell you who is playing in which team.

After the game you'll see a detailed final account: the Postgame Carnage Report (Fig. 2). You'll find a lot of information on the game you just played shown here, like Kills, Deaths, Hit Stats and Medals.

Looking at the Player vs Player screen will show you in detail who killed whom and how often. Just highlight one of the names in the table to see how often a player killed every other player, or how often he or she was killed by other combatants.

The criteria for scoring and securing a good place in the final standings is defined by the game type. In Slayer matches, for example, this would be Kills; for a CTF game, it's

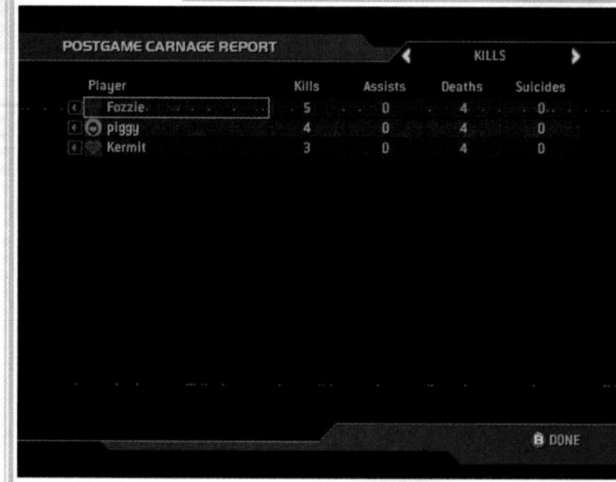

02

points accrued by taking the enemy flag to your base. If you find yourself in a draw at the end of a match, a secondary criteria will be taken into consideration before the winner is declared. Initially, this will be judged by the number of times each player has been killed, with the victor having the lowest total. In the unlikely event that players are still neck-and-neck, the conflict will be won by the participant with the most "assists" – instances where you've fought and wounded an enemy who was subsequently dispatched by another player.

Medals

Medals will be awarded for certain achievements. They are displayed during the game on the upper left of the screen for a short time, and you'll see them in the Postgame Carnage Report as small symbols. They'll also appear in your statistics on www.bungie.net. They can be given when:

- You kill several opponents without another player getting a shot: Killing Spree, Running Riot, Rampage, Berserker, Overkill.
- You kill several opponents in rapid continuous succession: Double Kill, Triple Kill, Killtacular, Kill Frenzy, Killtrocity, Killimanjaro.
- You kill an opponent in a specified way: Sniper Kill, Road Kill, Melee Kill, Stealth Kill, Grenade Stick.
- You've boarded an enemy vessel or destroyed it: Carjacking, Destroyed Vehicle.
- You've done something heroic (depending on which Game Variant you're playing): Killed Flag Carrier, Killed Bomb Carrier,Flag Taken, Bomb Planted, Flag Return

Communication

Use your Xbox Communicator headset to communicate before, after and – most importantly – during matches. Don't forget everybody in your vicinity can hear you when your microphone is activated, and that includes your enemies. Pressing ○ will allow your teammates all over the map will hear you.

Keep ○ held down for about one second, and you'll open a channel and be heard by every teammate on the map – but also by every enemy within your vicinity. When you stop talking, the channel will close again.

Pause Menu

Press ▶ in a multiplayer match to open the Pause Menu. You can depart with the Leave Game option and return to the Main Menu, or conclude a round with End Game.

If you want to, you can change the **Settings** for the Xbox Controller (find out more on page 10).

The **Handicap** menu will allow you to lower your maximum shield energy and damage in Custom Games. If you're far more skilled than the people you play with, you can level the playing field here. This setting is temporary, and will not be saved to your player profile.

In every Custom Game you can change the distribution of players in teams. Use **Select Team** to defect to the other side.

You can lock the current Party by selecting **Party Privacy** to prevent uninvited guests from gate-crashing.

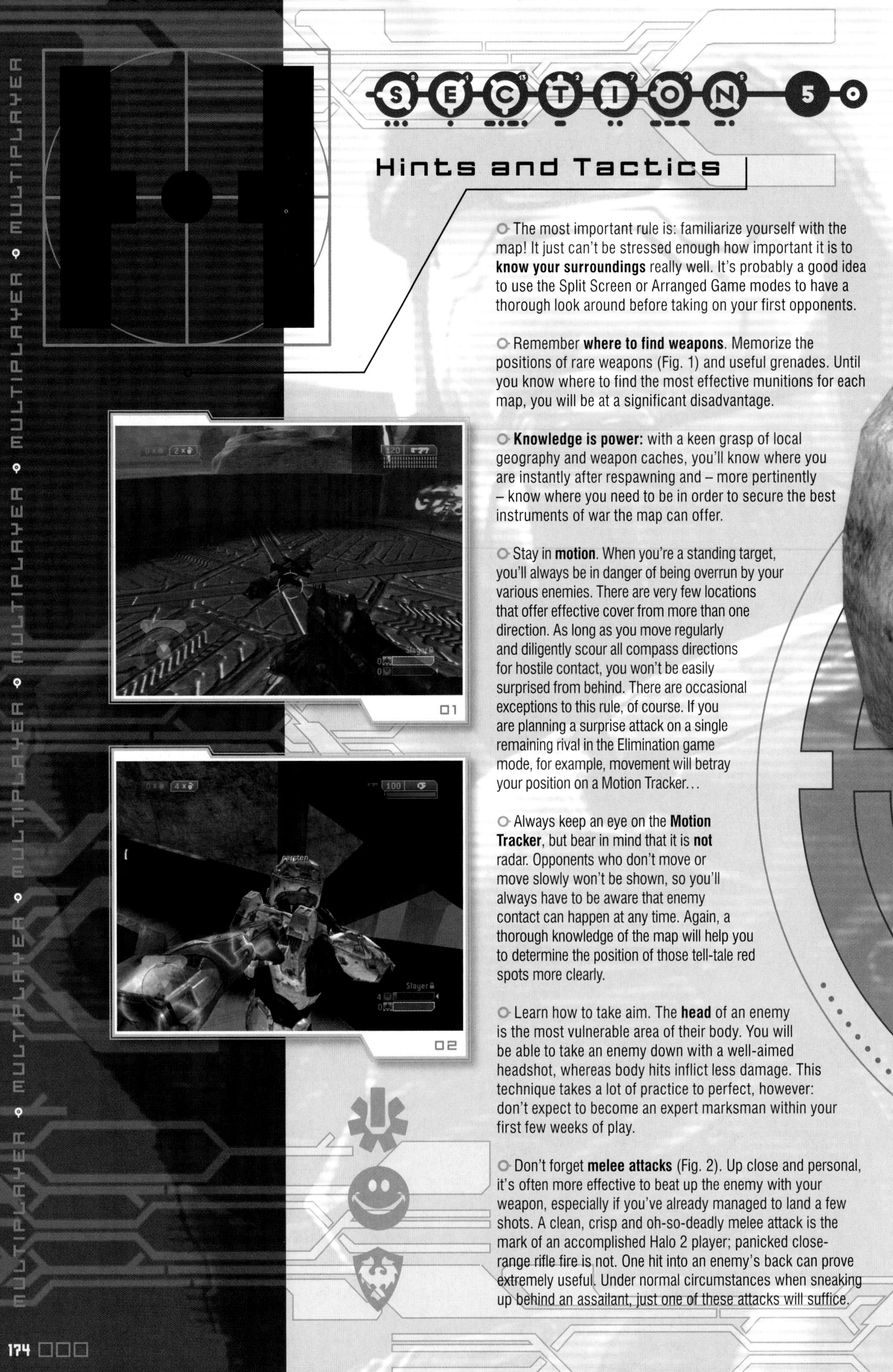

SECTION 5

Hints and Tactics

- The most important rule is: familiarize yourself with the map! It just can't be stressed enough how important it is to **know your surroundings** really well. It's probably a good idea to use the Split Screen or Arranged Game modes to have a thorough look around before taking on your first opponents.

- Remember **where to find weapons**. Memorize the positions of rare weapons (Fig. 1) and useful grenades. Until you know where to find the most effective munitions for each map, you will be at a significant disadvantage.

- **Knowledge is power:** with a keen grasp of local geography and weapon caches, you'll know where you are instantly after respawning and – more pertinently – know where you need to be in order to secure the best instruments of war the map can offer.

- Stay in **motion**. When you're a standing target, you'll always be in danger of being overrun by your various enemies. There are very few locations that offer effective cover from more than one direction. As long as you move regularly and diligently scour all compass directions for hostile contact, you won't be easily surprised from behind. There are occasional exceptions to this rule, of course. If you are planning a surprise attack on a single remaining rival in the Elimination game mode, for example, movement will betray your position on a Motion Tracker...

- Always keep an eye on the **Motion Tracker**, but bear in mind that it is **not** radar. Opponents who don't move or move slowly won't be shown, so you'll always have to be aware that enemy contact can happen at any time. Again, a thorough knowledge of the map will help you to determine the position of those tell-tale red spots more clearly.

- Learn how to take aim. The **head** of an enemy is the most vulnerable area of their body. You will be able to take an enemy down with a well-aimed headshot, whereas body hits inflict less damage. This technique takes a lot of practice to perfect, however: don't expect to become an expert marksman within your first few weeks of play.

- Don't forget **melee attacks** (Fig. 2). Up close and personal, it's often more effective to beat up the enemy with your weapon, especially if you've already managed to land a few shots. A clean, crisp and oh-so-deadly melee attack is the mark of an accomplished Halo 2 player; panicked close-range rifle fire is not. One hit into an enemy's back can prove extremely useful. Under normal circumstances when sneaking up behind an assailant, just one of these attacks will suffice.

01

02

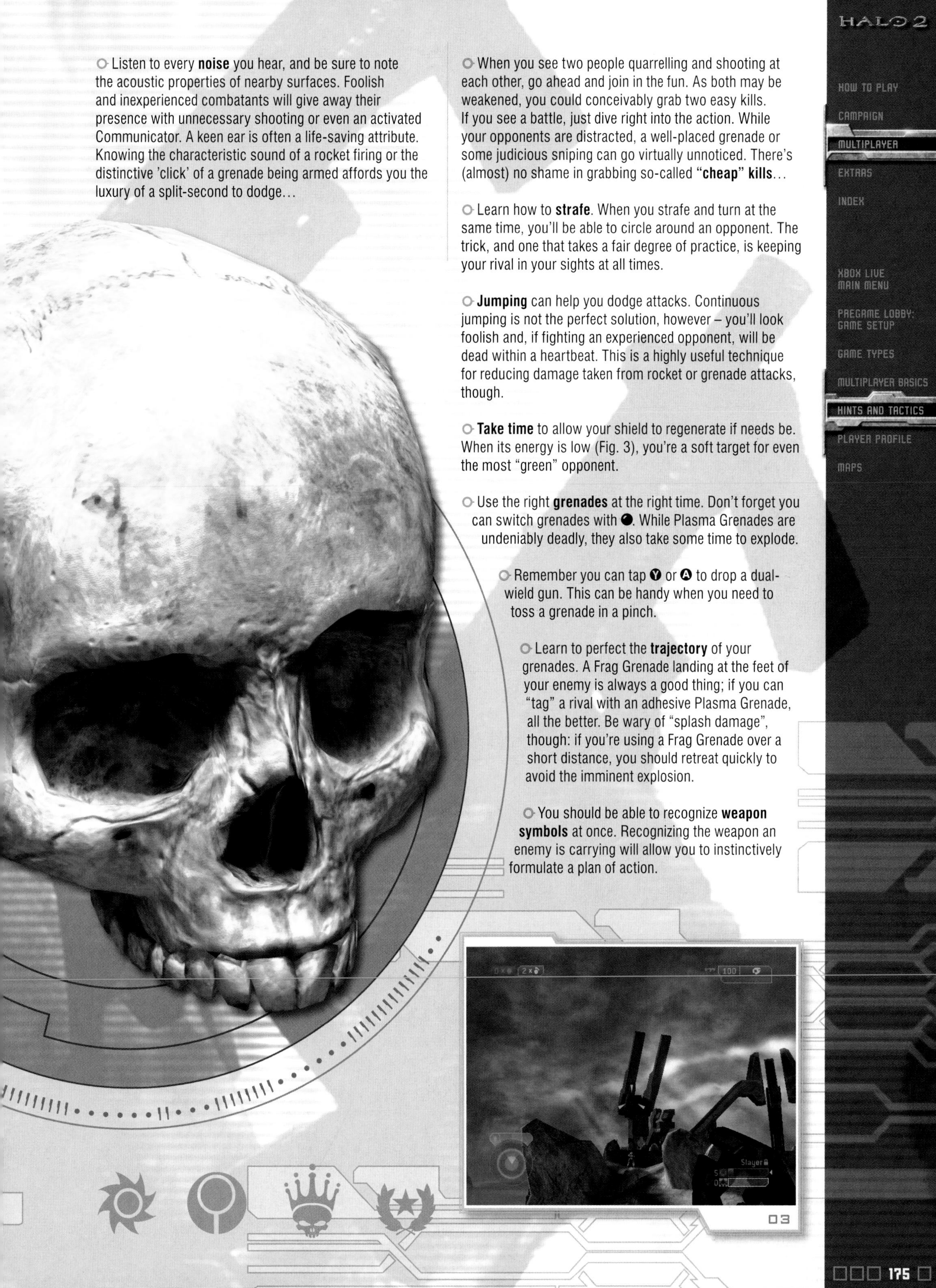

- Listen to every **noise** you hear, and be sure to note the acoustic properties of nearby surfaces. Foolish and inexperienced combatants will give away their presence with unnecessary shooting or even an activated Communicator. A keen ear is often a life-saving attribute. Knowing the characteristic sound of a rocket firing or the distinctive 'click' of a grenade being armed affords you the luxury of a split-second to dodge...

- When you see two people quarrelling and shooting at each other, go ahead and join in the fun. As both may be weakened, you could conceivably grab two easy kills. If you see a battle, just dive right into the action. While your opponents are distracted, a well-placed grenade or some judicious sniping can go virtually unnoticed. There's (almost) no shame in grabbing so-called **"cheap" kills**...

- Learn how to **strafe**. When you strafe and turn at the same time, you'll be able to circle around an opponent. The trick, and one that takes a fair degree of practice, is keeping your rival in your sights at all times.

- **Jumping** can help you dodge attacks. Continuous jumping is not the perfect solution, however – you'll look foolish and, if fighting an experienced opponent, will be dead within a heartbeat. This is a highly useful technique for reducing damage taken from rocket or grenade attacks, though.

- **Take time** to allow your shield to regenerate if needs be. When its energy is low (Fig. 3), you're a soft target for even the most "green" opponent.

- Use the right **grenades** at the right time. Don't forget you can switch grenades with ●. While Plasma Grenades are undeniably deadly, they also take some time to explode.

- Remember you can tap Ⓨ or Ⓐ to drop a dual-wield gun. This can be handy when you need to toss a grenade in a pinch.

- Learn to perfect the **trajectory** of your grenades. A Frag Grenade landing at the feet of your enemy is always a good thing; if you can "tag" a rival with an adhesive Plasma Grenade, all the better. Be wary of "splash damage", though: if you're using a Frag Grenade over a short distance, you should retreat quickly to avoid the imminent explosion.

- You should be able to recognize **weapon symbols** at once. Recognizing the weapon an enemy is carrying will allow you to instinctively formulate a plan of action.

03

Practice makes perfect. In Halo 2, **a little knowledge really is a dangerous thing**: you'll need to learn many tricks and tactics before you become a respected multiplayer veteran. You can learn a lot from observing other people. Oddly enough, the most instructive events you'll encounter are your own deaths. Observe how accomplished foes perform: the way they move, their choice of weaponry, their general technique. Take note of surprise assaults, how your opponent evades your attacks, and instances where your team has been completely overrun by an opposing force. What kind of tactics were used? Forewarned is forearmed, after all...

Whenever you find the time, **reload** your weapon using X (Fig. 4). Running headlong at an opponent in a deadly, high-speed duel, nothing is more embarrassing (and invariably fatal) than your character automatically reloading a weapon – leaving you momentarily vulnerable. This is especially important when wielding a slow-loading weapon like the Rocket Launcher or Shotgun. You should switch to another weapon in such situations or, if possible, try for a melee attack.

Learn to **use the flag, ball and bomb** as close combat weapons – it's not pretty, but if it hurts, it works. Sometimes, though, it's better to just drop the item and break out the heavy artillery. Just press L or R to do so.

You can **use explosions** to blast the Oddball out of the reach of enemies.

When playing Territories, **learn the name of each area**. This will allow you to know at once which Territory has fallen into enemy hands.

The Overshield will lose its energy gradually – use the advantage it gives you immediately. In the short time it takes the shield to build up, you're actually **invincible**.

Overshield and Active Camo power-ups **do not combine** well. The blue charges of the Overshield will flash all over your body, so your camouflage won't be particularly effective (Fig. 5).

Don't forget that one charged shot of the Plasma Pistol is enough to **disable an Overshield**.

04

05

06

07

Use **stealth** whenever possible (and, of course, appropriate). When you press L down, you'll move forward steadily in a crouching position (Fig. 6). Granted, this is very slow, but it renders you invisible on enemy Motion Trackers. Using this technique, you could slip in through an undefended entrance to an enemy base and, for example, initiate a devastating pincer attack.

You can block **Teleporters**. As long as a vehicle is parking in the destination teleporter, it can't be used.

Choose your choice of weapons to suit your surroundings. "**Bigger**" **isn't necessarily a synonym of** "**better**", as a close-quarters rocket explosion will soon teach you.

Don't forget that you can seize any vehicle that is moving slowly enough. Press and hold down X to throw an enemy driver from their seat.

You can even begin this maneuver with a jump. If you want to board a Scorpion, for example, you could also climb onto the tank and throw a grenade into the driver's compartment (Fig. 7).

The **Rocket Launcher** is most definitely not a weapon for short distances because of the disastrous self-immolation that can ensue from hasty shots. It also has its fair share of disadvantages over longer distances as well: being so slow, each rocket will only catch the most distracted or dim-witted enemy unawares. You should also exploit the fact that every explosion is accompanied by "splash damage" inflicted on nearby players. Aim for the ground in front of your opponent's feet, as one body alone is a very small and easily-missed target. If you're firing on something or someone close to you, jump back to avoid the worst effects of the blast.

The controller setting **Look Sensitivity** determines how fast you can turn around. It wouldn't be a good idea to adjust it several steps at once, because you may well find your character impossible to control. It's better to adjust this setting in small steps over time.

Be sure to read the **general hints** in the How To Play chapter on page 48 and the descriptions of each weapon from page 22.

Tips For Teams:

If you've just started playing the game, don't be confused by all the colored Waypoints (Fig. 8). The colors are related to the Emblem over the head of a player, or they say something about that individual's current condition. Additionally, anyone wearing a symbol over his or her head is definitely a member of your team. It's undiplomatic (not to mention impolite) to shoot these guys intentionally, and will frequently offend. It may even lead to sanctions in the form of time penalties before respawning.

08

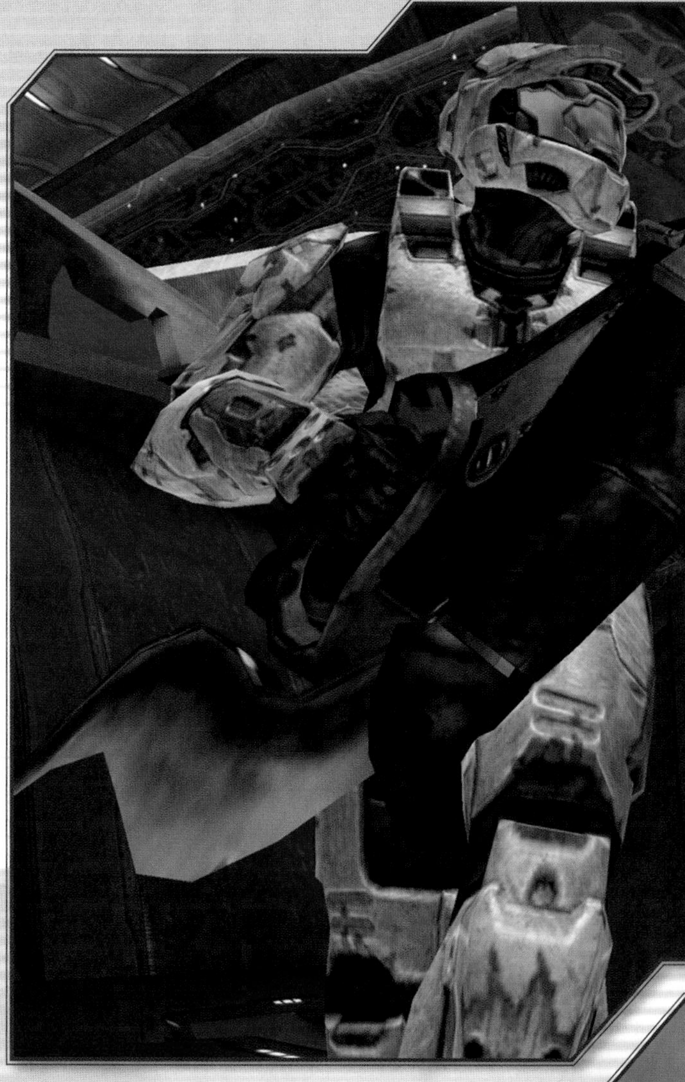

Pay close attention to the colors of your **teammates' indicators**. Chances are, they are not just firing their weapon because they like the particle effects, and might need a little support. You can quickly assess the battlefield if you pay attention to these.

Don't leave your base unguarded. At least one team member should stay at home to **defend your flag**.

When playing team games like Capture the Flag you should **coordinate** your actions. Four "lone wolves" adhering to their own individual agendas don't stand a chance against a well-tuned collective. Of course, this doesn't mean that you must practically hold hands en route to an objective. Working as a close-knit strike team and making a concentrated charge through enemy lines is a very effective tactic... though, obviously, it's more easily said than done.

Coordination means **communication**. Use the Voice Communicator to lead your team, or to advise your colleagues of particular threats. Just press O. Don't forget that nearby enemies can hear you!

Use the **names of the Territories** while communicating, so you can describe the places and everyone can understand you. For example, if you're all hunting down the Juggernaut, panicky calls like, "He's up there, hiding on the small platform at the slope with the thingy..." are not really helpful. When you say: "He's at the Sniper Roost", everybody should know where he is.

Develop a **strategy**. Try attacking the enemy base at the same time from two different points, or luring the enemy out from a hideout with a fake attack... only to land a fatal blow from another position. Good commanders will think on their feet and adapt according to the situation in hand, but don't be shy to speak up if you have a particularly novel idea: innovation could turn the tide of a particular battle.

Don't forget your goals when playing objective-based games (Assault, CTF, Oddball). For example, very organized enemies can set up bait-and-switch situations to lure you away from defending your flag. Additionally, if your flag is gone, you had better find out where it is and take care of it as soon as possible.

Everybody in the team should have a **task**, and do something he or she does best. It won't help anyone if all rush to grab the most popular vehicles, or if everyone tries to grab the most technically challenging but fun weaponry. Give the Rocket Launcher or the Banshee to people who can actually utilize them effectively. Above all, know your limitations: if you're a marksman of moderate ability, wouldn't the crack shot of your squad be better suited to the role of sniper?

Guard your flag carrier or the bearer of the bomb with some **bodyguards**.

When you're playing a game variant like Team Slayer, it is absolutely vital that you stick together. A lone warrior doesn't stand a chance of survival if he runs into a team of two or three well-drilled assailants.

09

- Under certain circumstances it can be necessary for opposing teams to form an alliance against another team that is only a few points away from victory. For example, if the team on the Hill (when playing King of the Hill) is a few seconds away from winning a round, the other teams should not waste time killing each other, but instead concentrate on their common enemy.

- Use your mates as stepladders (Fig. 9). Standing on their heads, you can jump on places you wouldn't normally be able to reach.

- There is no such thing as "The Most Perfect Strategy in the World, Ever" in any team game. Too many factors can influence the outcome: the size of the team, the map, the exact rules of the game, the available weapons and vehicles, the reactions of the other team, the abilities of the players… the list could go on. There are also less tangible variables, like luck – you'll soon come to appreciate that a single, casually-tossed grenade can sometimes be the solitary deciding factor between victory and defeat. Only practice will furnish you with the instincts and the ability to know the right thing to do in any given situation. Even then, victory is never truly assured…

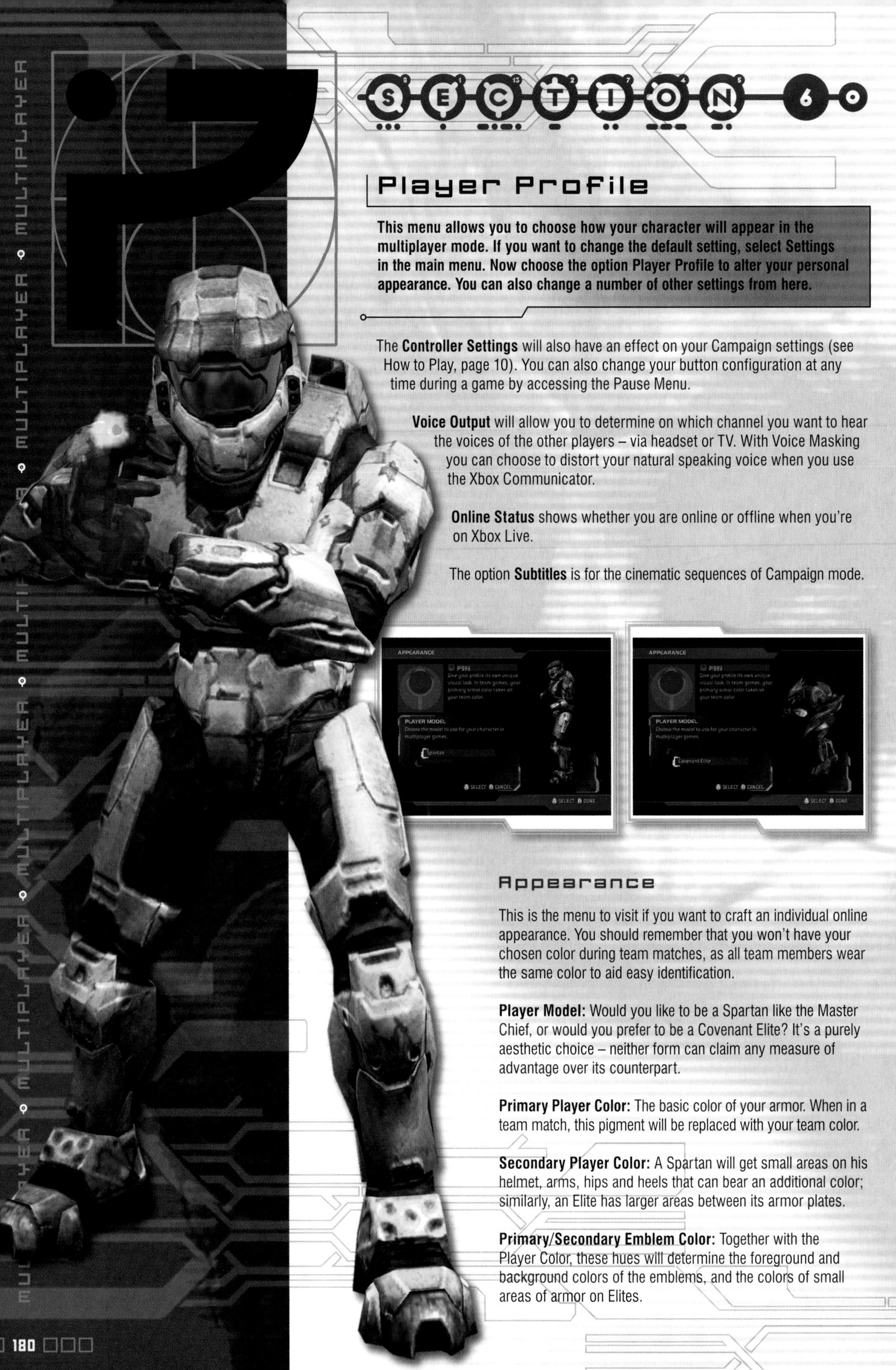

SECTION 6

Player Profile

This menu allows you to choose how your character will appear in the multiplayer mode. If you want to change the default setting, select Settings in the main menu. Now choose the option Player Profile to alter your personal appearance. You can also change a number of other settings from here.

The **Controller Settings** will also have an effect on your Campaign settings (see How to Play, page 10). You can also change your button configuration at any time during a game by accessing the Pause Menu.

Voice Output will allow you to determine on which channel you want to hear the voices of the other players – via headset or TV. With Voice Masking you can choose to distort your natural speaking voice when you use the Xbox Communicator.

Online Status shows whether you are online or offline when you're on Xbox Live.

The option **Subtitles** is for the cinematic sequences of Campaign mode.

Appearance

This is the menu to visit if you want to craft an individual online appearance. You should remember that you won't have your chosen color during team matches, as all team members wear the same color to aid easy identification.

Player Model: Would you like to be a Spartan like the Master Chief, or would you prefer to be a Covenant Elite? It's a purely aesthetic choice – neither form can claim any measure of advantage over its counterpart.

Primary Player Color: The basic color of your armor. When in a team match, this pigment will be replaced with your team color.

Secondary Player Color: A Spartan will get small areas on his helmet, arms, hips and heels that can bear an additional color; similarly, an Elite has larger areas between its armor plates.

Primary/Secondary Emblem Color: Together with the Player Color, these hues will determine the foreground and background colors of the emblems, and the colors of small areas of armor on Elites.

Emblem Foreground: You can choose from a variety of symbols to sit proudly in the foreground of your emblem. You can customize them further by pressing ⊗ during the emblem selection to show or hide secondary colors.

EMBLEM FOREGROUND

Seventh Column	Frowney Spearhead	Diamonds	Grunt Head
Bullseye	Sol	Hearts	Brute Head
Vortex	Waypoint	Wasp	Runes
Halt	Yin Yang	Mark of Shame	Trident
Spartan	Helmet	Snake	Number 0
Da Bomb	Triad	Hawk	Number 1
Delta	Grunt Symbol	Lips	Number 2
Rampancy	Cleave	Capsule	Number 3
Sergeant	Thor	Cancel	Number 4
Phoenix	Skull King	Gas Mask	Number 5
Champion	Triplicate	Grenade	Number 6
Jolly Roger	Subnova	Tsantsa	Number 7
Marathon	Flaming Ninja	Race	Number 8
Cube	Double Crescent	Valkyrie	Number 9
Radioactive	Spades	Drone	
Smiley	Clubs	Grunt	

Emblem Background: There are a number of patterns that you can choose to compliment your emblem.

EMBLEM BACKGROUND

Blank	Quadrants 1	Cross	Four Rows 2
Vertical Split	Quadrants 2	Square	Split Circle
Horizontal Split 1	Diagonal Slice	Dual Half-Circle	One Third
Horizontal Split 2	Cleft	Triangle	Two Thirds
Vertical Gradiant	X1	Diagonal Quadrant	Upper Field
Horizontal Gradiant	X2	Three Quarters	Top and Bottom
Triple Column	Circle	Quarter	Center Stripe
Triple Row	Diamond	Four Rows 1	Left and Right

Emblem Color Choices:

SECTION 8

Maps

You'll find maps of every area in Halo 2's multiplayer mode over the following pages. These environments are invariably complex and typified by a wealth of features and nuances, though time spent on each will reveal just how thoughtfully designed they are. The places marked on the map show where you can find weapons (according to the map defaults).

You can play matches with up to 16 players on every map. The recommended number of players and the suggested game variants in this book have been suggested by the Halo 2 developers themselves. Learn these maps by heart! A perfect knowledge of exactly where you are at every moment of a match is vital, and it is this that separates the raw Halo 2 recruit from the hard-bitten veteran…

Ascension

The relay station is part of a network that has kept Delta Halo functioning smoothly for untold centuries.

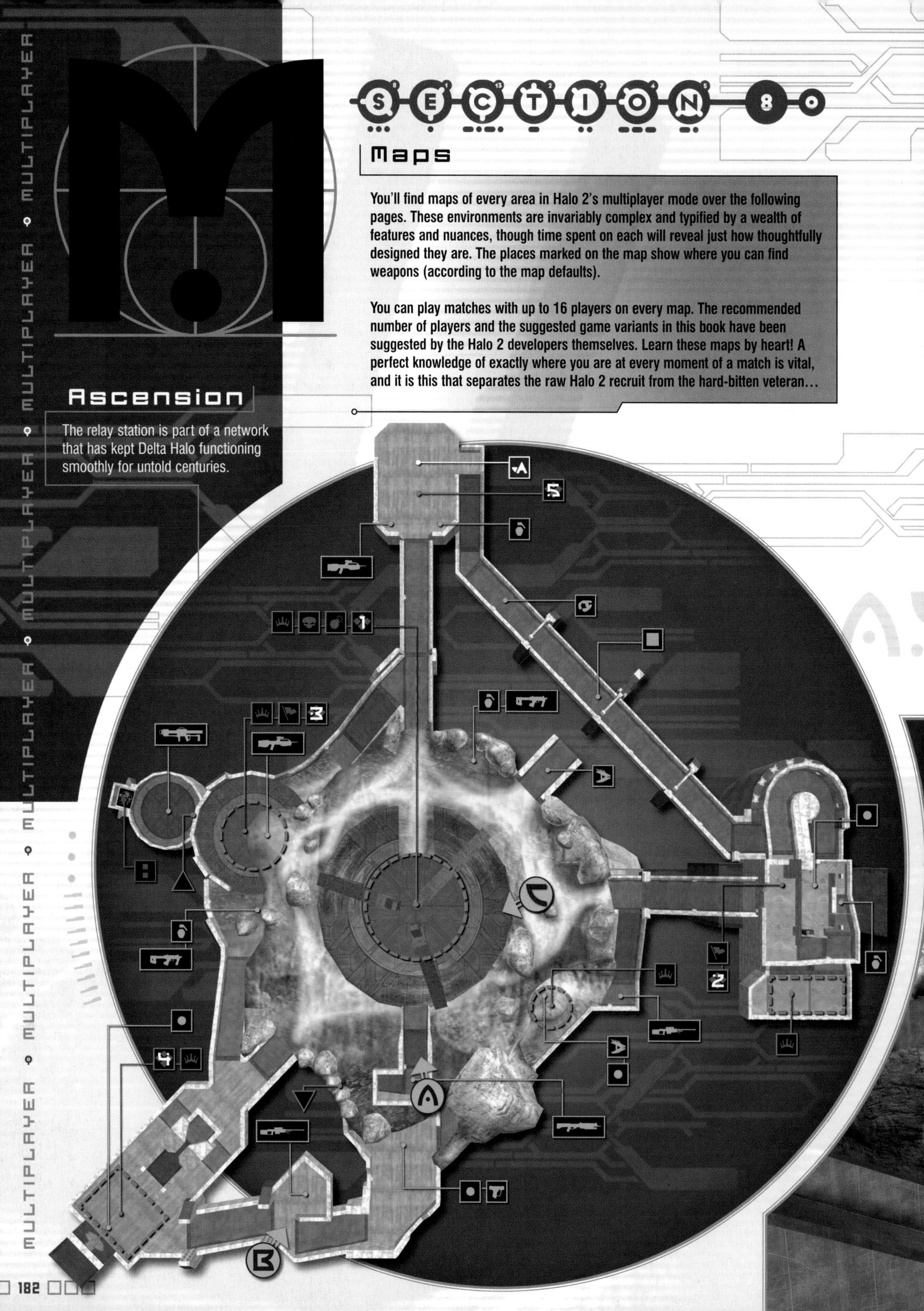

A
CENSION
B

Take a leap of faith at the place of the same name and jump over the rail to a round platform even further down (Fig. 1). A Rocket Launcher is the reward for your troubles.

You can get away from this spot via two different routes: you can use the one-way teleporter, or you can take the shining disk to speed up to the Dish.

There are only a few entrances to the Command Center building. If you've chosen a game variant in which you have to defend the base, the scarcity of ammunition could become a problem – there are next to no weapons in the vicinity of the tower.

01

Tips:

- There is an Overshield on the walkway between the Banshee and the Command Center. You can reach it when you jump on it from the ledge close to the Dish (Fig. 2).
- The Banshee is a mighty weapon on this map. As a pilot you should always keep moving if someone has got a Rocket Launcher.
- Remember the spot where you can jump over the parapet and be serene in the knowledge that you'll land nicely on a safe level under it. During fast, object-based games like Oddball, this trick can be the difference between victory and defeat.
- When playing Oddball and death is imminent, drop the ball into the abyss. After disappearing into the distance, it will reappear at its point of origin (in the middle of the Dish).

ASCENSION

Recommended Number of Players:	4-8
Recommended Game Variants:	1 vs 1 Slayer, King of the Hill, Juggernaut, Oddball
Vehicles:	Banshee
Territories:	1. Dish, 2. Command Center, 3. Leap of Faith, 4. Sniper Roost, 5. Landing Pad

Beaver Creek

These forgotten structures were once the site of many bitter battles but have since been reclaimed by nature.

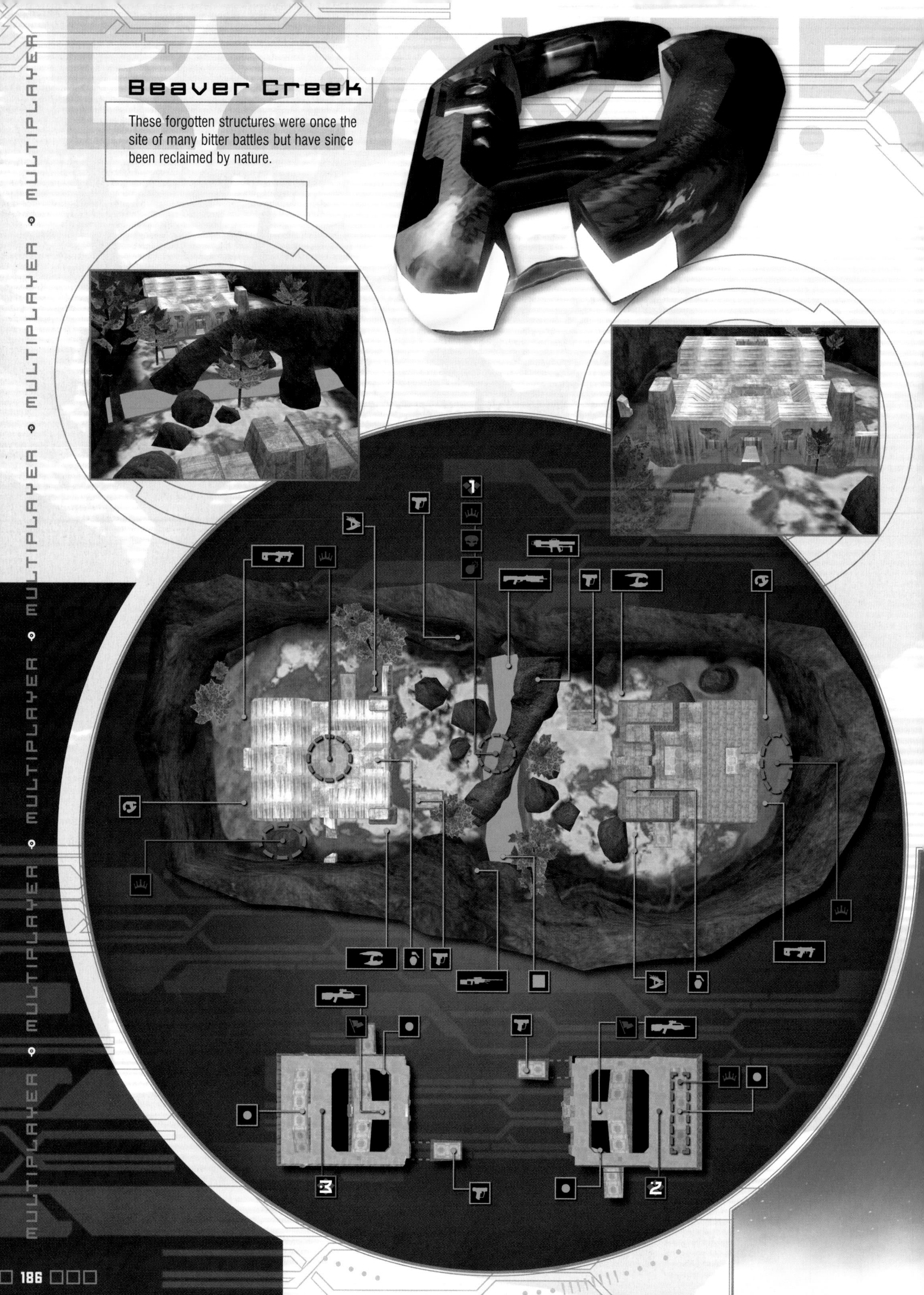

There are two bases in the small basin, separated by a small creek. Players of Halo: Combat Evolved will remember this map fondly by its former name of Battle Creek. You'll find several differences to the original in terms of detail.

On each side of the base there is a slope leading up into the rock face above. On the top you'll find a Sniper Rifle. Above the archway over the stream you'll find the most powerful weapon on this map: the Rocket Launcher (Fig. 1).

There are large openings on top of the bunkers. The glass pane will break under strain, betraying the position of an attacker in the most embarrassingly loud manner possible.

02

BEAVER CREEK

Recommended Number of Players:	4-8
Recommended Game Variants:	2 Flag CTF, Neutral Bomb, Slayer, Juggernaut, Oddball
Vehicles:	none
Territories:	1. River, 2. Blue Base, 3. Red Base

01

Tips:

- Use the walls and rocks close to the bunker to jump on the roof (Fig. 2) and get into it through the openings on top.

- As the teleporters on the backs of the bases are connected to each other, you can use them to warp back and forward quickly. In games like Oddball or Juggernaut you can confuse your pursuers by doing that for a while. In games like CTF or Assault it's more important to guard the teleporter so that your enemies won't be able to sneak up on you.

- The two small openings in the side walls of the base will give attackers the opportunity to put some pressure on the defenders inside. Coordinate this action with good communication via voice transmissions and combine it with an advance on the base.

- You can push the rocks over the ledges (Fig. 3). If you hit an opponent with one, the effect will be fatal.

- In CTF games, the flag can be thrown through the opening in the roof to a teammate above once the glass is smashed. You can also drop down on unsuspecting defenders this way.

- Get the Rocket Launcher, as it can sway the balance of power. It can be found on top of the rock bridge in the middle of map.

03

BURIAL

Burial Mounds

This makeshift Heretic camp on Basis is littered with wreckage from the destruction of Installation 04.

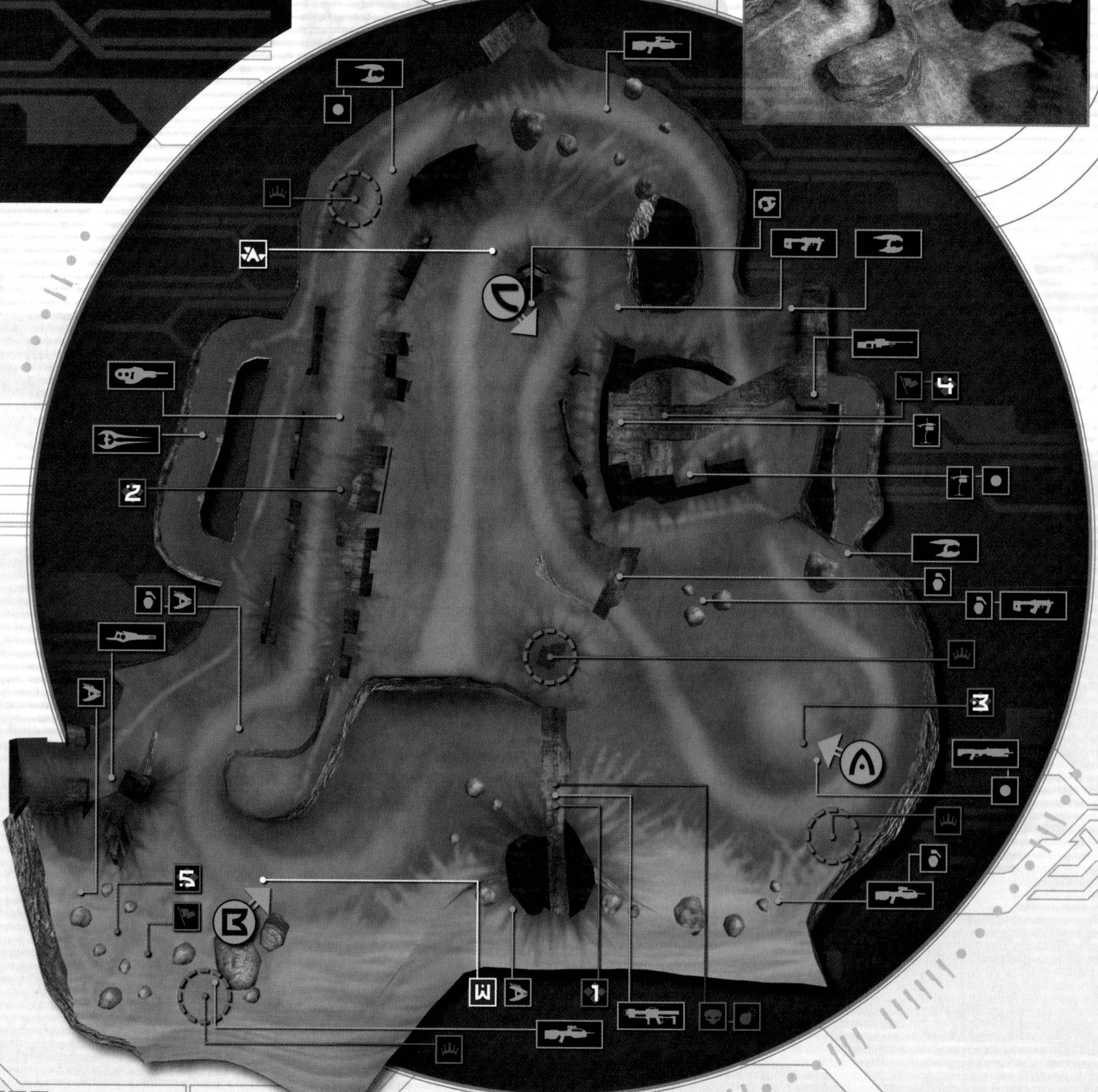

The underlying concept of Burial Mounds is somewhat similar to Zanzibar: one base is in a building (a ramshackle affair built with stone plates), while the opposing team will begin in an exposed area. The layout of the map differs quite a bit from Zanzibar, though; your survival and success here require a different set of strategies.

The big field offers many ways to approach the base, but most of them don't offer any useful amount of cover – apart from the path leading through the cave. In the other direction, two turrets can provide some cover (Fig. 1). A Ghost and a Warthog provide fast transport.

BURIAL MOUNDS

Recommended Number of Players:	4-8
Recommended Game Variants:	1 Flag CTF, Territories, Crazy King, Lowball
Vehicles:	Warthog, Ghost
Territories:	1. Bridge, 2. Ribs, 3. Generators, 4. Base, 5. Boulder Field

Tips:

- On both sides of the map you'll find a Sniper Rifle or a Beam Rifle. The important thing is to get the Rocket Launcher that is lying on the bridge in the middle. The Energy Sword in one of the tunnels should not to be ignored, either.

- In team games, you can drive a Warthog up to the front window, jump right into the base and catch defenders off guard. You can also do this without a vehicle if you carefully walk along the metal wall just in front of the base and jump over (Fig. 2). If the gun emplacement is manned, doing so will probably not be very successful.

- A moat between the generators and the base will limit access. With a crouch jump – press the left thumbstick button at the highest point of your leap – you can climb up. Start from the right rim on the left side of the tunnel (Fig. 3).

01

02

03

Coagulation

Recent excavations have failed to shed light on the true purpose of the outposts in this bloody gulch.

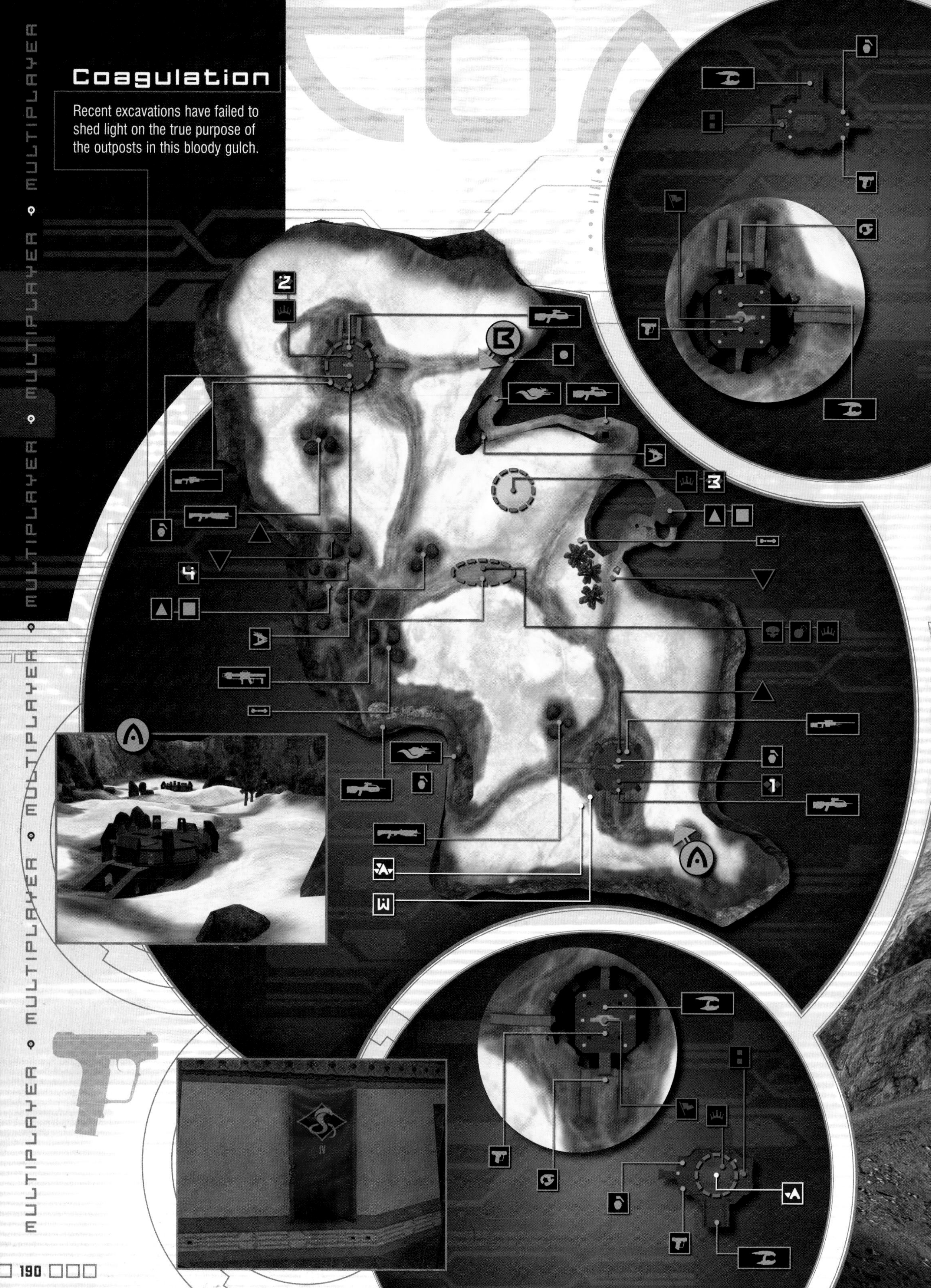

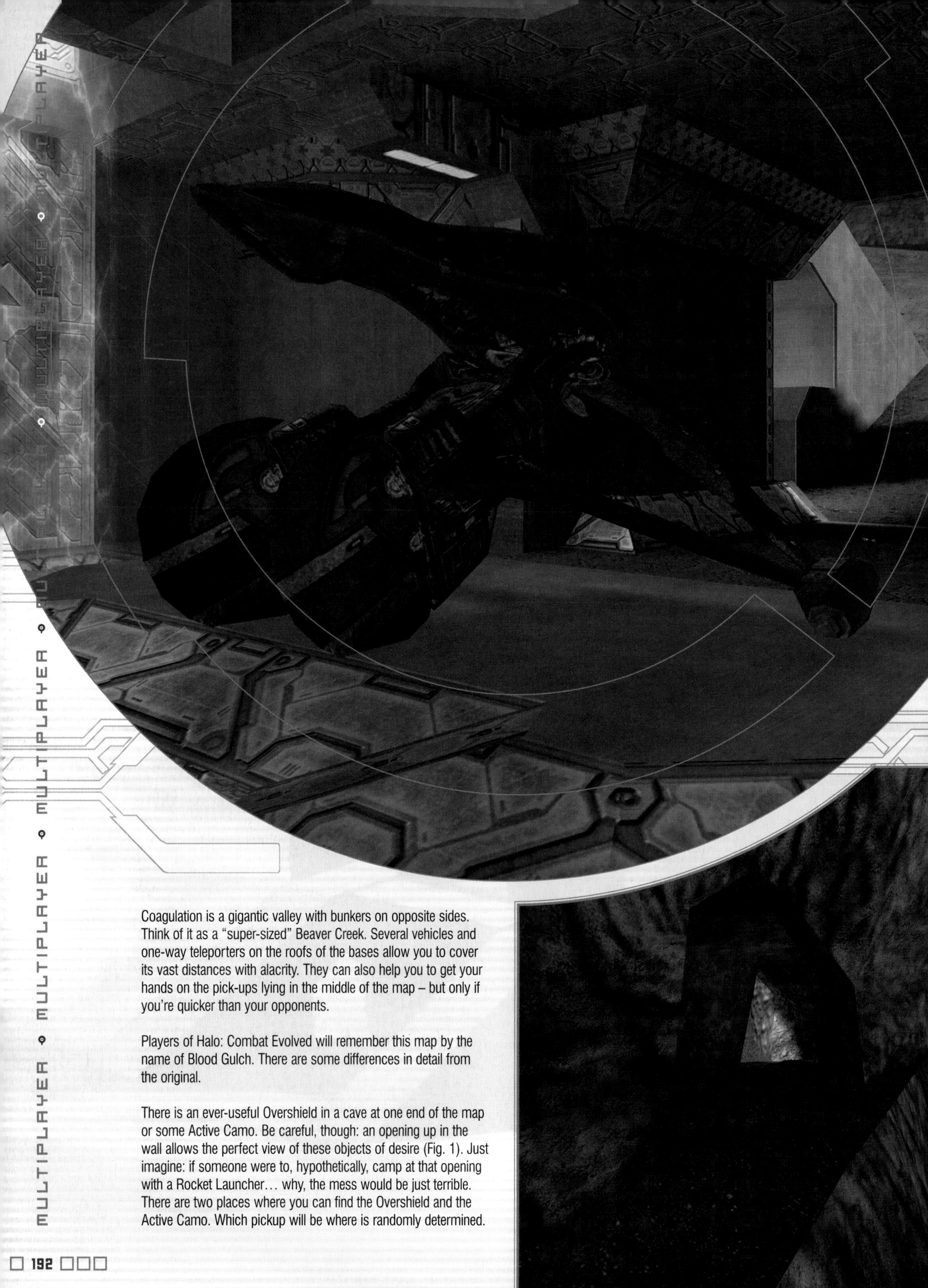

Coagulation is a gigantic valley with bunkers on opposite sides. Think of it as a "super-sized" Beaver Creek. Several vehicles and one-way teleporters on the roofs of the bases allow you to cover its vast distances with alacrity. They can also help you to get your hands on the pick-ups lying in the middle of the map – but only if you're quicker than your opponents.

Players of Halo: Combat Evolved will remember this map by the name of Blood Gulch. There are some differences in detail from the original.

There is an ever-useful Overshield in a cave at one end of the map or some Active Camo. Be careful, though: an opening up in the wall allows the perfect view of these objects of desire (Fig. 1). Just imagine: if someone were to, hypothetically, camp at that opening with a Rocket Launcher… why, the mess would be just terrible. There are two places where you can find the Overshield and the Active Camo. Which pickup will be where is randomly determined.

Tips:

- This is a map where an experienced sniper can be worth a dozen rifle-toting cowboys. You can see the whole area rather nicely from the base. Apart from that, you can reach some practical lookout points up in the rocks (Fig. 2). Use the Ghost to drive as far up on the walls as possible. The most important thing here is not to forget the tunnel at the edge of the area.

- Keep in mind that the central room of the base is not easily defended. There are entrances on all sides. The opening in the ceiling as well as the elevator coming up from the cellars makes this a logistical nightmare for a defending commander. On the other hand, it's far from easy to get the flag from A to B in a game of CTF, simply because the area is so huge. Be sure to make good use of the available vehicles and don't forget about the teleporter on the roof. When defending the interior, grab a plasma rifle and a pistol – or some similar combination – so you can drop a foe in a few quick shots.

- When you're trying to grab the flag, have your teammates drive in the lower level with a Warthog. All you need to do is throw the flag down the hole to their waiting arms below, allowing a quick getaway...

- When you're playing a Custom Game, you could also choose to unlock heavy vehicles and turrets. Control the skies. Use your Banshees – they are the best counter to Wraiths. Finally, grab the Rocket Launcher! Someone needs to have it at all times during team games.

01

02

COAGULATION

Recommended Number of Players:	10-16
Recommended Game Variants:	2 Flag CTF, Neutral Bomb Assault
Vehicles:	2 x Banshee, 2 x Ghost, 2 x Warthog
Territories:	1. Red Base, 2. Blue Base, 3. Hill, 4. Rockslide

Colossus

Numerous scientific expeditions have failed to reveal what the Forerunners intended with all this damn gas.

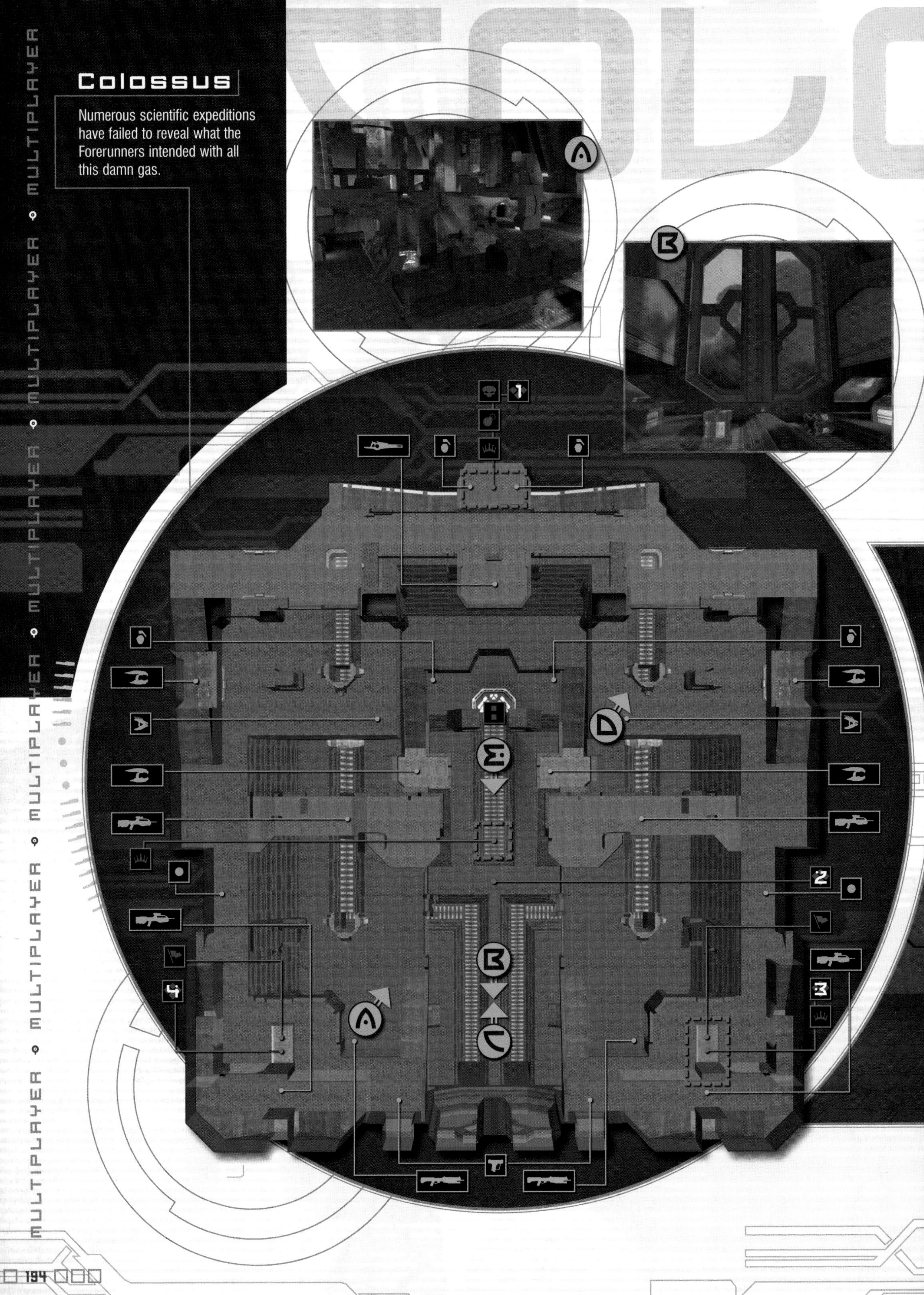

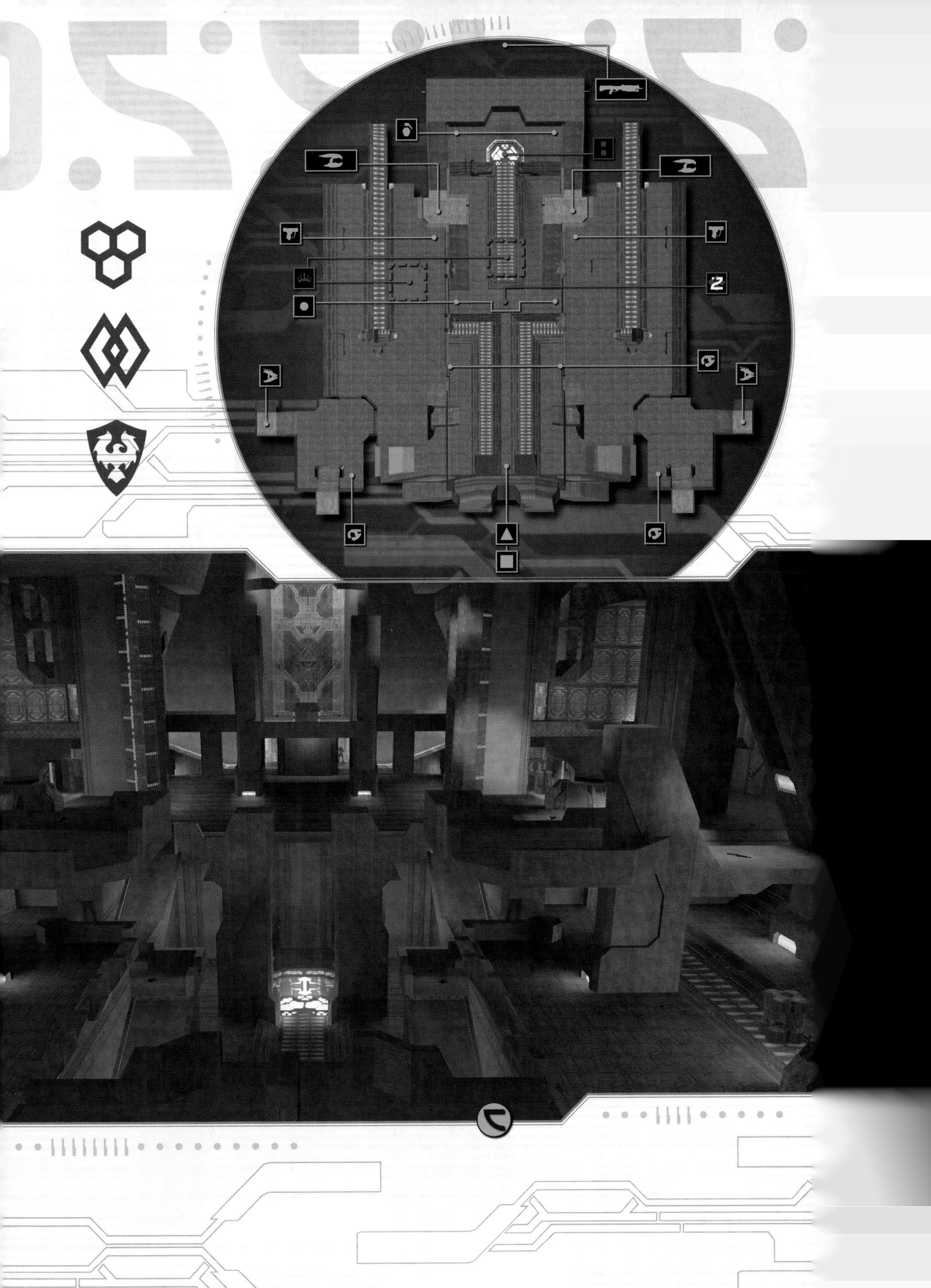

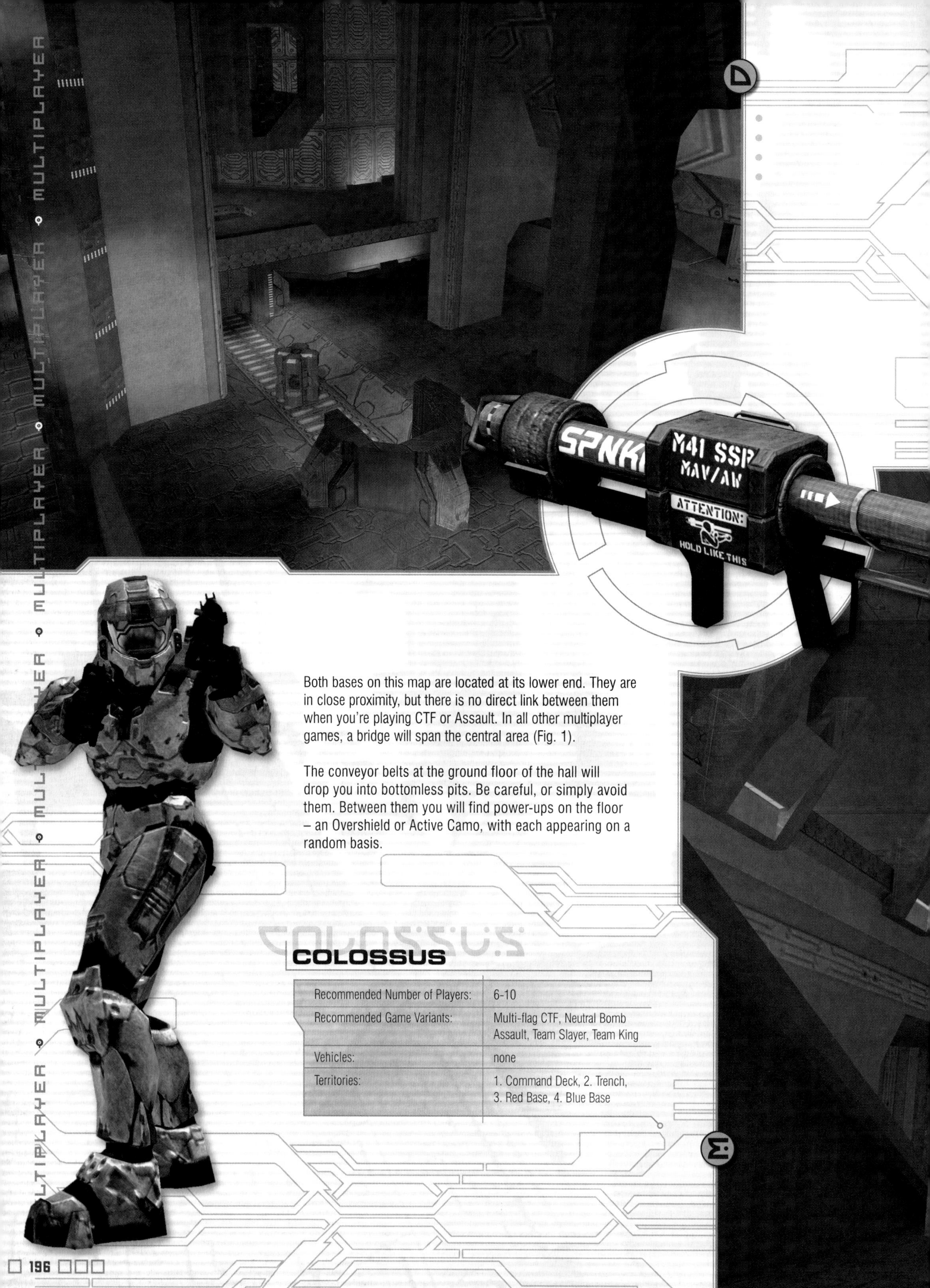

Both bases on this map are located at its lower end. They are in close proximity, but there is no direct link between them when you're playing CTF or Assault. In all other multiplayer games, a bridge will span the central area (Fig. 1).

The conveyor belts at the ground floor of the hall will drop you into bottomless pits. Be careful, or simply avoid them. Between them you will find power-ups on the floor – an Overshield or Active Camo, with each appearing on a random basis.

COLOSSUS

Recommended Number of Players:	6-10
Recommended Game Variants:	Multi-flag CTF, Neutral Bomb Assault, Team Slayer, Team King
Vehicles:	none
Territories:	1. Command Deck, 2. Trench, 3. Red Base, 4. Blue Base

Tips:

- The conveyor belts are especially useful for flag and bomb carriers – they allow you to run faster and will accelerate your jumps. Memorize where the holes will drop you at the end of the conveyor belts.

- Just as in the level The Arbiter, the conveyor belts transport containers. If they contain blue gas, you can shoot them to instigate an explosion.

- The Gravity Lift (Fig. 2) will hurl you from the trench right up to the Command Deck. If you're entering the lift from the other side, it'll hurl you up to the sniper platform. This elevator is generally quite handy for escaping pursuers.

01

02

Headlong

Although during the day Section 14 monitors almost all harbor traffic, at night it's one of the city's most notorious hangouts.

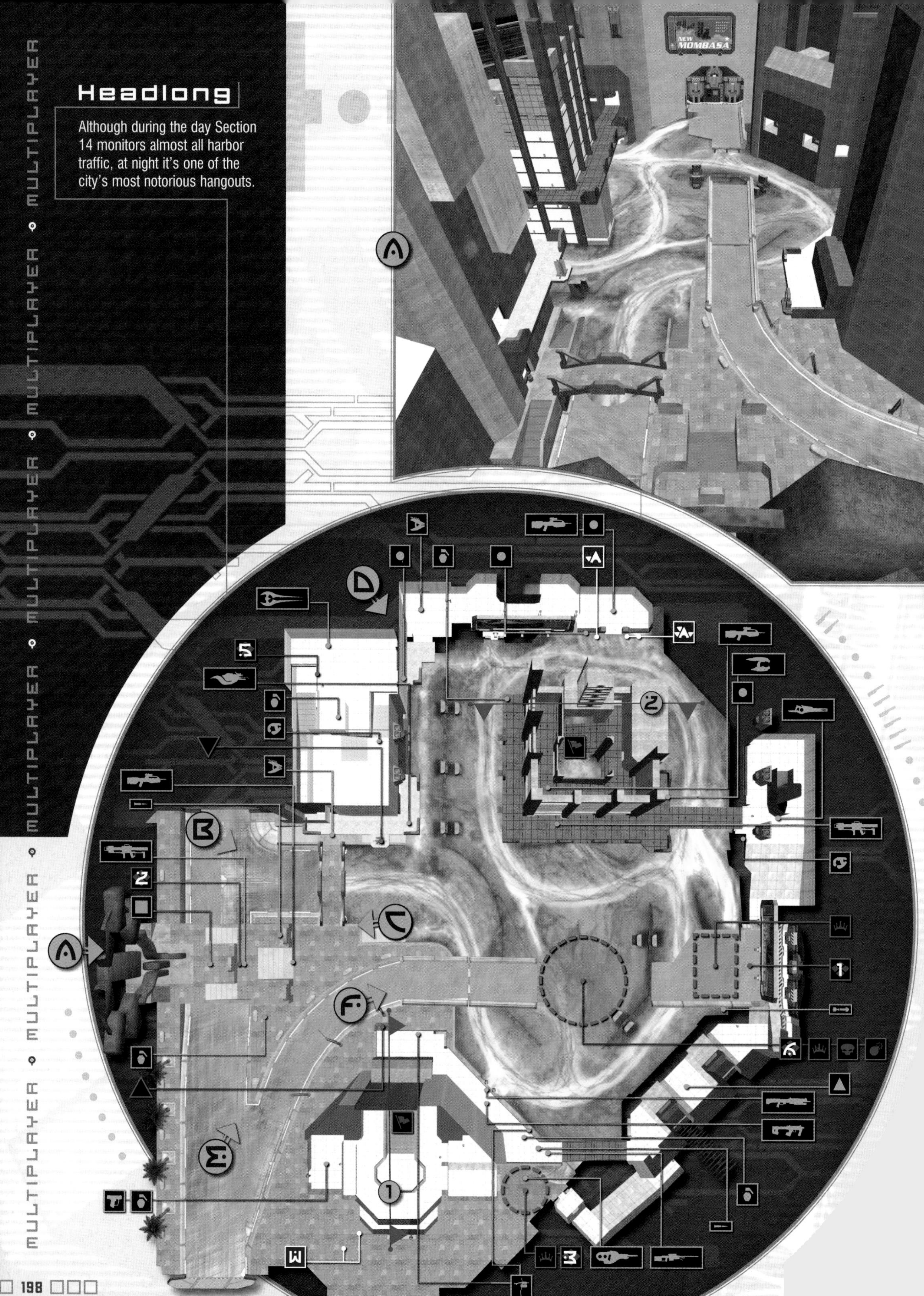

1
B
C
2
4
D
5

Colossus is made for CTF or Assault games, with one team defending and the other attacking. This construction site is huge, so take the time to familiarize yourself with its layout (Fig. 1). It's best enjoyed with really large teams.

On one side you'll find the copper office tower; behind the building, two Warthogs are waiting to be used. On the opposite side is the tower under construction. There are two Ghosts and a Banshee parked behind it.

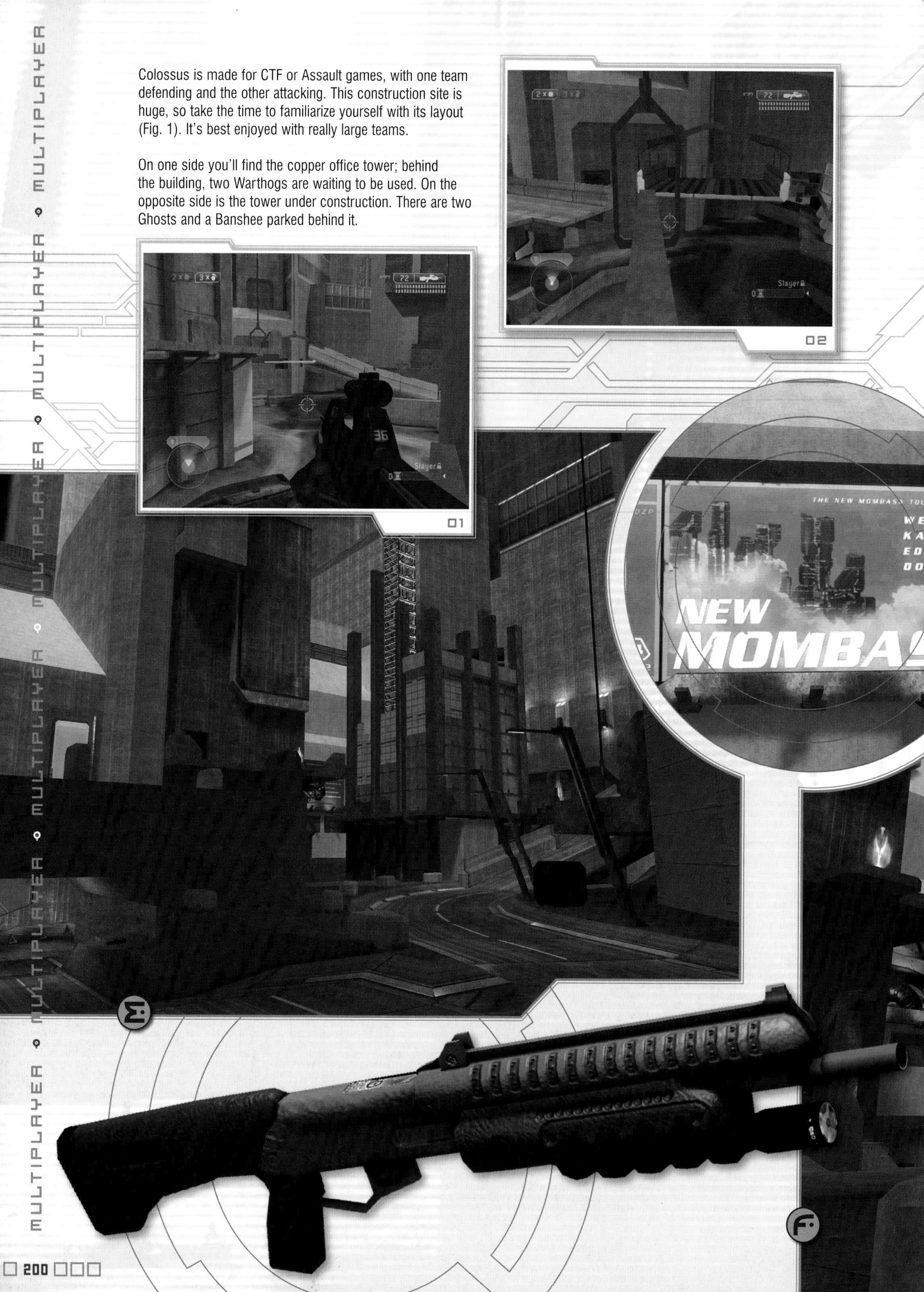

01

02

HEADLONG

Recommended Number of Players:	10-16
Recommended Game Variants:	1 Flag CTF, Team Oddball, Territories
Vehicles:	Banshee, 2 x Ghost, 2 x Warthog
Territories:	1. Gate Bridge, 2. Statue, 3. Alley, 4. Building Site, 5. Corner Building, 6. Construction Pit

Tips:

- In the middle of the area, a huge steel girder is dangling. You can cross it with big jumps (Fig. 2). A section of highway is also hanging – and can be moved...

- Use the teleporter on the human side to get into the abandoned building where you'll find a Brute Shot and an Energy Sword.

- If you begin close to the Ghost, take it and rush to the Active Camo. Keep to the left, drive up the ledge and into the building. The other power-up will be close to the statue.

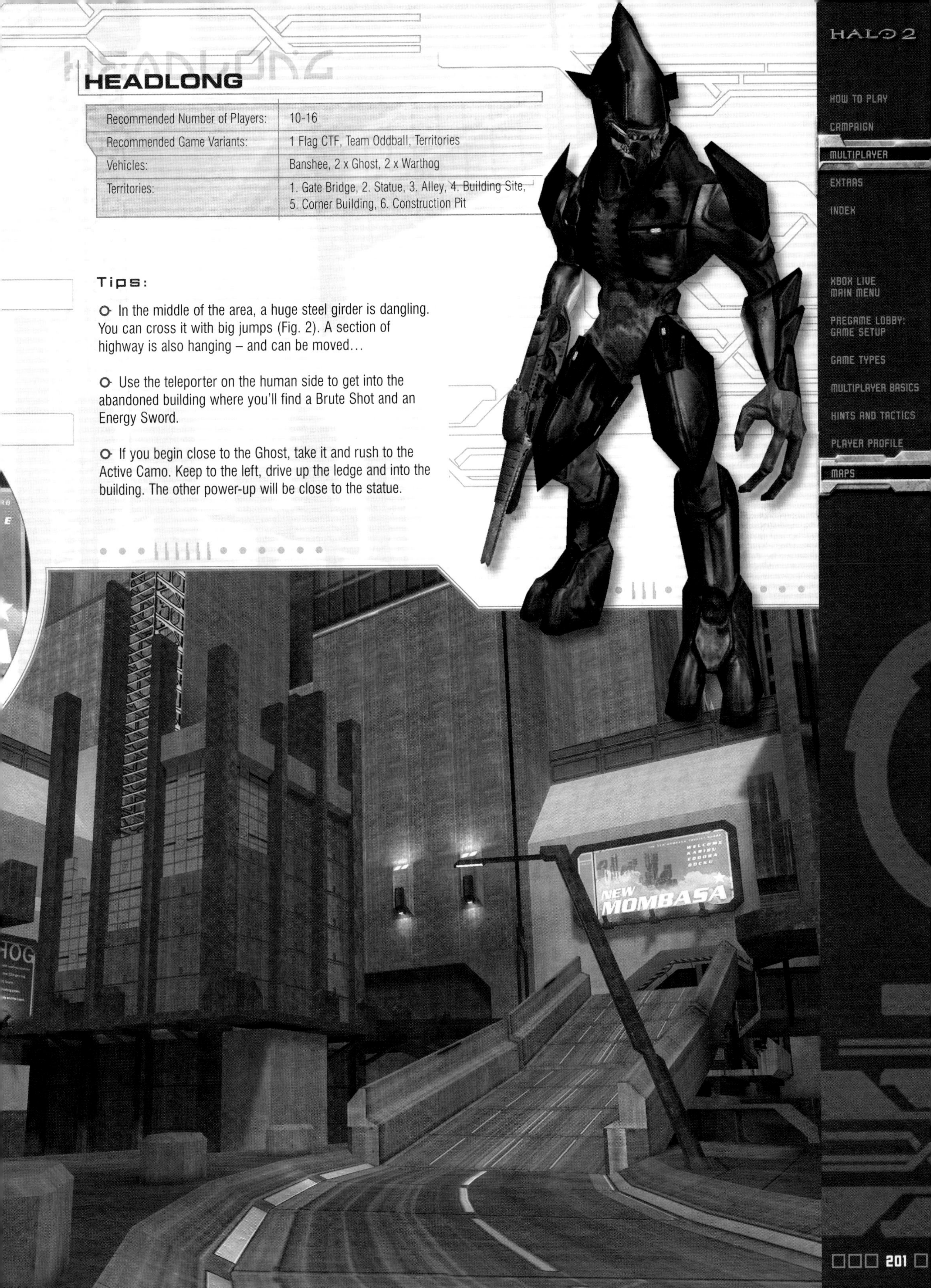

Ivory Tower

Once the home to famous socialite Lance O'Donnell, the top floor of this building is now a public park.

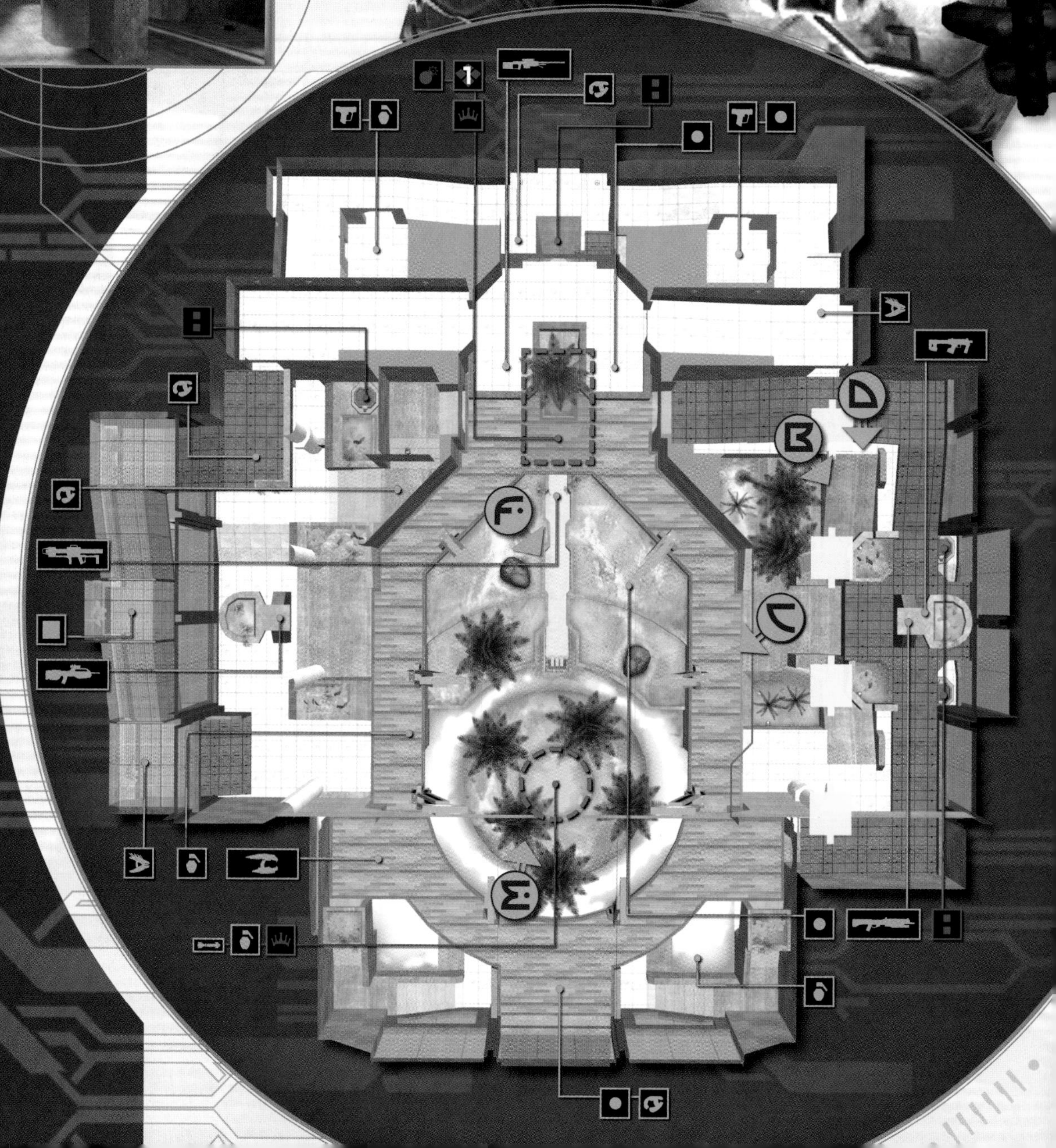

3
4
5
2

IVORY TOWER

Recommended Number of Players:	6-8
Recommended Game Variants:	Slayer, 1 Flag CTF, 1 Bomb Assault
Vehicles:	none
Territories:	1. Walkway, 2. Elevators, 3. Tunnel, 4. Crossroads, 5. Air Lifts

This map is one of Halo 2's smaller multiplayer maps. The building is rather asymmetric and doesn't really offer any safe hiding places when you're playing Slayer. You'll find three strong air streams rising from grids on the ground that you can use as elevators to climb upward (Fig. 1).

The walkway through the hall shouldn't be used too often: you'll be an easy target as you cross, as it doesn't offer much cover. It is, however, a good place for a surprise attack in CTF, as it often lies unguarded.

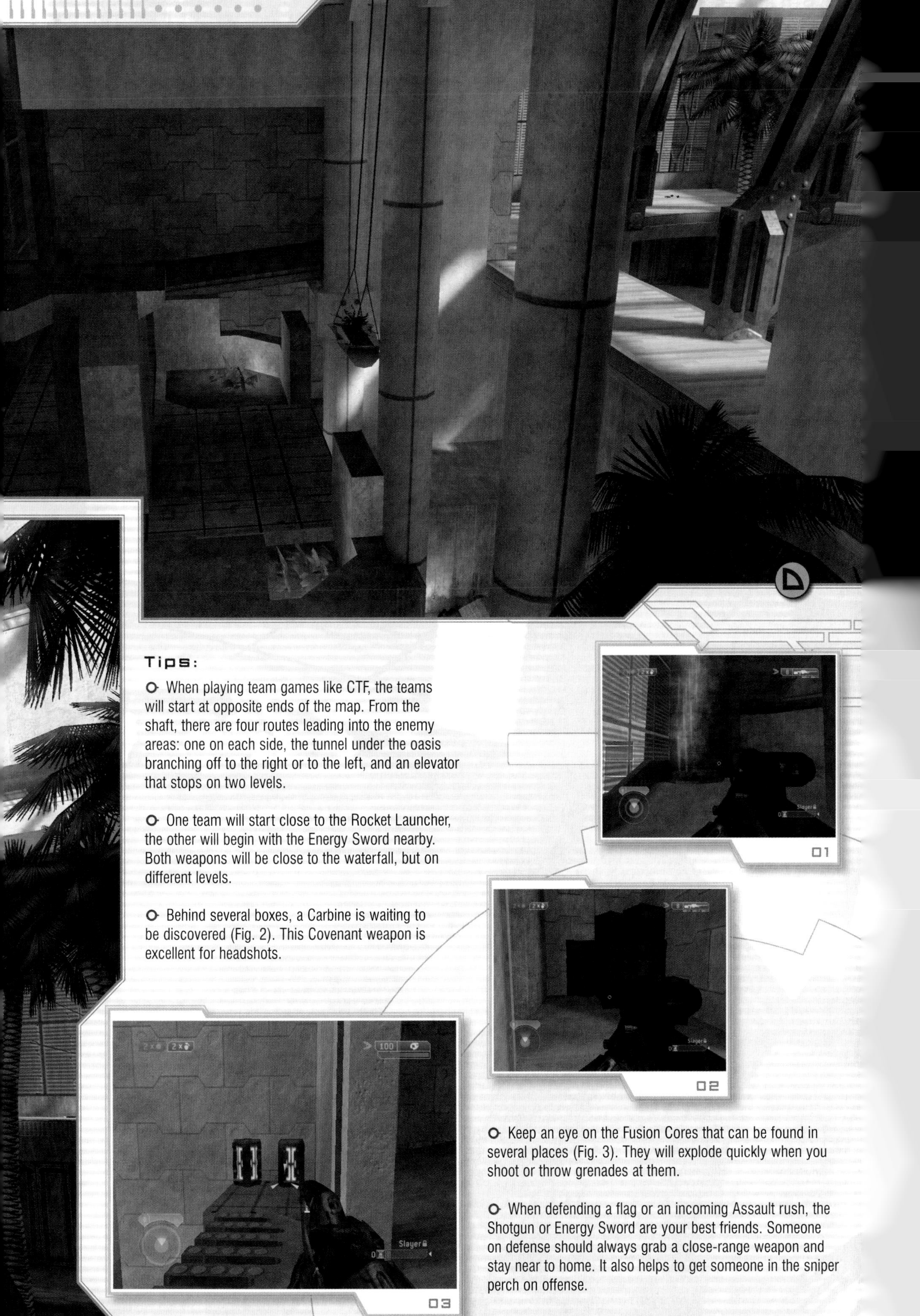

Tips:

- When playing team games like CTF, the teams will start at opposite ends of the map. From the shaft, there are four routes leading into the enemy areas: one on each side, the tunnel under the oasis branching off to the right or to the left, and an elevator that stops on two levels.

- One team will start close to the Rocket Launcher, the other will begin with the Energy Sword nearby. Both weapons will be close to the waterfall, but on different levels.

- Behind several boxes, a Carbine is waiting to be discovered (Fig. 2). This Covenant weapon is excellent for headshots.

01

02

03

- Keep an eye on the Fusion Cores that can be found in several places (Fig. 3). They will explode quickly when you shoot or throw grenades at them.

- When defending a flag or an incoming Assault rush, the Shotgun or Energy Sword are your best friends. Someone on defense should always grab a close-range weapon and stay near to home. It also helps to get someone in the sniper perch on offense.

Lockout

Some believe this remote facility was once used to study the Flood. But few clues remain amidst the snow and ice.

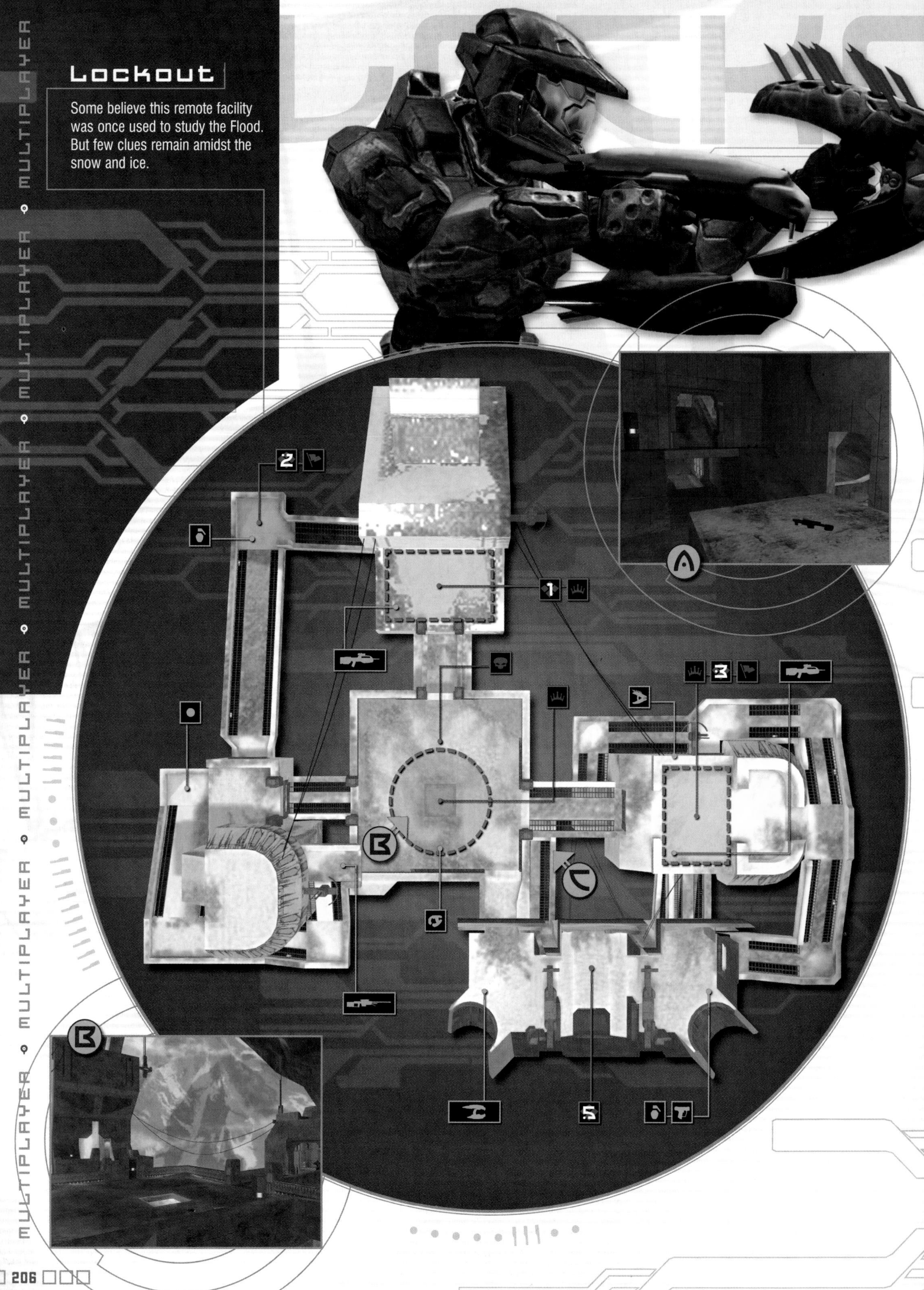

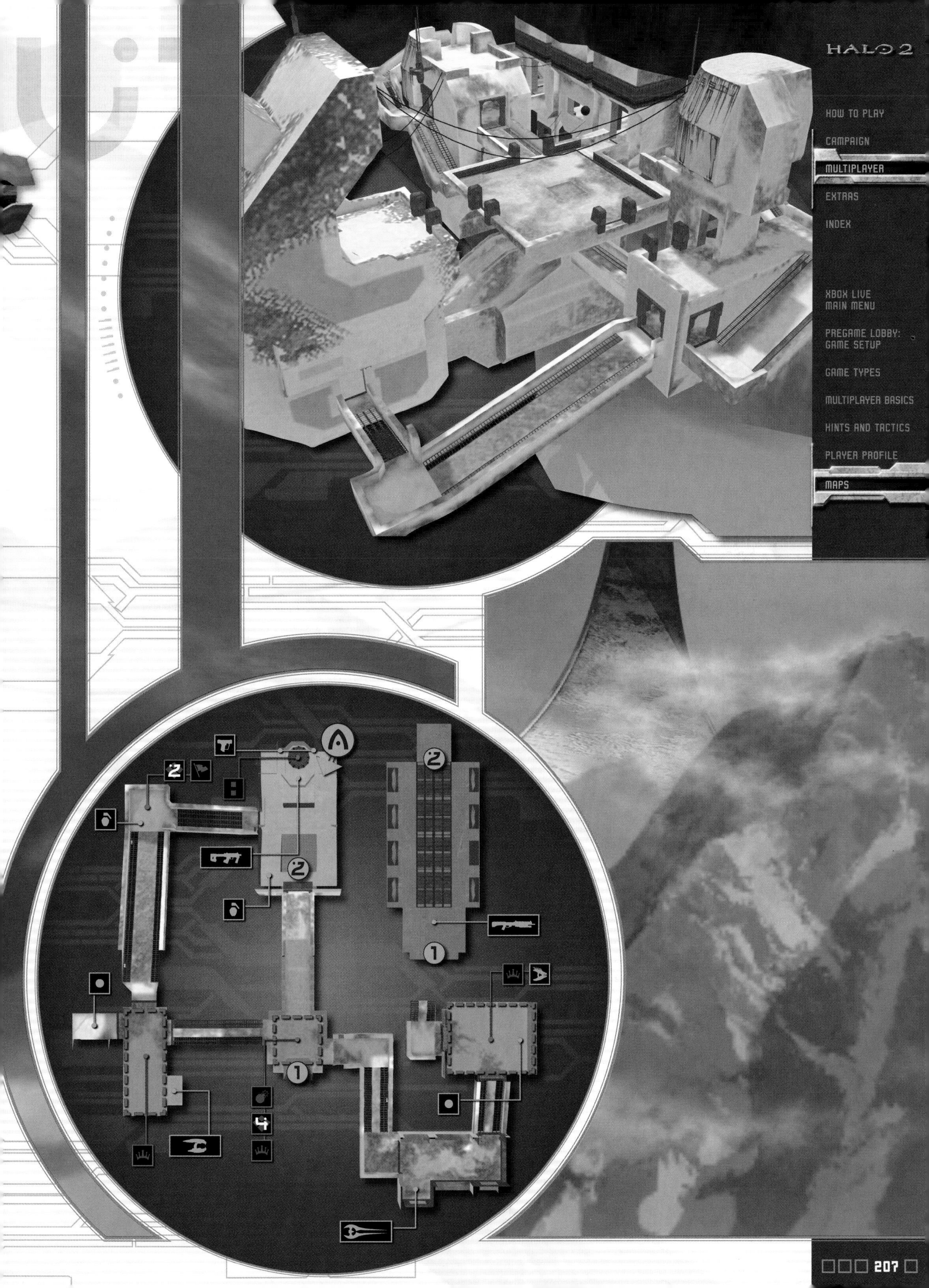

Lockout is best used for Slayer variants or fast-paced CTF battles. Leaping over the rail will, of course, be viewed as suicide. The central platform can be seen clearly from absolutely everywhere, which makes it a very dangerous place to be.

A Gravity Lift in the southern tower will take you from the ground level to the top floor. Always consider that you might already be expected before you use it...

The tower in the east is a position favored by snipers. You should be aware that this balcony is easily reached with well-aimed grenades (Fig. 1), and that the explosive containers also make this position rather unsafe.

01

02

03

Tips:

- Memorize the complex layout of the map as quickly as possible. You should additionally be aware of the position of every hole in the ceiling and floor. They often facilitate unexpected visits from unwelcome guests – but that works both ways, of course. Jumping will allow you to take unusual paths. For example, you could jump from the corner under the sniper post to the left and jump on the slope (Fig. 2).

- Initially, it seems that there is only one access point – the ramp at the rear – to the flag on the roof. Don't be lulled into a false sense of security. Skilful players will soon realize that, with a courageous jump from the nearby rail, you can actually reach the platform quite easily (Fig. 3).

- As there are always numerous battles over short distances on Lockout, the Energy Sword is a weapon you shouldn't underestimate. You can hide in the Center Room right on the top of a slope (Fig. 4) and surprise careless victims. The Shotgun is equally valuable here.

LOCKOUT

Recommended Number of Players:	2-8
Recommended Game Variants:	1vs1 Slayer, Rockets, Juggernaut, Oddball, 1 Flag CTF
Vehicles:	none
Territories:	1. Lift, 2. Walkway, 3. Roof, 4. Center Room, 5. Cliff Room

04

MULTIPLAYER • MULTIPLAYER • MULTIPLAYER • MULTIPLAYER • MULTIPLAYER • MULTIPLAYER • MULTIPLAYER

Midship

Don't let its luxury fool you – the Pious Inquisitor is one of the fastest ships in the Covenant fleet.

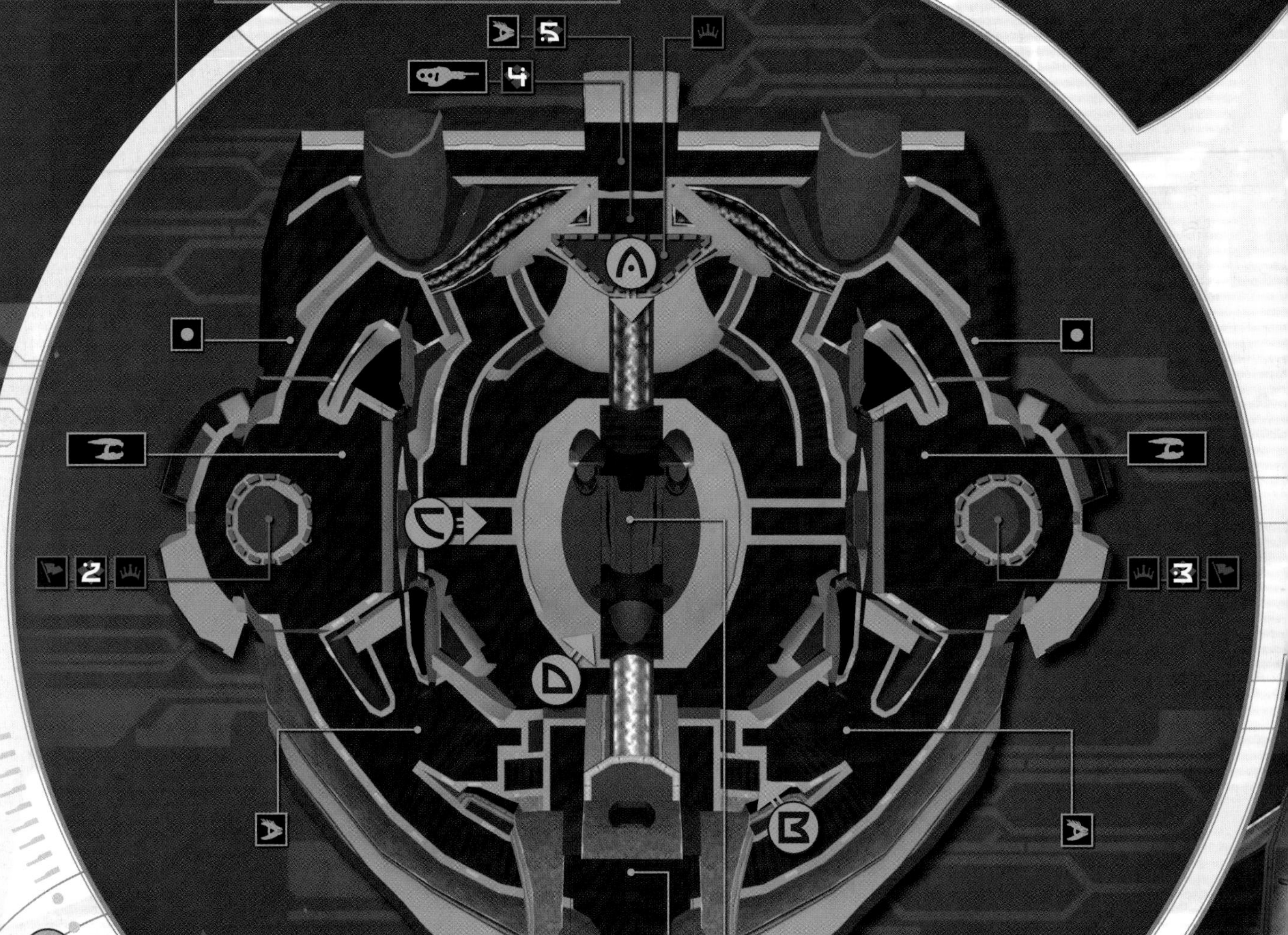

A

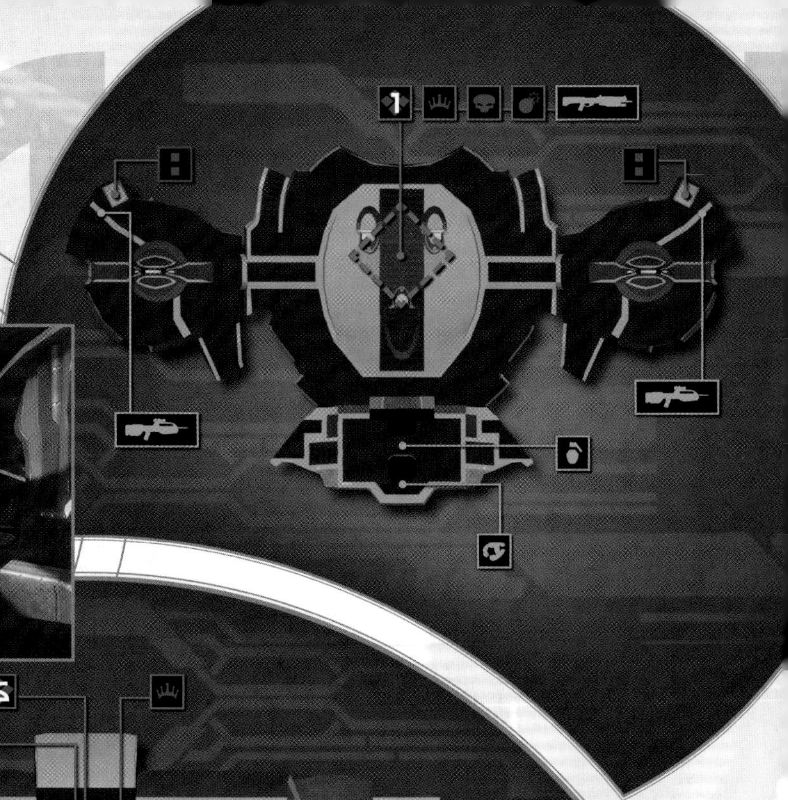

C

1

2

3

4

5

A

B

C

D

At the back end of both bases you'll find gaps in the floor that are difficult to see from above (Fig. 1). The gravity elevators one level below will take you up again. Defenders should always train an eagle eye on this route into their base.

This map is rather small, but as its color scheme and construction don't offer many recognizable spots, it may take a while for you to feel completely comfortable when navigating from one point to the next. Your first task should be to learn which ramp leads where.

Keep an eye on the "space crates" situated in various spots. These things can blow up quite nicely (if you catch an opponent in the explosion), or very annoyingly (should someone else do the same to you).

MIDSHIP

Recommended Number of Players:	4-6
Recommended Game Variants:	Slayer, 2 Flag CTF, Territories, Juggernaut
Vehicles:	none
Territories:	1. Center, 2. Planetside Deck, 3. Moonside Deck, 4. Batteries, 5. Walkway

Tips:

- You can reach the bases via the windows, too. Jump on the wall outside and, from there, to the balcony (Fig. 2). You can also use the container on the one side as a platform.

- Look out of the windows of the base: you'll see the Moon from one window and the Earth from the other. The view will help you find your bearings on the spaceship.

- On the very top of the base you'll find an Energy Sword. To reach it, you'll have to run across the platform in the center – but it offers no cover…

- In team-oriented games like CTF and Assault, have someone grab a suitable long-range weapon – a Battle Rifle or Sniper Rifle, for example. They can act as a support sniper from inside your base.

01

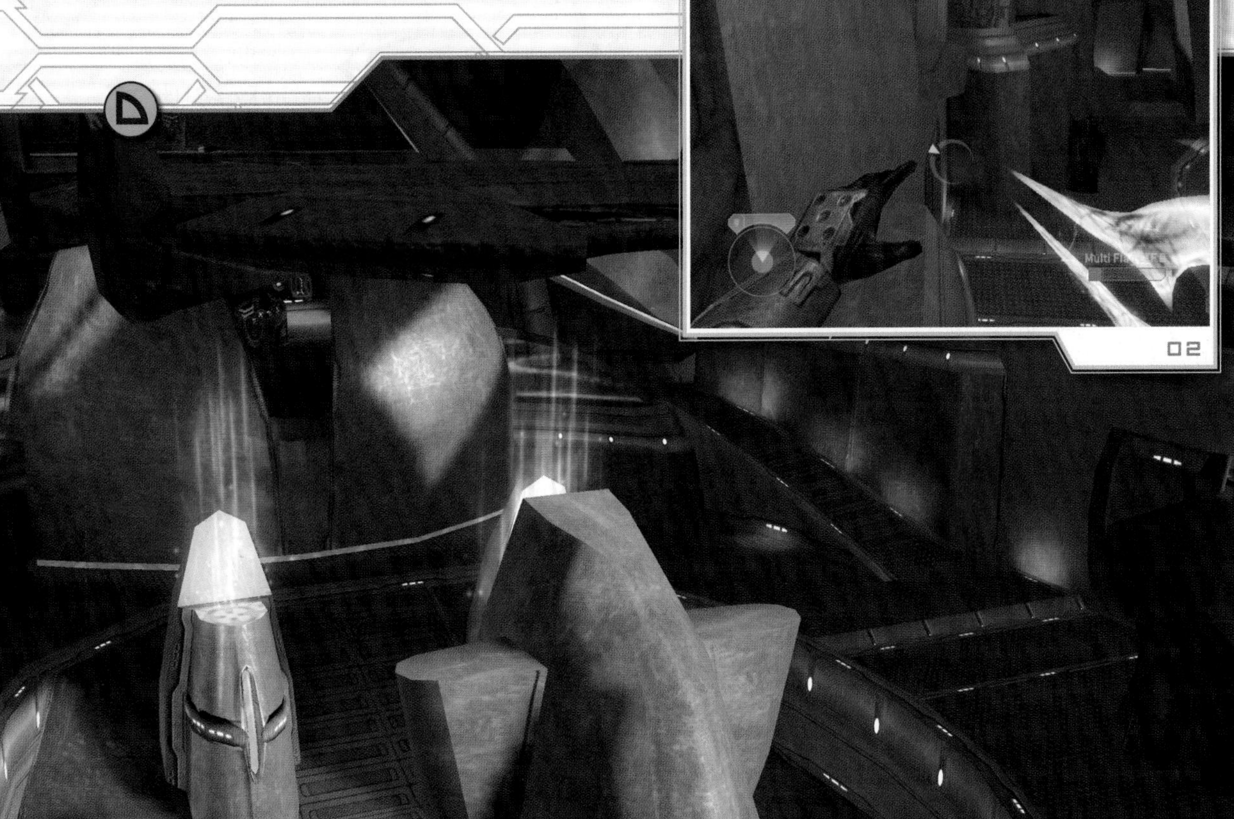

02

Waterworks

While the Forerunners excelled at mimicking natural beauty, the machinery in this cavern exemplifies their true genius.

4
5
2
1
2
3
B
A
W

Waterworks is a large map with a useful selection of vehicles. Wraith is the default setting for the map, but you could change that to Scorpions if you want to. You can even have four teams of four competing in enjoyable CTF matches here.

01

The many vehicles in the base might lead ill-disciplined teams to scatter into small groups or even set off individually. You'll usually find that they compound that error by committing the cardinal sin of leaving their home base unguarded. The key to this map is to own the tower structure in the center. You and your teammates will then have absolute knowledge of all vehicular traffic on the map, and will also be able to quickly cut off the flag carrier if necessary.

You should also take note that there are ladders leading from the central bridge up into the tower (Fig. 1). The sniper ledge will give you a good view across the whole area. A good sniper can be very dangerous in this spot, but will be particularly vulnerable to attacks from the rear. Jumping down from up there shouldn't be difficult, but consider the beckoning abyss very carefully before you leap.

02

Tips:

- You can shoot the stalactites off the ceiling (Fig. 2). If there's someone standing under one, it can do considerable damage.

- The Rocket Launcher is close to the teleporter exits. Keep in mind that the teleporters work in one direction only.

- At a glance, the flag seems easy to defend here, but the window and the hole in the ceiling make this base rather susceptible to grenade attacks. The large containers are not mere decoration – use them to jump on the roof of the base. As a defender, you can prevent this by pushing the crates somewhere else with a vehicle.

- Snipers placed on the rock ledges in the center can see the bases rather well. You should be aware that the gigantic machine close to the center of the construction will disturb a sniper's scope at regular intervals.

WATERWORKS

Recommended Number of Players:	10-16
Recommended Game Variants:	Multi Flag CTF, Snipers, Team Oddball
Vehicles:	2 x Banshee, 2 x Ghost, 2 x Warthog, 2 x Wraith
Territories:	1. Center Bridge, 2. Red Base, 3. Blue Base, 4. Blue Bridge, 5. Red Bridge

Zanzibar

Wind Power Station 7 sits as a mute reminder of the EAP's late 25th-century attempt at re-nationalization.

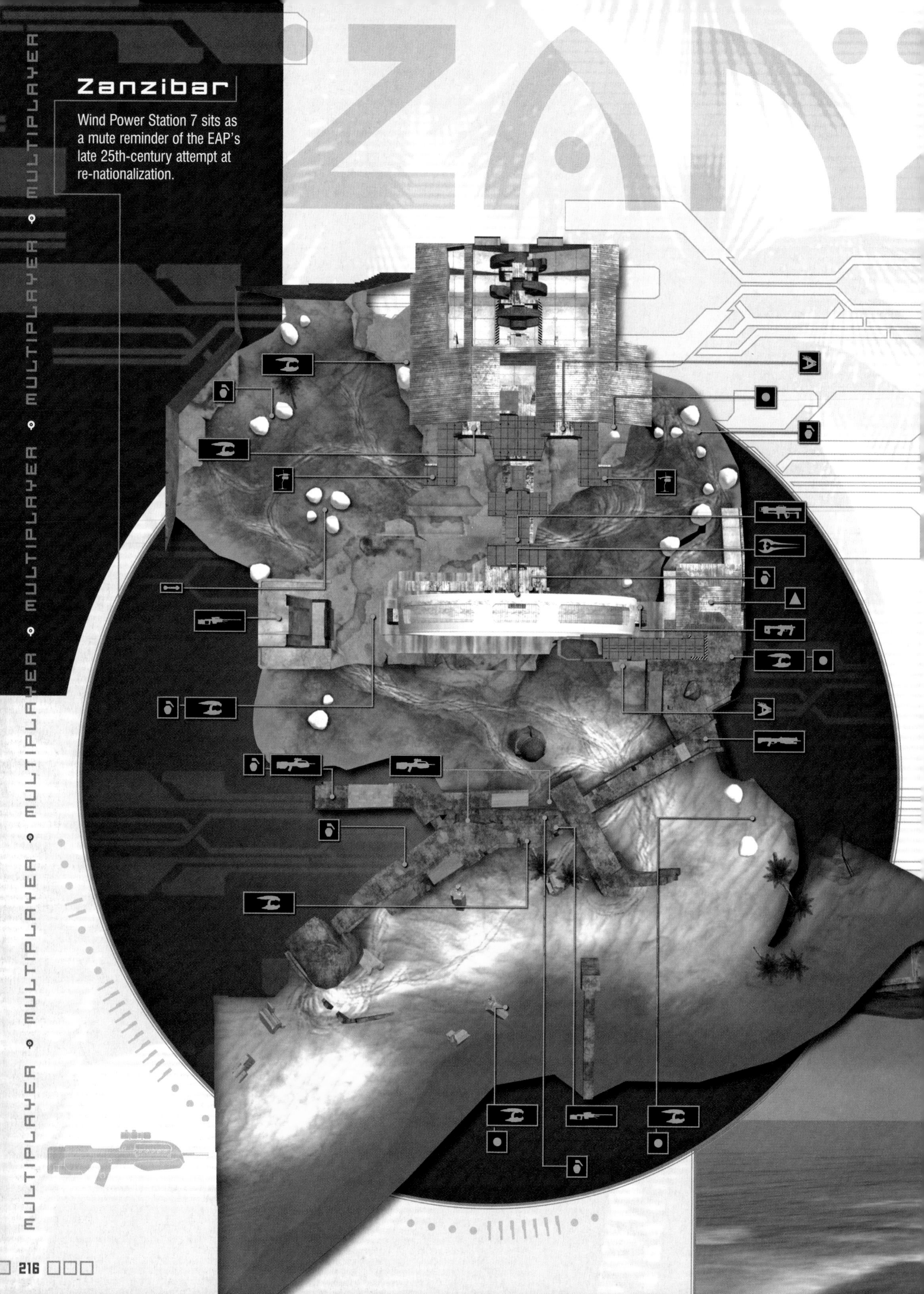

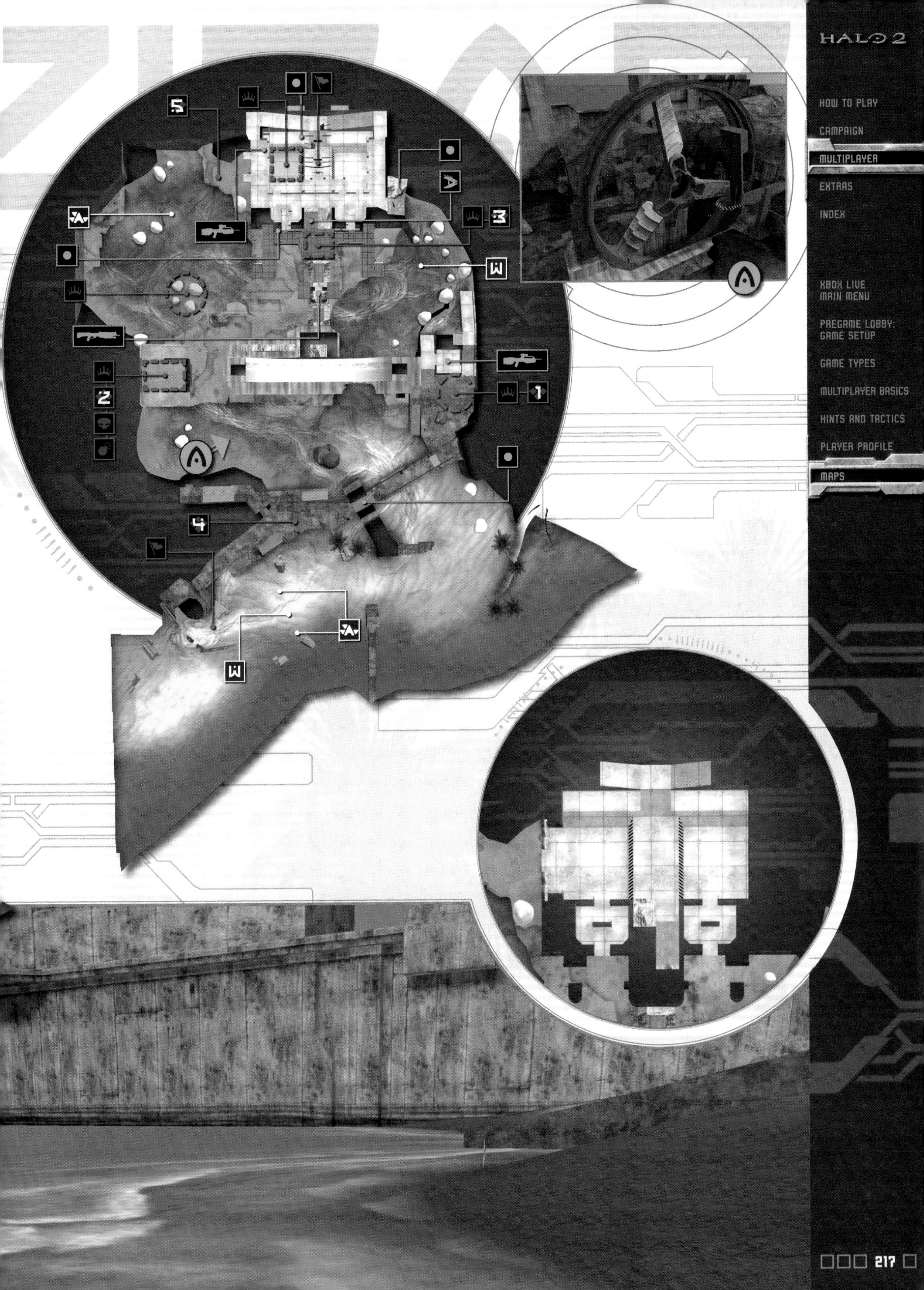
5
3
2
1
4

ZANZIBAR

Recommended Number of Players:	8-10
Recommended Game Variants:	1 Flag CTF, Assault, Territories
Vehicles:	Ghost, 2 x Warthog
Territories:	1. Control Tower, 2. Camp Froman, 3. Base, 4. Sea Wall, 5. Gate

Zanzibar is a very versatile map which is best used for object-based team games. How enjoyable it is depends on the exact game variant and the number of participants, but it offers a lot of space for highly strategic encounters.

There is a raised metal ramp between the Control Tower and the fan. Shoot at the mounting to lower the ramp (Fig. 1). Inside the building you'll find a switch (Fig. 2) on the upper level that opens the gate downstairs (Fig. 3). You can destroy the windowpanes on the second floor.

You can't turn the two turrets on the canopy to face the inside, so their effectiveness is often limited to the initial stage of a successful assault. You can definitely welcome attackers with them, but you should leave them immediately once there are no available targets – go make yourself useful elsewhere!

01

02

03

Tips:

- Under the center of the fan you'll find an Energy Sword waiting for you. Use the holes in the fan construction (Fig. 4) to drop down and grab it.

- Attackers in vehicles can launch a concentrated and extremely fast attack here. If you want to prevent this, you should find more suitable weapons as soon as possible – especially the Rocket Launcher, which is invaluable. (The vehicles close to the building will only be there in neutral game types.)

- Controlling the central sniper perch "Camp Froman" is an excellent strategy for both offense and defense – you have a vantage point that allows you to view almost the entire map. It's especially effective when offensive teams come pouring over the wall... and right into your crosshairs!

- When attackers are on their way back to their base with a flag they will only have the choice to go through the archway, the ramp above it or the steps to the right. The opening in the wall close to the sniper post can't be reached from down there – unless, that is, you park a Warthog under it and use it as a stepladder to get up.

- Experiment with Custom Variants and add the Wraith, turrets and other vehicles to spice things up.

04

4 EXTRAS

Spoiler alert!

If you have yet to finish the level entitled "The Arbiter", leave this chapter immediately! You have been warned...

EXTRAS

Spoiler alert! • Spoiler alert! • Spoiler alert!

Difficulty Settings

When you play Halo 2 on a new difficulty level, you will find many tangible differences. The higher the setting, the more aggressive your adversaries become: they will be tougher, and their weapons might have a higher rate of fire. Additionally, their positioning and numbers may vary. In places where you encountered little or light resistance on Normal, you might (and often will) experience a frantic battle on Legendary.

Halo 2, like its predecessor, is a game you should complete at least twice. Fans have opined that the Normal setting in Halo: Combat Evolved was, in a sense, an introduction; the true game, the most enjoyable challenge, was conquering the Legendary mode. The same can be said of this sequel. You should also look out for subtle changes that occasionally appear when you play on different difficulty levels. After the crash landing at Old Mombasa, for example, Cortana's address to the Master Chief varies according to the mode you are playing on.

You can find or share tips on variations between play modes, swap anecdotes, and join the hunt for Bungie's Halo 2 Easter Eggs at the **www.bungie.net** and **www.piggybackinteractive.com** forums.

On Top of the World

Always take the time to examine and explore your surroundings: you can sometimes find secret (or simply subtle) pieces of scenery that allow you to leave the beaten path. There are occasions when you can jump on top of surrounding buildings or structures – like in Old Mombasa, for example, or outside the Umbilicals at Cairo Station (Fig. 1). Don't miss the opportunity to have a good look around. As was the case with Halo: Combat Evolved, it's enjoyable to attempt to reach areas that Bungie's designers did not expect you to see. However, be aware that invisible "walls" may eventually block your progress.

01

Additional Firepower

Did you know that you can "unlock" additional turrets for some of the multiplayer maps? Access the Vehicle Options in the Game Variants menu and turn the setting for turrets to "on". By doing this, you can add:

- **Ascension:** a primary turret upstairs in the base (Fig. 2)
- **Coagulation:** a primary turret on the roof of each base
- **Colossus:** primary turrets in the bases
- **Headlong:** a secondary turret next to the Warthog poster
- **Lockout:** a primary turret on the roof (Fig. 3) and a secondary turret on the sniper stand
- **Waterworks:** secondary turrets on the sniper ledges
- **Zanzibar:** a secondary turret on the sea wall

02

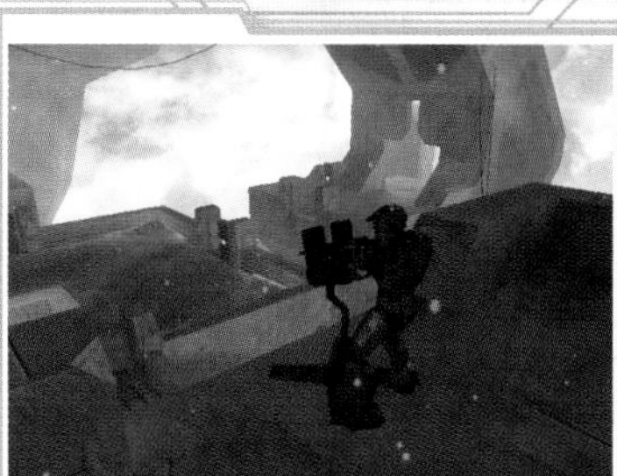

03

Power-ups

Here is a list of all the power-ups available on the multiplayer maps. You should be aware of their location and note that, in some cases, the type of pickup is random:

- **Ascension:** Overshield on the long walkway
- **Beaver Creek:** Overshield at one end of the creek
- **Coagulation:** random Overshield or Acitve Camo within reach of each teleporter destination
- **Colossus:** a random Overshield or Active Camo down below by the "pits of death"
- **Headlong:** Overshield by the statue and Active Camo in the hallway at the opposite side of the map
- **Ivory Tower:** Overshield on the outer walkway
- **Zanzibar:** Active Camo in the control tower

Weapons on Map

You can define the type of armaments found on the multiplayer maps by changing the setting Weapons on Map in the Equipment Options at the Game Settings menu. The first column of the following table states the weapon you would usually find on the map – that is, the default configuration. In the columns to the right, you can see which weapon you will find should you change the setting. While some are very obvious (like Rockets or Shotguns, where the only weapons are Rocket Launchers and Shotguns respectively), the differences when you choose others (like Halo Classic and New Classic) are not immediately apparent. The following reference table is an at-a-glance guide to what you'll find with each option.

DEFAULT	ROCKETS	SHOTGUNS	BRUTE SHOTS	HALO CLASSIC	NEW CLASSIC	HEAVY WEAPONS	ALL DUALS
Magnum	Rocket Launcher	Shotgun	Brute Shot	Magnum	SMG	Rocket Launcher	Magnum
SMG	Rocket Launcher	Shotgun	Brute Shot	Magnum	SMG	Rocket Launcher	SMG
Battle Rifle	Rocket Launcher	Shotgun	Brute Shot	Battle Rifle	Carbine	Rocket Launcher	SMG
Shotgun	Rocket Launcher	Shotgun	Brute Shot	Shotgun	Energy Sword	Rocket Launcher	Magnum
Sniper Rifle	Rocket Launcher	Shotgun	Brute Shot	Sniper Rifle	Beam Rifle	Rocket Launcher	Magnum
Rocket Launcher	Rocket Launcher	Shotgun	Brute Shot	Rocket Launcher	Brute Shot	Rocket Launcher	Needler
Plasma Pistol	Rocket Launcher	Shotgun	Brute Shot	Plasma Pistol	SMG	Brute Shot	Plasma Pistol
Plasma Rifle	Rocket Launcher	Shotgun	Brute Shot	Plasma Rifle	Brute Plasma Rifle	Brute Shot	Plasma Rifle
Needler	Rocket Launcher	Shotgun	Brute Shot	Needler	SMG	Rocket Launcher	Needler
Carbine	Rocket Launcher	Shotgun	Brute Shot	Battle Rifle	Carbine	Brute Shot	Plasma Rifle
Brute Shot	Rocket Launcher	Shotgun	Brute Shot	Rocket Launcher	Brute Shot	Brute Shot	Needler
Beam Rifle	Rocket Launcher	Shotgun	Brute Shot	Sniper Rifle	Beam Rifle	Rocket Launcher	Plasma Rifle
Energy Sword	Rocket Launcher	Shotgun	Brute Shot	Shotgun	Energy Sword	Brute Shot	Plasma Pistol

NO DUALS	RIFLES	SNIPING	NO SNIPING	PISTOLS	PLASMA	HUMAN	COVENANT
Battle Rifle	Battle Rifle	Sniper Rifle	Magnum	Magnum	Plasma Pistol	Magnum	Plasma Pistol
Battle Rifle	Battle Rifle	Sniper Rifle	SMG	Magnum	Plasma Rifle	SMG	Needler
Battle Rifle	Battle Rifle	Sniper Rifle	Battle Rifle	Magnum	Plasma Rifle	Battle Rifle	Carbine
Shotgun	Battle Rifle	Sniper Rifle	Shotgun	Magnum	Plasma Rifle	Shotgun	Needler
Sniper Rifle	Sniper Rifle	Sniper Rifle	Battle Rifle	Magnum	Brute Plasma Rifle	Sniper Rifle	Beam Rifle
Rocket Launcher	Battle Rifle	Sniper Rifle	Rocket Launcher	Magnum	Brute Plasma Rifle	Rocket Launcher	Brute Shot
Shotgun	Carbine	Beam Rifle	Plasma Pistol	Plasma Pistol	Plasma Pistol	Magnum	Plasma Pistol
Carbine	Carbine	Beam Rifle	Plasma Rifle	Plasma Pistol	Plasma Rifle	Battle Rifle	Plasma Rifle
Carbine	Carbine	Beam Rifle	Needler	Plasma Pistol	Plasma Rifle	SMG	Needler
Carbine	Carbine	Beam Rifle	Carbine	Plasma Pistol	Plasma Rifle	Battle Rifle	Carbine
Brute Shot	Carbine	Beam Rifle	Brute Shot	Plasma Pistol	Brute Plasma Rifle	Rocket Launcher	Brute Shot
Beam Rifle	Beam Rifle	Beam Rifle	Carbine	Plasma Pistol	Plasma Rifle	Sniper Rifle	Beam Rifle
Energy Sword	Carbine	Beam Rifle	Energy Sword	Plasma Pistol	Brute Plasma Rifle	Shotgun	Energy Sword

Experience Points and Levels

When you play Halo 2 multiplayer via Xbox Live, the "skill" of every player is indicated by his or her level. New players start at level one, and the highest level is 50. Your level is determined by experience points. As the system is not shown on screen, we'll provide a explanation of how it works. The basic principle is very simple: if you win a "ranked" game, you earn experience points. If you lose a "ranked" game, points are deducted. The more points you have, the higher your level will be, as the following chart demonstrates.

EXPERIENCE POINTS

LEVEL	EXP.
1	0-100
2	100-199
3	200-299
4	400-599
5	600-899
6	900-1199
7	1200-1599
8	1600-1999
9	2000-2499
10	2500-2999
15	5000-5499
20	7500-8149
30	20750-22899
40	49000-52649
50	92250-...

The number of points you earn depends on the score of the game. Let's say you are playing a game of Slayer with four people. The result of the game is as follows:

- **1st place:** Player 1 (John, level 10)
- **2nd place:** Player 2 (Paul, level 7)
- **3rd place:** Player 3 (George, level 8)
- **4th place:** Player 4 (Ringo, level 5)

John will earn points for beating the other three. Paul will earn points for beating George and Ringo, but lose points for being beaten by John. The number of experience points earned or lost is based on the level of the players. You'll get a bonus for beating "better" players, and there's a point deduction penalty for losing against players that are not as experienced as you are.

Let's calculate the experience change for John. John (level 10) beat Paul (level 7). They are three levels apart, so the third row of the table shows us that John gains 85 points. John also beat George (level 8), so John earns 90 points because they are two levels apart. Finally, John earns 75 points for beating Ringo (level 5). The total for John is 250 points. The total is divided by the number of enemies (three), so the experience point change is +83.

Let's have a look at Paul. He lost to John, who was higher in level. We consult row four of the table and have a look at the "lower loss" column. According to this, he loses 55 points. However, he won against George, who has a higher level. Row two of the chart shows us that a "lower win" earns 115 points. Finally, Paul picks up 90 experience points for beating Ringo. So overall, his experience point change is (-55 + 115 + 90) = 150, divided by 3 = +50. The calculation for George is (-70 -105 +85): 3 = -30. He loses 30 points. Ringo loses 53 points ((-35 -70 -55): 3).

Finally, there is another factor. Players with low levels get a helping hand. Their loss of points is divided by a factor, so that they will not lose their rank as quickly as an experienced player will. Furthermore, you will only lose a level if your experience points drop below the midpoint experience required for the previous level. This helps avoid the frustration of hovering right at the boundary between two levels, constantly switching back and forth. It also offers you peace of mind when you reach a new level – you know you won't be slipping back down immediately.

Luckily, it's not a requisite that you understand how this system works. Just be assured that it is not arbitrary, or even random, but calculated by hard facts. It is possible that Bungie may modify or optimize this system at a later date. The information provided here is correct at the time of this guide going to press, but don't rely on it to calculate your points for every match you play in. Besides, any time you might spend fooling around with numbers and statistics could be better spent honing your Slayer skills...

POINTS BASED ON LEVEL DIFFERENCE

LEVEL DIFFERENCE	HIGHER WIN	HIGHER LOSS	LOWER WIN	LOWER LOSS
0	100	100	100	100
1	95	105	115	85
2	90	110	130	70
3	85	115	145	55
4	80	120	155	45
5	75	125	165	35

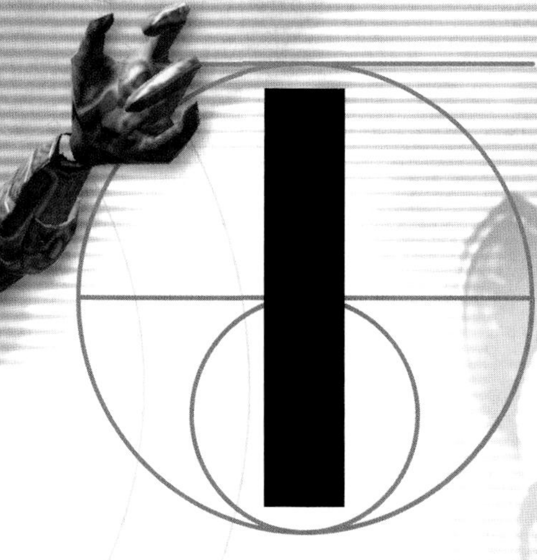

Introduction

This alphabetical listing gives direct page numbers for various points of interest throughout the Halo 2 guide. Be warned: depending on your current position in the game, these locations may contain spoilers. For that reason, all entries that lead to the Campaign walkthrough are colored **red**. For quick reference, maps for both multiplayer and Campaign modes are **blue**. A "C" denotes that the map in question is part of the Campaign mode; unsurprisingly, "M" is used to highlight those found in multiplayer matches.